# Acts Analyzed

The Key Book, the Beginning Book
of the Executed New Testament of
Our Lord and Saviour Jesus Christ

. . . BY . . .

ADAM KENNEDY ADCOCK, M.A., LL.D.

Author of "The Glorious Gospel" and "At the Feet of Paul"

THE STANDARD PUBLISHING COMPANY

CINCINNATI, OHIO, U. S. A.

Printed in U. S. A.

# DEDICATION

To the blessed memory of his sainted mother, Mahala Archer Adcock, the most beautiful and the most intuitive person he has ever known, to whom, under the Lord Himself, he owes more than to anybody else he has ever seen, this volume is most gratefully and affectionately inscribed by the author.

# AUTHOR'S FOREWORD

To see Christ as the Correlative of the Scriptures is essential to the appreciation of the immense, unique, infinite value of the Bible as the revelation of the will of the Deity. It puts no strain on faith that Philip began at a certain Scripture, and preached Jesus to the Ethiopian eunuch: all roads and all highways and all bypaths in the Word of God lead in a straight line to the Lord Jesus Christ, with reference to whom both Testaments should be read and studied by everybody. The relationship of the Old Testament, from Genesis to Malachi, inclusive, to the Lord Jesus Christ is, *Coming up to Christ;* of Matthew and Mark and Luke and John, *The Coming of Christ;* of Acts of Apostles, *Coming into Christ;* of the Epistles, or Church Letters, from Romans to Jude, inclusive, *Living in Christ, Continuing in Christ;* of Revelation, *Reigning with Christ, Living with Christ Forever.* The Old Testament prophesied that He would come; the Gospels declare that He did come; Acts of Apostles makes plain and particular the way out of the world into Christ; Revelation gives a picture of the saved in heaven with Him forever.

This volume shows, according to the text, that the New Testament did not actually go into effect till the first Pentecost following the resurrection of the Lord Jesus Christ from the dead. The New Testament was purely theoretical till that day, when the great God Himself nailed it to the ground. Let no man now go behind the cross of Christ to find the answer to the

5

sinner's question what to do to be saved. Nobody knew this adequate and final answer when the Old Testament was written, as it had not then been revealed. Neither was it possible or germane for Matthew and Mark and Luke and John, save in the terms of the Great Commission, to incorporate this answer for the Christian Dispensation, which did not really begin till after the Life about which they wrote was fully lived. Now, while Acts of Apostles is echoed and re-echoed in the Old Testament and in all the other books of the New Testament, yet it is the key book and the first book to make simple and specific and imperative the way out of the world into the church, the way out of death into life.

It is generally agreed that there are three kinds of preaching—topical, textual, expository. Any discourse not based on the truth of God, ignoring the Word of God, with whatever graces it may have or can possess, can not possibly be a sermon. The risen Lord has Himself given preaching its only authority. Any unbeliever in Him as the unique, the only begotten Son of God, should vacate the sacred desk forever, call nothing he produces a sermon, quit presuming to preach and abandon meddling with his fellows. Expository preaching should prevail. It is the most profitable both to the preacher and to people, and more faithful to the text than mere textual preaching, and a safer guide than simple topical preaching. Expository preaching helps the preacher to find topics and to discover sermons in the Word of God itself, and educates both him and his hearers in the Bible.

ADAM KENNEDY ADCOCK.

# CONTENTS

## I

CONTENTS 9

V

Lost World Struck Back at Paul (10-15). *The Body
Doomed; Spirit Ultimate Reality* (16-34).—Heathen
Curiosity May Spawn Idols and Abstract Theories, But
Recoils on Itself in Pitiable Helplessness (16-21); There
Is No Eternal Life, No Ultimate Reality, in Physical Cul-
ture or in Mere Intellectual Development (22-34).

# XVIII

# XIX

# XX

# XXI

# THE AUTHORITY OF THE APOSTLES

## (Acts 1)

*Authority is an absolute necessity; anarchy is its only alternative.* All independent authority is divine. Yet there must be human vestment or enduement of power in this world, because here God operates through man. But all actual authority, or all constant control, or all practical power, must inhere in its agent; if it merely hangs like a garment about the person of an actor, being artificial and affected, it is false and futile. The Creator made men equal, and no man should assume authority over his associates. But any man may lead among his fellows who has the requisite gifts of patience and sympathy and understanding and energy and foresight. Now the most amazing authority ever vouchsafed to mortal man was given to His apostles by the Lord Jesus Christ Himself. In the first chapter of Luke's inspired record of Acts of these wonderful men, let us discover that their authority is real and genuine, yet delegated and limited withal, and practical. We always speak of their authority in the present tense, because they are apostles forever, and their power is coextensive with the Christian era.

### The Apostles Have Real Authority (vs. 1-5)

*The apostles have real authority, because the Lord Jesus Christ Himself chose them and commanded them* (1, 2). Luke makes Acts of Apostles a continuation of the life of Jesus in this world; but since Jesus was "received up" into heaven, His apostles are left in the center of the stage. Perhaps the greatest achievement of the Lord in His earthly ministry was the selection and training and commanding of these twelve men to represent Him and interpret His life and exemplify His teaching and execute His will to the whole world forever. Jesus called these men at the very beginning of His work. They went everywhere with Him; they heard what He said and saw what He did. When He chose them, they were honest, manly men, and capable of receiving His teaching and understanding His heart. The statement that they were illiterate and uneducated is false and slanderous. They went to school to the Lord Jesus Christ. Jesus was bigger than all the educational institutions on the face of the earth. Real education is active rather than passive; everybody has to educate himself. A school is nothing but an opportunity—and the opportunity is the teacher. The apostles had the greatest Teacher and the best opportunity for training and leadership and inspiration of any men that ever lived or ever shall live! To them Jesus showed the vital, and revealed the innerness of things. He bore with their weaknesses, wept over them and prayed for them. He planted the seed of His kingdom in their hearts, and knew that they would bear fruit—His fruit! He gave "commandment through the Holy Spirit" unto them. He honored them with responsibility for His own work, and glorified them with His own authority and power. Their training was neither technical nor perfunctory, but it was adequate and successful. It is always a liberal education to be associated with a great man; the apostles were the most highly favored of all men in their association with Jesus.

*The direct, immediate association of the apostles with the person of the Lord Jesus Christ also made their authority real and original* (3). To them "he also showed himself alive after his passion by many proofs, appearing unto them forty days, and speaking the things concerning the kingdom of God." While Christianity rises infinitely above this test, which is convincing if even crude, yet the Christian religion submits itself to the testimony of the bodily senses; and let us thank God for this test, through whose door no vagary can pass. History admits frankly that Jesus lived, but many men balk at His resurrection. His resurrection is a fact. The only way to prove a fact is by the testimony of competent, credible witnesses who saw the fact done or happen. Either Jesus arose from the dead, or the apostles and their associates imagined He did and deliberately lied about Him. When they saw Him expire on the cross, hope also died in their hearts and the resumption of His life was infinitely beyond them, as heaven is high above earth. He arose, and they knew it. Subsequent to His resurrection from the dead, He appeared unto them repeatedly for forty days, and submitted Himself to every conceivable test. They saw Him with their eyes and heard Him with their ears and handled Him with their hands (1 John 1:1-4) and loved Him with their hearts and served Him with their lives and sealed their testimony with their blood. Even if His resurrection body were not under the necessity of food, yet He ate with them, as if further to assure them of His identity. He gave them every proof of Himself after His passion that He had given them before; and if they had not been convinced then of His resurrection from the dead, they would have been idiots or fools or lunatics or devils. The death of His body of flesh did

not change the heart of the Lord Jesus Christ; after
He arose, He still talked about "the things concerning
the kingdom of God." Verily, truth inheres in the
simplicity and the honesty of the witness of the apostles.
And their story of Him is really timeless, and must be
told and retold to all the generations forever. If the
time is out of joint with the New Testament, that is bad
for the time; break its bones and reset them, but never
trifle with the Word of God, or modify in the slightest
degree the inspired teaching of the apostles of the Lord
Jesus Christ.

*That the apostles were "baptized in the Holy Spirit"
likewise assures the genuineness of their authority* (4, 5).
With all the richness and glory of their direct and immediate and personal association with Jesus in this world,
the apostles were not ready to begin their work, the
most momentous task ever assigned to mortal men. And
so Jesus "charged them not to depart from Jerusalem,
but to wait for the promise of the Father, which, saith
he, ye heard from me." As long as the Lord was with
them in a body that they could see and hear and touch,
the apostles seemed unable to realize the essential spiritual character of the divine kingdom. They themselves
had to be baptized, and overwhelmed, and taken possession of, and dominated, and inspired, by the Holy Spirit,
before they could bear effective, powerful witness of
their risen Lord. And this "promise of the Father"
of the baptism of the Holy Spirit, about which Jesus
had spoken to His apostles, is evidently limited to them.
The Holy Spirit gave them their message mysteriously
and enabled them to work miracles. But it is not necessary that the Holy Spirit should do that for the ordinary minister or the common Christian. We can read
the divine message in the New Testament, and miracles

have served their purpose. But it is just as necessary for us to have the Holy Spirit as it was for the apostles to have Him. He inspired them and their colleagues to create the New Testament. For ten days they prayed and did nothing else. Everybody that obeys the gospel is promised "the gift of the Holy Spirit," which is the Holy Spirit given. The apostles emptied themselves that the Holy Spirit might come into them, and we must do a similar thing. They prayed, and we must pray incessantly and fervently. The reason why the church is being flooded by waves of worldliness, which drown its power to save the lost, is that it has forgotten to pray and does not have the Holy Spirit to inspire the power and passion of the Lord Jesus Christ. The Holy Spirit made the witnesses of the apostles irresistible, and assured their authority forever. The baptism of the Holy Spirit enabled them to set the Roman empire on fire; the gift of the Holy Spirit in the church today will enable the church to take their witness of the Lord and save the world.

### The Authority of the Apostles Is Delegated and Limited (vs. 6-14)

*The authority of the apostles is delegated and limited, because they were finite and could not pry into divine secrets* (6, 7). All human power is limited by the finiteness of man; the apostles are no exception to this rule. "They, therefore, when they were come together, asked him, saying, Lord, dost thou at this time restore the kingdom to Israel? And he said unto them, It is not for you to know times or seasons, which the Father hath set within his own authority." Evidently, when they saw Jesus in their midst, alive from the dead, the old hope of a material Jewish kingdom revived in their hearts. Yet

Jesus did not argue against this false expectation, because He knew that they would soon give it up as an impossible dream. However, till they did give it up and see the reign of Jesus as essentially spiritual and radically different from David's sovereignty, their authority was so limited that they could not even begin their work as the witnesses of the risen Lord. The authority of the apostles did not originate in them; it was delegated to them by the Lord Jesus Christ through the inspiration and control of the Holy Spirit. This is the source of all power in the church of Christ forever.

*That the apostles are the deputies of the Lord Jesus Christ is seen again in the special purpose for which the Holy Spirit empowered them to act* (8-11). Here Luke gives the fifth, and the briefest, record of the Great Commission, in summarizing what Jesus said to His apostles: "But ye shall receive power, when the Holy Spirit is come upon you: and ye shall be my witnesses both in Jerusalem, and in all Judæa and Samaria, and unto the uttermost part of the earth." The apostles never claimed universal knowledge for themselves; no men ever lived humbler or freer of pretense or assumption or affectation or arrogance than they did. They frankly avowed the limitation of their knowledge. But they deliberately claimed for themselves the inspiration of the Holy Spirit. They knew Jesus of Nazareth as no other men ever knew Him. They heard all His discourses and sermons and debates and speeches and conversations; they witnessed all His miracles and deeds of mercy and kindness. They saw Him arrested and condemned without guilt or testimony. They beheld Him die on Golgotha's heights, and knew that He was buried in the new tomb of a rich man. The Holy Spirit inspired them to report to the world every essential thing in their knowledge of Him, and led them into the understanding of all the truth necessary to save the sinful and the lost forever. Their authority is spiritual and special—to bear witness of the life and teaching and preaching and death and resurrection and ascension and coronation and glorification of the Lord Jesus Christ. And this they do boldly, daringly, heroically, exclusively, successfully! Let all the preachers and all the churches in all the world follow their example, and never be turned aside to deal with other things. The apostles saw Jesus ascend to heaven in a cloud of glory and heard the angelic promise of His second coming. This significant story has reached us; let it ring down through the years and centuries and millenniums and ages and cycles forever!

*This power of the apostles opened their eyes to their own weakness and dependence, and impelled them to pray as never before* (12-14). "Both Peter and John and James and Andrew, Philip and Thomas, Bartholomew and Matthew, James, the son of Alphæus, and Simon, the Zealot, and Judas, the son of James. These all with one accord continued stedfastly in prayer with the women, and Mary, the mother of Jesus, and with his brethren." Prayer is itself the great mark of dependence. The great eternal God has absolute, independent authority, and He is above the necessity of prayer. Prayer is impossible to God; indeed, there is no other being in the whole universe to whom "the King eternal, immortal, invisible, the only God" (1 Tim. 1:17) could pray. Jesus *prayed to keep in touch with God,* in whom all power inheres. The apostles prayed ten days before they were baptized of the Holy Spirit, and they continued to pray the rest of their lives in this world. No doubt, if they had neglected to pray,

they would have become indifferent, and would have
lost their authority. Prayer is hard work, but it is also
sweet and satisfying and exhilarating. Have we lost
the art and power of prayer in these modern days?
Prayer keeps all followers of the Lord Jesus Christ,
whether apostles or preachers or evangelists or elders
or deacons or teachers or members of the church, in
touch with Him; and He gives them His own grace and
the love of God, through the communion of the Holy
Spirit (2 Cor. 13:14). We can never do His work
without His passion and power, and we can never have
His passion and power unless we read His Word and
pray.

### The Authority of the Apostles Is Practical (vs. 15-26)

*The authority of the apostles is practical, because
they saw that the vacancy among themselves should be
filled* (15-20). Some have assumed that, because another man was selected to take the place from which
Judas had fallen, before the apostles were baptized by
the Holy Spirit, this selection was without authority
and divine approval. Now, this conclusion is a mere
supposition, a bad guess, without one iota of Scriptural
support. Let us keep in mind that real authority can
not be mechanical or artificial or affected; it must always
have a basis of character and knowledge and power. It
is true that before the Holy Spirit came upon them on
Pentecost, the authority of the apostles was incomplete
to execute the Great Commission; but Jesus, under the
first commission, had given them power to cast out
unclean spirits and to heal all kinds of disease (Matt.
10:1). And the Eleven, led by Peter, most certainly
had the character and knowledge and power to do what
they did to restore their number to the original twelve.

Moreover, it was absolutely necessary that this new member of the apostolic Group should have been chosen before the Day of Pentecost came, that he might be present with the original Eleven, and receive the baptism of the Holy Spirit just as they did and when they did. And both Peter and Luke give satisfactory Scriptural support of this selection of Matthias, and of the original choice, and of the terrible fate of Judas.

*Moreover, the utility of the apostles' prerogative is emphasized by the qualifications essential to their office* (21, 22). They ruled, ''Of the men therefore that have companied with us all the time that the Lord Jesus went in and went out among us, beginning from the baptism of John, unto the day that he was received up from us, of these must one become a witness with us of his resurrection.'' Now this decision of the eleven apostles commends itself to the common sense and fairness of mankind, and is acceptable in any court of justice in the world. That the apostles had belonged to the original company that saw Jesus go in and out among the people from the time John baptized Him in the Jordan till the day a cloud of glory received Him out of their view —this made it possible for them to identify Him, beyond question and above doubt, after His resurrection from the dead. Judas had enjoyed this wonderful and glorious privilege; and surely no other man could fill the office to which Judas was originally chosen without this same intimate and direct and immediate and personal association with Jesus of Nazareth. This rule holds and governs the original apostles forever, and makes it impossible for Paul or any other man to belong to the original group of apostles. Paul's apostolate is real and genuine, but it is special—to the Gentiles. If Judas had been faithful, and there had never been any va-

cancy in the original group of apostles, Paul would have
been called just the same as he was called. His office
originates with himself, and he takes nobody's place.
In some respects, Paul surpasses the original Twelve;
but they have priority and precedence over him and all
other men forever.

*Finally, the reality of the apostles' function is glori-*
*fied by their idealism* (23-26). They did not dare to
take things into their own hands; they always looked
heavenward for guidance. They could find only two
men that had been with their original group—''Joseph
called Barsabbas, who was surnamed Justus, and
Matthias''; and they put both these men ''forward.''
Evidently, either one of these men could have honored
the position that Judas disgraced, but there was place
for only one of them. And the eleven apostles, not
knowing how to make a choice between these two good
and faithful and efficient and qualified brethren, bowed
their hearts in the prayer, remarkable for its brevity and
directness and simplicity, ''Thou, Lord, who knowest
the hearts of all men, show of these two the one whom
thou hast chosen, to take the place in this ministry and
apostleship from which Judas fell away, that he might
go to his own place.'' Then it is written of them by
Luke, ''And they gave lots for them; and the lot fell
upon Matthias; and he was numbered with the eleven
apostles.'' This shows that the apostles believed in the
special providence of God and the risen Lord, and let
the Master, of whom witness was to be borne, select
Matthias, instead of Joseph Barsabbas Justus, to be one
of His original witnesses forever. A long time after
Pentecost, when the Lord Jesus Christ created His
church in the twelve original apostles by the mysterious
power of the Holy Spirit, Luke wrote of Matthias, ''And

he was numbered with the eleven apostles.'' It was necessary that the number of the apostles should be twelve,
because, during the Christian era, which began on Pentecost and shall close when Jesus Christ has conquered
all enemies and will turn all things back to God, the
apostles, according to type, are to sit on twelve thrones,
judging the twelve tribes of Israel (Matt. 19: 23-30).
During the forty days when the Lord appeared repeatedly to the apostles subsequent to His resurrection, He
may have talked to them about the choice of the succes-
sor of Judas; and they saw to it that this election was
made before Pentecost when the church was to be created
in them.  Here is an interesting parallel: Jacob had
twelve sons.  But he adopted the two sons of Joseph,
and that made thirteen sons of Jacob.  There is no tribe
named for Joseph, but out of Joseph really came two
tribes.  And so there were ''twelve tribes of Israel,''
and yet there were thirteen tribes; and there are twelve
apostles of the Lord Jesus Christ, and yet there are
thirteen apostles—the original group, and Paul whose
mission was particularly to the Gentiles.

## II

## THE POWER OF PENTECOST

### (Acts 2)

*Pentecost produced the new creation; it brought
forth the greatest beginning in all the history of time.*
On Pentecost, nothing was simply born, nothing was
merely established, nothing was organized; on that day
something flashed into existence, something sprang into
being (Rom. 4:17) by the fiat of the great God and of the
risen Lord. We are not saying that Pentecost is in nowise
related to its antecedents or precedents; we are saying
that Pentecost sounded and shone and glowed and
gleamed and signaled directly from the Deity, as the acme
of the divine plan of salvation, by the creative power of
the Holy Spirit. When nothing exists, only God can originate it by creation. To form the human race out of
nothing, God had to *make* the first man and the first
woman; to bring the church of Christ into being, the
Lord *created* the first Christians on Pentecost by the supernatural power of the Holy Spirit. It is no wonder that
"the multitude were confounded" and "were all amazed
and marveled," and "were perplexed"! Nothing like this
occasion ever happened before or again since God rolled
the world into space. To speak of Pentecost as the
"birthday" of the church is a misnomer, improper; nothing can be born without antecedents or precedents in
kind. Adam and Eve had no antecedents in kind; neither had the church. The church is the new creation.
The human race was *originated* in the first pair; the

church was *created* in the first Christians, the original
twelve apostles. To say that the church was "born" on
Pentecost is to use an inadequate figure; to say that the
church was *created* is to give a proper description of its
origin. But the Lord creates only when it is necessary.
Creation in process is not identical with birth. There
is no indication that the Twelve ever had any baptism
in water but John's. The first father and the first
mother had to be *created;* all other human beings are
*born*. The church was *created* in the apostles as the
first Christians; all other Christians come into being by
*the new birth. Creation* is essentially miraculous; *birth,
old or new,* is always by the operation of law.

## Pentecost Was Powerful (vs. 1-13)

*Pentecost was powerful, because it "came from
heaven"* (1-4). Pentecost was both special and sensa-
tional and spectacular and spiritual. The Holy Spirit
might have filled the apostles without sounding like wind
or looking like fire, and He might have re-created them
on an ordinary occasion; but this emotional spectacle
assembled thousands in Jerusalem from all parts of the
world on the special day of Pentecost, to hear the gospel
in fullness the first time it was ever preached. Here
heaven compelled attention. Pentecost "came from
heaven" both in its outward manifestation and in its
inward significance. Inwardly, it made new creatures
of the apostles; outwardly, it drew the multitude to hear
what they had to say. The church now should use
every legitimate means to force the world to consider
the Lord Jesus Christ as the only Saviour. Jesus said,
"For the sons of this world are for their own generation
wiser than the sons of the light" (Luke 16:8). Every
enterprise among men is exploited. The pre-eminent

purpose of the church is to evangelize and save the lost; this is the first love of the church (Rev. 2:4). The church must work and advertise and pray and read the Word of the Lord and move heaven and earth to get the attention of alien sinners to Jesus Christ, that He may save them. That is why the church came into existence on Pentecost. When God created Adam and Eve, He gave them a passion for one another, and commanded them to multiply and replenish the earth. When Jesus Christ created His church in the apostles as the first Christians, He gave them His own passion for the lost; and they brought 3,000 sinners to Him in one day.

*Another striking element in the force, in the effectiveness, of Pentecost was its multitudinous assembly* (5-13). The death of Jesus was witnessed by the world at the great Passover feast; Pentecost likewise made a multitude accessible when His church was created. Nothing like this Pentecost was ever before or since exhibited to public view. And yet Pentecost was climactic; it roots itself in the past. The Patriarchal and the Jewish dispensations—one was enlargement of the other—were preliminary to the Christian era in which the Lord made His invitation to every lost soul. When Jehovah God sentenced the serpent through whose subtlety the race was lost, He set out for Pentecost; when He called Abraham and Moses, He was developing His plan to wrench His creatures out of the clutches of the devil; when He sent John the Baptist and Jesus of Nazareth, "the kingdom of heaven was at hand"; "and when the day of Pentecost was now come," the clock of time and eternity struck, and the Holy Spirit came and created the church in the apostles. And the newly created church hit the enemy with all the power of God and man. The multitude that "came together" on Pentecost was composed of Jews and proselytes, the latter being Gentiles converted to the Jews' religion. Luke enumerates nearly a score of countries outside of Jerusalem from which these hearers had come; indeed, they were "devout men" from "every nation under heaven"; they were strangers in Jerusalem, and asked if the apostles whom they heard speaking were not all "Galileans." The apostles were "Galileans," and they did not know the various tongues spoken and understood by the many members of their audience; but the Holy Spirit knew these languages, in which He really preached the gospel to this vast assembly through Peter and his associates. What has always seemed to me the greatest sermon I ever heard was preached by the incomparable Z. T. Sweeney at our great Jubilee Convention in Cincinnati in 1899, in the St. Paul M. E. Church, to a great audience. The minister of that congregation said, "There are three kinds of oratory: That of an ordinary speaker on an ordinary occasion, that of an ordinary speaker on an extraordinary occasion, and that of an extraordinary speaker on an extraordinary occasion; and I am sure we have heard the last today." Pentecost was the most extraordinary occasion in the history of the world; only the second coming of Jesus can surpass it. But the honor of the sermon on Pentecost rises above Peter and the Eleven with whom Peter stood up. The Holy Spirit was the preacher on Pentecost. And the Holy Spirit should always be the preacher and in the preacher, and He would be if the preacher would marry himself to the Bible and write the New Testament in essence on his heart and incarnate it in his life and "pray without ceasing" (1 Thess. 5:17), and crowd out false human ideas and "preach the word" (2 Tim. 4:1-8).

## The Sermon on Pentecost Was Epochal (vs. 14-36)

*The sermon on Pentecost was epochal, because it ushered in a new day and marked the greatest age in the history of the world* (14-21). Sermons are called good, fine, great, striking, powerful, wonderful, marvelous; all the adjectives in the dictionary could not do justice to the Pentecostal message. The Lord Jesus Christ created this new day and greatest of all ages, but He lived all His life in this world under the Jewish dispensation. He was born and lived and died a Jew. It was He who gave the law to Moses, under which He was born, which He obeyed and fulfilled and set aside at His death on the cross. The books that tell the story of the life of Jesus, therefore, belong in the Old Testament, under which He lived all the days of His life among men. He had to return to heaven to create and execute His New Testament, the very first book of which is Acts of Apostles. A testament is a covenant, an agreement between two or more parties. The Old Testament is an agreement between God and the Jews. The New Testament is an agreement between Christ and all who accept Him. The death of Jesus ended the Old Covenant; the coming of the Holy Spirit on the first Pentecost after His resurrection from the dead actually began the New Covenant or the New Testament. If Matthew and Mark and Luke and John were classified in the Old Testament or between the two Testaments, and Acts of Apostles stood at the very beginning of the New Testament, that would help Bible readers to see more clearly that Pentecost is the very beginning day of the Christian dispensation, which the sermon on Pentecost ushered in and set the pattern of the Lord forever. Peter answered the charge that he and his

associates were filled with new wine, and explained
to his hearers the phenomenon of Pentecost, which none
of them understood, by a quotation from the Old Testament—from Joel. This prophecy is descriptive both of
Pentecost and the age it began. The outstanding, and
the overshadowing, characteristic of this era is the Holy
Spirit Himself, which the Lord is to "pour forth upon
all flesh." The Holy Spirit created the church of Christ
in the apostles, and He dwells in the heart and life of
every newborn creature, who is "added to the church."
Indeed, the Christian dispensation is the dispensation
of the Holy Spirit; the New Testament is the inspiration,
the creation, the message, the power, the instrument, of
the Holy Spirit, to save sinners, to grow Christians.
Here is the simplest, profoundest, most inclusive, most
wonderful, of all benedictions: "The grace of the Lord
Jesus Christ, and the love of God and the *communion*
of the Holy Spirit, be with you all" (2 Cor. 13:14).
Now we receive the "grace of the Lord Jesus Christ"
and "the love of God" by the "communion of the Holy
Spirit" through the Word that He inspired.

*The sermon on Pentecost was Christocentric* (22-36).
Jesus became known as the Christ during His ministry
in the flesh, but He forbade that He should be preached
as the Christ till after He was raised from the dead.
But since the day of Pentecost, no sermon can be real
and genuine and profitable and powerful that does not
begin and run its course and have its being and end
in the Lord Jesus Christ as the Son of the living God
and the only Saviour of sinners. If this be dogmatism,
make the most of it! Today the world is perishing for
the lack of this clear, positive, dogmatic preaching!
Hear what Peter preached, or rather what the Holy
Spirit preached through Peter, on Pentecost: "Ye men

of Israel, hear these words: Jesus of Nazareth, a man approved of God unto you by mighty works and wonders and signs which God did by him in the midst of you, even as ye yourselves know; him, being delivered up by the determinate counsel and foreknowledge of God, ye by the hands of lawless men did crucify and slay: whom God raised up, having loosed the pangs of death: because it was not possible that he should be holden of it.'' When at last the Lord released His message on Pentecost, He had something to make known, something for His church to tell and proclaim and preach to the lost race of man forever! No wonder Paul pronounced a curse upon any messenger, angel or man, that preaches anything else! God approved Jesus of Nazareth as His Man, as His Son, as the Christ. Jesus was not merely overcome by His enemies. He had the power to protect Himself, but He was ''delivered up by the determinate counsel and foreknowledge of God''; ''whom God raised up, having loosed the pangs of death: because it was not possible that he should be holden of it.'' The glorious light of noonday can not be imprisoned in the cellar of midnight darkness! The thousands to whom Peter preached on Pentecost believed the Old Testament, out of which the apostle quoted from David the prophecy of the resurrection of the Christ, exclaiming, ''This Jesus did God raise up, whereof we all are witnesses. Being therefore by the right hand of God exalted, and having received of the Father the promise of the Holy Spirit, he hath poured forth this, which ye see and hear. Let all the house of Israel therefore know assuredly, that God hath made him both Lord and Christ, this Jesus whom ye crucified.'' Once a good friend chided me, ''Brother Adcock, you do not preach the Holy Spirit enough.'' Immediately I replied, ''The Holy Spirit

does not preach Himself; He glorifies the Lord Jesus
Christ.'' There is no commission to preach God in the
abstract, the great, eternal, immortal, invisible God,
because the finite mind, unaided, can not lay hold on
God, or comprehend such preaching; neither is there any
divine command to proclaim a mere spirit, even the Holy
Spirit, because that would open a door through which
vagaries could pass. But heaven charges the church to
declare Jesus to the world. Men can believe in Him.
He was a man, and now He is both Lord and Christ on
the celestial throne forever. He reveals the great God
to us, and when we obey Him He gives us the Holy
Spirit to live in us. It is utterly impossible for anybody
to have any adequate faith in God, or the Holy Spirit
as his indwelling Guest, who rejects the revelation of
the Lord Jesus Christ.

## Pentecost Was Phenomenal (vs. 37-47)

*Pentecost was phenomenal, because it discovered and
declared the law of pardon and, in one day, grounded
the arms of three thousand rebels against the divine
government* (37-42). Mounting up in the enthusiasm
and inspiration of the Holy Spirit, Peter was equal to
the magnitude of Pentecost. And when the vast audience that stretched out before Peter and the other apostles heard him denounce the crucifixion and proclaim
Jesus Lord and Christ, ''they were pricked in their
heart,'' and asked what they should do to be saved.
''And Peter said unto them, Repent ye, and be baptized
every one of you in the name of Jesus Christ unto the
remission of your sins; and ye shall receive the gift of
the Holy Spirit.'' Pentecost was the first time this
answer was ever given. Now it is the only answer, and
must be preached forever; ''for to you is the promise,

and to your children, and to all that are afar off, even as many as the Lord our God shall call unto him,'' added Peter. The Pentecostans saw the blood of Jesus on their hands, and they could not resist Peter's testimony and exhortation; and about three thousand ''were baptized'' and ''added unto them in that day''; that is, unto the apostles who were created Christians and constituted the church originally. The apostles had to be created Christians, because they had no antecedents, nobody to father them, to beget them ''through the gospel,'' as Paul begat the Corinthians (1 Cor. 4:14, 15) or as Peter and the other apostles begat the three thousand on Pentecost, and as every other ''new creature'' is begotten by whoever preaches the gospel to him. These twelve men that were in charge on Pentecost were re-created on that day to be the first Christians and the first preachers and the first apostles and the first fathers of all the ''new creatures'' to whom the gospel shall be preached forever! Evidently, Peter told the Pentecostans how to keep themselves saved, for Luke wrote of them, ''And they continued stedfastly in the apostles' teaching and fellowship, in the breaking of bread and the prayers.'' Pentecost witnessed the first execution of the Great Commission, or of the law of pardon, and the beginning of the church of the Lord Jesus Christ. Again and again we shall meet the law of pardon in Acts, which, in its simplest, briefest form, is this: *What to Do to Be Saved*: (1) Hear the Gospel; (2) Believe on Christ; (3) Repent of Sin; (4) Confess Christ Before Men; (5) Be Baptized; (6) Live Faithful Till Death. Peter did not instruct the Pentecostans to believe on Christ, because they did believe on Him; and out of this faith came their repentance and baptism.

*And so out of Pentecost came the church of the Lord
Jesus Christ, sacred and supernatural in its conception,
miraculous in its creation, marvelous in its growth,
unusual, prodigious in its life* (43-47).   What Luke
describes here is neither a commune nor a socialistic
club, but a church, the very first church, the great model
church of the Lord Jesus Christ, in Jerusalem: "And
fear came upon every soul: and many wonders and signs
were done through the apostles.   And all that believed
were together, and had all things common; and they
sold their possessions and goods, and parted them to all,
according as any man had need. And day by day, continuing stedfastly with one accord in the temple, and breaking bread at home, they took their food with gladness and
singleness of heart, praising God, and having favor with
all the people.   And the Lord added to them day by day
those that were saved."   This is the unity for which
Jesus prayed, practical unity, because it was doctrinal
unity; if the church had this unity all over the earth
today, it would speedily take the world for Christ.   Why,
this church made conquest of its community and recruit-
ed its membership every day.   New people did not "join
the church" in Jerusalem, they were "added" to the
church by the Lord Himself.   Children do not "join"
the family, they are born into the family; nobody "joins
the church," he is born into the church as a "new creature."   "Join the church" is an un-Scriptural phrase
that should never be used.   I read a tract, "Why Every
Christian Should Join the Church," based on a fundamental misconception.   There are not two processes revealed in Acts of Apostles—one leading to salvation and
the other to church membership.   There is only the answer to the question what to do to be saved, which is
given under all circumstances; and it is always the same

as the law of pardon, summarized in the preceding paragraph. We are to receive one another in fellowship on the same conditions on which Christ forgives us. What saves one also makes him a member of the church at the same time, whether his name is on a roll or not. Of course, every Christian should be identified with a local congregation or beget one.

## III

## THE HIGHEST NAME

### (Acts 3)

*A name is the description or picture of the original.*
Sometimes it is speciously remarked that there is nothing in a name. Why, without names there would be
utter confusion in the world; but there has been order
from the beginning. God created things; man originated
their names (Gen. 2:19). The distinction or difference
in beings or creatures attaches to their names; like their
originals, names may be good or bad, strong or weak,
wise or foolish, attractive or repellent, elevating or de-
grading, living or dead, high or low. There is one name
that is absolutely good, with the strength and wisdom and
attraction and elevation and life of the great God
Himself; yea, that name is transcendent of any mere
description, any bare picture or any simple appellation.
Through the dim vistas of time, Isaiah saw the Original
of this name, and called Him "Wonderful, Counsellor,
Mighty God, Everlasting Father, Prince of Peace" (Isa.
9:6). Paul saw Him enthroned, and pronounced His
name supreme on earth and in heaven (Eph. 1:15-23).
Now, let us revolve Acts 3 around this name, that this
chapter may yield us its glory of teaching and soundness
of doctrine and thrill of inspiration.

### Jesus Is the Highest Name (vs. 1-10)

*Jesus is the highest name, because it unlocks the
gates of heaven* (1). "Peter and John were going up

into the temple at the hour of prayer.'' It is always wonderful and blessed to pray. The prayerless are superficial and worldly and godless. Prayer breaks up the depths of the heart and cultivates the vision of the spirit and leads the soul into refreshing experiences. The high name of Jesus unlocked the gates for Him, and became His passport back into heaven as ''the King of glory'' (Ps. 24: 7-10). Prayer has taken on new meaning during our era, the Christian dispensation. Jesus has underwritten prayer by the power and glory of His own name (John 16: 24). He came out of the loins of Abraham, and His name is intercessory (Genesis 18). He was after the order of Melchizedek, and His name is mediatorial. Prayer is not limited to words; it may come out of the heart, as sincere desire and worship without words. Prayer takes tribute of action and life. The big thing in prayer is the recognition of divine strength and the confession of human weakness. The impulse to pray must not be limited to craven fear, but must abound in intercession and supplication and thanksgiving; that will relieve us of anxiety, bless others all around us and manifest our concern for the sons of men everywhere. Indeed, prayer should be the very atmosphere of the life of every Christian and of the whole church of Christ; without this the lost world can never be saved. (Jesus, His name, means Saviour; Christ, His title, means ''The Anointed, the Messiah.'')

*The supreme exaltation of the name of Jesus Christ was magnified and glorified by the startling, miraculous healing at the Beautiful Gate of the temple of the man that was born lame* (2-10). The relatives or friends of this unfortunate, innocent sufferer carried him and laid him every day ''at the door of the temple which is called Beautiful, to ask alms of them that entered into the temple; who seeing Peter and John about to go into the temple, asked to receive an alms. And Peter, fastening his eyes upon him, with John, said, Look on us. And he gave heed unto them, expecting to receive something from them. But Peter said, Silver and gold have I none; but what I have, that give I thee. *In the name of Jesus Christ of Nazareth, walk.* And he took him by the right hand, and raised him up: and immediately his feet and his ankle-bones received strength. And leaping up, he stood, and began to walk; and he entered with them into the temple, walking, and leaping, and praising God. And all the people saw him walking and praising God: and they took knowledge of him, that it was he that sat for alms at the Beautiful Gate of the temple; and they were filled with wonder and amazement at that which had happened unto him.'' What a classic writer was Luke! We have quoted this perfect passage as the simplest, best way to get before us all the essential details of this marvelous miracle. The apostles' healing here of the man born lame suggests the Lord's giving eyes to the man born blind, to which the entire ninth chapter of John is devoted. And Jesus, when His disciples asked Him why this man was born blind, because he sinned or his parents sinned, said, ''Neither did this man sin, nor his parents: but that the works of God should be made manifest in him.'' The same God that sent Jesus into the world also sent this man into the world without eyes, that Jesus might prove Himself the Son of God by giving eyes to a man that never had had eyes. And perhaps the Lord sent this beggar into the world, who had been lame all his life, that Peter and John might enable him to walk, and thus prove themselves His apostles forever. In any case, that is precisely what this wonderful healing did. Verily, the

only way to save the world now is to preach the over-
whelming testimony of the original witnesses of Jesus
that He is the Christ, the Son of the living God and the
Saviour of all that accept Him! Jesus healed the lame
man, because He yearns to save the sinner from eternal
death. This is only one of the "many wonders and
signs done through the apostles" (Acts 2:43). The
miraculous healing of the body, wonderful in itself, is
still more remarkable as a sign pointing to the exalted
name of Jesus Christ and salvation of the lost soul,
through His name.

### But Height Demands Depth (vs. 11-26)

*Humility gives depth and leads to height* (11-18).
As they seemed to him the source of his great blessing,
the healed lame man, out of sheer gratitude, "held Peter
and John"; and "all the people ran together unto them
in the porch that is called Solomon's, greatly wondering." Peter was quick humbly to disclaim for himself
and John any power or godliness to make the lame man
walk; and he also hastened, in the explanation of this
miracle of healing, which had drawn together a great
audience, to preach the gospel: "The God of Abraham,
and of Isaac, and of Jacob, the God of our fathers, hath
glorified his Servant Jesus; whom ye delivered up, and
denied before the face of Pilate, when he had determined to release him. But ye denied the Holy and
Righteous One, and asked for a murderer to be granted
unto you, and killed the Prince of life; whom God
raised from the dead; whereof we are witnesses. *And
by faith in his name hath his name made this man
strong,* whom ye behold and know: yea, the faith which
is through him hath given him this perfect soundness
in the presence of you all. And now, brethren, I know

that in ignorance ye did it, as did also your rulers. But the things which God foreshadowed by the mouth of all the prophets, that his Christ should suffer, he thus fulfilled.'' Faith was both ''common'' and uncommon. This lame man was healed by the miraculous faith of the apostles; no one else had supernatural faith to whom it was not imparted by the laying on of the apostles' hands. The apostles and any others that had this kind of faith always worked signs and wonders in the name of the Lord Jesus Christ and by the power He delegated to them; Jesus did whatever He would by the strength that inhered in Him as the Son of God, and His authority as the Christ is dominant forever! The Scriptures, as Peter does here, often place the will or sovereignty of God and the will or choice of man side by side. God's prophecy ''that his Christ should suffer'' was fulfilled by the ignorant, wicked will of His enemies, because He foresaw what they would do. The divine will prevails ultimately. The foundation of a skyscraper must penetrate the earth deeply and rest upon solid rock; Jesus Himself is the rock upon which He built His church in the depths of this world! Emptying Himself of His eternal glory, He sounded the depths by His incarnation. His own favorite appellation of Himself was ''the Son of man.'' With power to save Himself or return to heaven by translation, ''he humbled himself, becoming obedient even unto death, yea the death of the cross. Wherefore also God highly exalted him, and gave unto him the name which is above every name; that in the name of Jesus every knee should bow, of things in heaven and things on earth and things under the earth, and that every tongue should confess that Jesus Christ is Lord, to the glory of God the Father'' (Phil. 2:5-11). Jesus was *lowly,* but not *low;* He measured all the

depths but those of sin and hell, left for the devil and
his angels and dupes, totally depraved, incorrigibly
wicked.

*But the love of the Lord Jesus Christ has both
"breadth and length and height and depth"* (19-26).
And so Peter, the spokesman of the Lord on this occasion, came straight to the point, and commanded the
enemies and murderers of Jesus what to do to be saved:
"Repent ye therefore, and turn again, that your sins
may be blotted out, that so there may come seasons of
refreshing from the presence of the Lord." Now this
mandate is substantially the same as Peter's answer on
Pentecost (Acts 2:38). In both instances, *faith* and
*confession* are taken for granted, but *repentance* and
*baptism* were both *specified* on Pentecost. Here, however, while *repentance* is *specified, baptism* is *indicated
by the generic word "turn."* When one repents, he
turns to obey the Lord; and the word "turn" points to
the first act of obedience, which is baptism. Of course,
"unto the remission of your sins" means "that your sins
may be blotted out"; and the clauses, "and ye shall
receive the gift of the Holy Spirit," and "that so there
may come seasons of refreshing from the presence of
the Lord," interpret one another. Acts of Apostles
makes plain and permanent the law of pardon, or the
terms of salvation, without any stereotyped statement of
these terms. In Acts, as we shall see, the preacher
always began with the sinner where he found him, and
led him on through the process of his deliverance from
sin. Every time Peter or anybody else preached, according to the Book of Acts, he told his hearers what
to do to be saved. And the sermon that does not do
that falls far short of the divine purpose in preaching.
The active phrase "turn again" in the American Revised

Version is a big improvement over the passive phrase
"be converted" in King James' Version. The sinner
is active rather than passive, in his conversion. It requires action to believe and repent and confess; and
while the body is passive in baptism, yet the heart,
through the will, is active in deciding to "be baptized."
Ever since Dr. McGarvey forbade us preacher boys to
use the old version in the College of the Bible, Lexington,
Ky., I have had the new version. I would not accept the
old version, printed on gold, as a gift, if I had to use
it. I want my Bible in up-to-date English. Evidently,
Peter here refers to the second coming of the Lord Jesus
Christ, which prophecy verifies but does not time. Jesus
said the knowledge "of that day or that hour" is locked
up in the heart of "the Father" (Mark 13:32). The
purpose of predictive prophecy is not to enable any man
to work with a detailed scheme of the future, but rather
to convince all men that the Bible is the Word of God
(John 14:29). Jesus is the prophet "like unto" Moses,
of whom all the prophets prophesied, and "the seed of
Abraham." He came to the Jews, but, as we shall see,
He came also to the Gentiles and to the whole wide world.
Verily, His love has all dimensions—it is broad and long
and high and deep.

# IV

## THE FIGHT OF FAITH

### (Acts 4)

*Marvel of marvels, the "Prince of Peace" is the world's weightiest warrior* (Matt. 10:34-39). What did Jesus mean when He said: "Think not that I came to send peace on the earth: I came not to send peace, but a sword. For I came to set a man at variance against his father, and the daughter against her mother, and the daughter-in-law against her mother-in-law: and a man's foes shall be they of his own household"? What He meant immediately follows: "He that loveth father or mother more than me is not worthy of me; and he that loveth son or daughter more than me is not worthy of me. And he that doth not take his cross and follow after me, is not worthy of me. He that findeth his life shall lose it; and he that loseth his life for my sake shall find it." Every text must be understood in the light of its context. Scripture explains Scripture; the Bible is its own best interpreter or expositor or commentary. The war that Jesus initiated is a wonderful war! It means downright physical passivity and strange spiritual activity. The sword Jesus came to send, or cast, is "the sword of the Spirit, which is the word of God." He did not come to disrupt the family, but the love of Him must have priority over every other attachment, because He is our Leader and Saviour. The devil precipitated war in heaven, and he and his angels were cast down to the earth (Rev. 12:7-9). Here he began his time-

long struggle to destroy man by deceiving Eve, the
mother of the human race; and Jehovah God declared
war between the seed of the woman and the devil, saying to the old serpent, "He shall bruise thy head, and
thou shalt bruise his heel" (Gen. 3: 15). Paul lays bare
the character of this Christian conflict, which "is not
against flesh and blood, but against the principalities,
against the powers, against the world-rulers of this darkness, against the spiritual hosts of wickedness in the
heavenly places" (Eph. 6: 10-20). And the Christian
soldier meets the enemy without any offensive weapon
at all; he has absolutely nothing in his hand or about
his person with which he could slay physically: he wraps
"the whole armor of God" about himself, he girds his
"loins with truth," he wears "righteousness" as a
"breastplate," and "the preparation of the gospel of
peace" for shoes; "faith" is his "shield"; "the Word
of God" is his "sword," and "prayer" is his passion.
Jesus had power to save Himself and slay His enemies,
but He refused to use it. He fought and won passively
—by submitting to persecution and false testimony and
mockery and ignominy and shame and crucifixion and
death!

### Faith Fights and Wins (vs. 1-37)

*Faith fought through the apostles, because it had
powerful enemies* (1-4). By this time, the apostles
may have begun to feel that the triumph of the truth
they preached about the Lord Jesus Christ was so complete that His old enemies were silenced; but the storm
of interference and persecution broke suddenly upon
them. While Peter was still preaching, he and John
were arrested by "the priests and the captain of the
temple and the Sadducees," because "they taught the

people, and proclaimed in Jesus the resurrection from
the dead.'' Peter and John were imprisoned all night.
''But many of them that heard the word believed; and
the number of the men came to be about five thousand.''
The Sadducees, rather than the Pharisees, led in this
persecution. In this world faith is always on trial and
fights for its life; unbelief is the sin that besets all men
(Heb. 12:1, 2). Faith fought in Peter and John,
because it was active; yea, the faith of the apostles, the
created Christians, the first Christians, had already begotten more than five thousand others through the gospel
they preached. ''The number of the men came to be
about five thousand.'' It is probable that many of the
three thousand that responded on Pentecost had returned
to their distant homes. Peter and John had ''faith and
a good conscience; which some, having thrust from them,
made shipwreck concerning the faith'' (1 Tim. 1:19).
Real, live faith always fights when it is attacked; nomi-
nal, inert, dead faith is in danger of destruction by
persecution or worldliness or indifference or neglect.
Faith must be fed and nurtured: faith eats the Word
of God. Faith exercises itself and grows in the work
of the Lord. Led by its Lord, faith has discovered that
the real enemy is the devil; and faith sees the Bible as
the inspired Word of God, and neglect as worse than
transgression or disobedience (Heb. 2:1-4). And whoever casts reflection on the sacred Scriptures, as the
revelation of God and of the Lord Jesus Christ, whether
he is conscious of it or not, is the servant of the devil.
The apostles did not fight ''the priests'' and the captain
of the temple and the Sadducees,'' who put them under
arrest; they fought the devil, who was back of these
men and in them. Faith never fights men; faith fights
to save men from sin and the great original sinner, Satan.

*Faith fights spiritually and intelligently* (5-12).
Here we see the attack on Peter and John assuming
large proportions: it drew together the "rulers and
elders and scribes," who constituted the main body of
the supreme court of the Jews, called the Sanhedrin;
and certain distinguished persons were present—"Annas
the high priest" and "Caiaphas," his son-in-law, "and
John and Alexander, and as many as were of the kindred
of the high priest." And Peter and John, who had
spent a quiet night as prisoners, were unabashed when
they were led into the presence of this august assembly.
They had been seized summarily without any charge;
and the indefinite question asked them, "By what power,
or in what name, have ye done this?" compromises
their judges in the weakness and irregularity and ille-
gality of their position. However, the Holy Spirit was
the apostles' marshal in this battle; and they knew how
to proceed and what to say. "Then Peter, filled with
the Holy Spirit, said unto them, Ye rulers of the people,
and elders, if we this day are examined concerning a
good deed done to an impotent man, by what means
this man is made whole; be it known unto you all, and
to all the people of Israel, that in the name of Jesus
Christ of Nazareth, whom ye crucified, whom God raised
from the dead, even in him doth this man stand here
before you whole." This answer is complete; but the
divine Captain, still in command of the battle, has more
to say, and hurls this at the enemy: "He [Jesus Christ
of Nazareth] is the stone which was set at naught of
you the builders, which was made the head of the corner.
And in none other is there salvation: for neither is there
any other name under heaven, that is given among men,
wherein we must be saved." Verily, the Holy Spirit
dominated Peter and John in this conflict, and He is

with and in every believer in the fight of faith. Faith always fights spiritually—with "the sword of the Spirit, which is the word of God." And the words of the apostles are always marked by the discernment of the Holy Spirit. The availability of the New Testament, which the Holy Spirit created through the apostles and their associates, makes faith the greatest intelligencer in the world. Faith surpasses science in understanding "that the worlds have been framed by the word of God, so that what is seen hath not been made out of things which appear" (Heb. 11:3). The humblest believer, reading the Word of God, praying, living faithful, in the world, knows more about the Creator and the Christ and creation than all the infidels on the face of the earth, however well schooled in human wisdom they may be.

### Faith Wins the Fight (vs. 13-37)

*Faith won the fight through the apostles Peter and John, with boldness and aggression* (13-22). Peter and John were absolutely fearless, and their boldness was evident to all that saw them. Since these apostles, according to the standard of the Sanhedrin, "were unlearned and ignorant men," the members of this court "marvelled"; "and they took knowledge of them, that they had been with Jesus." The healed impotent man had come into the council, and stood with Peter and John, his benefactors, against whom no charge or case could be made at all. But the members of this court, sending these apostles out of their presence, "conferred among themselves, saying, What shall we do to these men? for that indeed a notable miracle hath been wrought through them, is manifest to all that dwell in Jerusalem; and we can not deny it. But that it spread no further among the people, let us threaten them, that

they speak henceforth to no man in this name. And
they called them, and charged them not to speak at all
nor teach in the name of Jesus. But Peter and John
answered and said unto them, Whether it is right in the
sight of God to hearken unto you rather than unto God,
judge ye: for we can not but speak the things which we
saw and heard. And they, when they had further
threatened them, let them go, finding nothing how they
might punish them, because of the people; for all men
glorified God for that which was done. For the man was
more than forty years old, on whom this miracle of healing was wrought.'' The members of this Jewish council,
finding themselves in an untenable position in regard
to Peter and John, whom they had arrested illegally,
extricated themselves the best way they could. If their
hearts had not been hardened and poisoned by the devil,
they would have been convinced and would have become
Christians themselves; but, as it was, only their fear
of the people saved Peter and John from punishment.
We shudder when we try to imagine what would have
been the result to the world if the apostles had been
afraid of these wicked judges, and had ceased ''to speak
at all nor teach in the name of Jesus.'' Every preacher
of the gospel should be bold and aggressive; the sacred
desk is no place for the time-server or the man-pleaser.
The church must not wait for sinners to come to Christ;
it must go after them in His power and passion. Evan-
gelism is more direct and more dynamic in saving the
lost than institutionalism.

*In winning the fight, faith joins its brethren, with
whom it fuses itself in prayer for further advance*
(23-31). As soon as this happy release came to them,
Peter and John reported ''to their own company all
that the chief priests and the elders had said unto them.''

This information blended all their hearts in the prayer,
intense, fervent, powerful: "O Lord, thou that didst
make the heaven and the earth and the sea, and all that
in them is: who by the Holy Spirit, by the mouth of our
father David thy servant, didst say,

"Why did the Gentiles rage,
　And the peoples imagine vain things?
　The kings of the earth set themselves in array,
　And the rulers were gathered together,
Against the Lord, and against his Anointed:

for of a truth in this city against thy holy servant
Jesus, whom thou didst anoint, both Herod and Pontius
Pilate, with the Gentiles and the peoples of Israel, were
gathered together, to do whatsoever thy hand and thy
counsel foreordained to come to pass. And now, Lord,
look upon their threatenings: and grant unto thy servants to speak thy word with all boldness, while thou
stretchest forth thy hand to heal; and that signs and
wonders may be done through the name of thy holy
servant Jesus. And when they had prayed, the place
was shaken wherein they were gathered together; and
they were all filled with the Holy Spirit, and they
spake the word of God with boldness." By shaking the
building in which the apostles were assembled, the Lord
immediately gave them a sign, a new sign, of His power
and presence with them in the Holy Spirit. The apostles
had no hatred toward their enemies, neither did they
presume to advise the Lord as to what should be done
to their persecutors; they simply prayed, "And now,
Lord, look upon their threatenings." Let there be no
question about the power, the efficacy, of prayer in saving souls, which the apostles demonstrated on a large
scale, and which every true evangelist knows well in his

own experience. Faith always wins the fight to save
the lost when the church preaches the gospel passion-
ately and prays on its knees with tears in travail of
soul.

*Faith wins the fight by the unity of the church*
(32-37). "And the multitude of them that believed were
of one heart and one soul: and not one of them said
that aught of the things which he possessed was his own;
but they had all things common. And with great power
gave the apostles their witness of the resurrection of the
Lord Jesus: and great grace was upon them all. For
neither was there among them any that lacked: for as
many as were possessors of lands or houses sold them,
and brought the prices of the things that were sold,
and laid them at the apostles' feet: and distribution was
made unto each, according as any one had need. And
Joseph, who by the apostles was surnamed Barnabas
(which is, being interpreted, son of exhortation), a
Levite, a man of Cyprus by race, having a field, sold it,
and brought the money and laid it at the apostles' feet."
This wonderful unity of the very first church in the
city of Jerusalem came from within and not from without; it can not be at all described by the modern terms
of socialism or communism. It was not the result of
theorizing; it happened because all the members of
this very first congregation of believers in the world
were led directly and immediately by the Holy Spirit
through the inspired teaching and preaching of the
apostles; and, consequent upon their obedience of the
same gospel, the Lord added them all to His church,
and gave them all the same Holy Spirit, not to enable
them to work miracles, as the apostles did, but to make
it possible for them to have "seasons of refreshing from
the presence of the Lord." The only way for any group

of human beings to be "of one heart and one soul" is for them all to have the same spirit; of course, their bodies and temperaments and the environment out of which each one came are inevitably different; but if they all have the same spirit, the Holy Spirit, they face the Lord and one another and the world in the fundamental spiritual unity for which Jesus prayed. They were not selfish; nobody can care only or chiefly for himself and have the Holy Spirit in his heart. Any Christian will sell his property, if necessary, before he will see his brother suffer. In the Jerusalem church, some had more than they needed, and others did not have enough to live; the former were the givers, the latter were the receivers. Out of the money "laid at the apostles' feet," "distribution was made to each, according as any one had need." And this unity of the church increased the force of the apostles' "witness of the resurrection of the Lord Jesus," and likewise augmented the power of the church, as it always does every-where and every-when, in its appeal to the lost of its own community. But early in its history, the devil crept into the church, destroying its unity with paralysis and strife and wickedness, and turned it into an instrument for his own use. And the church will never be able to save the world till it recovers the unity of the very first congregation in Jerusalem; the unity for which the Lord Jesus Christ prayed. Now we have classified what Luke wrote of Barnabas here as an illustration of the benevolence and unity of the original church in Jerusalem, as a part of this paragraph. That Barnabas was a great exhorter is indicated by the Hebraism, "son of exhortation." This man had a rare gift, and we shall meet him again.

## V

# THE APARTNESS OF THE APOSTLES

## (Acts 5)

*Webster defines "apart" to mean "separately in regard to space or company," and "apartness" as signifying "the quality of standing apart."* Even an inanimate thing, like the tabernacle, was sanctified for a holy purpose; and its vessels could not be used as ordinary utensils. And the priest was consecrated, or set apart, to his sacred office, and could not pursue any ordinary vocation. The individual, the unit of life, is apart and lonely even in the midst of his fellows. Every person is born alone, and vanishes solitary in death. Jesus was the loneliest pilgrim that ever crossed the desert of time; He was homesick for heaven (John 14:28). He set Himself apart to save the lost, and no influence could swerve Him a hairsbreadth from His divine course. His church He likewise sanctified and consecrated to the achievement of His original purpose; and of His church, His most wonderful, most unique, most characteristic creation, He declared that the gates of hell shall not prevail against it. The church, like the apostles, in whom it was originally created, is "in the world," but not "of the world." It is fatal for any Christian to be "of the world." "Love not the world, neither the things that are in the world. If any man love the world, the love of the Father is not in him. For all that is in the world, the lust of the flesh and the lust of the eyes and the vainglory of life, is not of the

Father, but is of the world. And the world passeth
away, and the lust thereof: but he that doeth the will
of God abideth for ever'' (1 John 2: 15-17). Of course,
the church must do its utmost to save the world for
which Jesus died; and yet it must stand apart from the
world in sin and wickedness, or be separated from God.
The church saves from sin, itself from worldliness.

### The Apostles Stand Apart in the Church (vs. 1-16)

*The apostles stand apart in the church, because*
*through the Holy Spirit the Lord Jesus Christ made*
*them His deputies and gave them His own authority*
(1-6). This energy, absolutely amazing on Penteocost,
was constantly in evidence through all the ministry of
the apostles. Here this power was exercised in a new
direction with startling effect; indeed, it is impossible
to read Luke's narrative now without excitement: ''But
a certain man named Ananias, with Sapphira his wife,
sold a possession, and kept back part of the price, his
wife also being privy to it, and brought a certain part,
and laid it at the apostles' feet. But Peter said, Ananias,
why hath Satan filled thy heart to lie to the Holy Spirit,
and to keep back part of the price of the land? While
it remained, did it not remain thine own? and after it
was sold, was it not in thy power? How is it that thou
hast conceived this thing in thy heart? thou hast not
lied unto men, but unto God. And Ananias hearing
these words fell down and gave up the ghost: and great
fear came upon all that heard it. And the young men
arose and wrapped him round, and they carried him out
and buried him.'' The admirable virtue of benevolence
was counterfeited by Ananias and Sapphira; it was not
real charity that moved them to sell their land and give
to the poor, but an inordinate desire for the praise of

men. If their sin had been only covetousness, they probably would not have sold their "possession," or, having
sold it, they would have laid nothing "at the apostles'
feet." Their offense, in effect, was that they lied "to
the Holy Spirit"—not "unto men, but unto God." The
transgressor is spiritually blind; if he saw clearly in his
heart, he would not sin! Ananias and Sapphira really
attacked the apostles, or the Holy Spirit that inspired
them, and compelled immediate exposure and punishment. Death came in this case as suddenly as it had
come to Nadab and Abihu (Lev. 10:1-7), and neither
weeping nor funeral nor any other show of sorrow was
allowed to interfere with the divine program. The sinner is also deceived: "Satan filled" Ananias' "heart to
lie to the Holy Spirit, and to keep back part of the price
of the land." Peter put side by side the power of the
tempter and the choice of man, saying also to Ananias,
"How is it that thou hast conceived this thing in thy
heart?" Man has two potential masters: one, the Lord,
calls man to save him; the other, the devil, seeks man
to destroy him. But neither the Lord nor the devil can
take man till he makes his own choice. The only way
to escape the devil is to accept the Lord and serve Him
faithfully. Worse than telling a lie is living a lie. Of
course, the Holy Spirit revealed to Peter this attempt
at deception, but there is no indication that Peter had
anything to do with Ananias' death. Everybody present, including the apostles, must have been horrified at
the sin and punishment of Ananias and Sapphira. But
now all can see the righteousness of the judgment that
fell swiftly upon them. If their fraud had succeeded
even temporarily, its later discovery would have shaken
the faith of the church in the spiritual leadership of the
apostles.

*The apartness of the apostles in the church is emphasized by the repetition of this miracle of punishment* (7-11): "And it was about the space of three hours after, when his wife, not knowing what was done, came in. And Peter answered unto her, Tell me whether ye sold the land for so much. And she said, Yea, for so much. But Peter said unto her, How is it that ye have agreed together to try the Spirit of the Lord? behold, the feet of them that have buried thy husband are at the door, and they shall carry thee out. And she fell down immediately at his feet, and gave up the ghost: and the young men came in and found her dead, and they carried her out and buried her by her husband. And great fear came upon the whole church, and upon all that heard these things." Of course, Luke, constantly seeking brevity and aiming only at essentials, leaves out many details in his story. The apostles, led by Peter, were in charge; and they must have commanded "the young men" to bury Ananias, and enjoined everybody present not to let Sapphira know about her husband's death that her complicity in the crime might be fairly tested and exposed. And when "the young men came in" from burying Ananias, and found his wife dead, without waiting for an order "they carried her out and buried her by her husband." We have become so accustomed to deeds of mercy or acts of healing that we are distinctly shocked by these deaths as signs of divine power; but this test was forced upon the Holy Spirit, who dominated the apostles. Evidently, the Lord prefers expressions of His love and forgiveness to declarations of His abomination of sin as signs of His power. But Luke assures us in the last sentence of this paragraph that this divine discipline accomplished its purpose: "And great fear came upon the whole church, and upon all that heard these things." Now Ananias and Sapphira sought their own credit and praise by representing that their offering to the Lord was more than it really was; if all the church members that commit this sin suffered a sudden, spectacular fate, a lot of people might drop dead in the churches. There is nobody in the church on earth now who can read the hearts of its members as the apostles did, but the New Testament provides for its proper discipline: *the church must be Christian.* Gross immorality in the church should cause mournful excommunication to save the church, and severe punishment to save the sinner. The discipline of the church, a matter of mind and spirit, makes the church, under Christ, supreme in its own affairs; but the church leaves the unbelieving world in the hands of God for judgment. Indifferent, frivolous matters may be overlooked in the church, but not the serious, such as fornication, covetousness, idolatry, reviling, drunkenness or extortion.

*The apartness of the apostles in the church increased both their time and leisure to do their real work and the praise of them by their brethren and the fruitfulness of the church* (12-16): "And by the hands of the apostles were many signs and wonders wrought among the people: and they were all with one accord in Solomon's porch. But of the rest durst no man join himself to them: howbeit the people magnified them; and believers were the more added to the Lord, multitudes both of men and women: insomuch that they even carried out the sick into the streets, and laid them on beds and couches, that as Peter came by at the least his shadow might overshadow some one of them. And there also came together the multitude from the cities round about Jerusalem, bringing sick folk, and them that were vexed

with unclean spirits: and they were healed every one.''
The terrible punishment of Ananias and Sapphira, instead of slowing down the increase of the church, as the
disclosure of crime in modern times seems to do, vastly
accelerated the growth of the congregation in Jerusalem
and reached out into adjoining communities. At this
time, ''Solomon's porch'' of the temple served as a
church building. It taxed the strength of the Lord to
heal (Mark 5: 25-34), and it must have been a constant
strain on the apostles to work ''many signs and wonders
among the people.'' It was happy for them, therefore,
that, as their burden increased, ''of the rest durst no
man join himself to them.'' They needed time for
prayer and rest. If any of the brethren of these holy,
spiritual leaders held back from them because they were
conscious of their own imperfection, that was wholesome,
too. The Lord excels all other beings in dignity; He
indulges no cheap disclosure. The preacher must guard
constantly against commonness; and his brethren must
have the very highest respect for his office. In these
modern days, there should be more preaching and less
of other performances in the church. ''It was God's
good pleasure through the foolishness of the preaching
to save them that believe'' (1 Cor. 1: 21). The church
in Jerusalem had a constant revival; the apostles
preached every day. No congregation will get very far
without revivals. The apostles drew people into Jerusalem from all directions. And, like their Lord and ours,
they turned nobody away; they healed all the ''sick
folk and them that were vexed with unclean spirits.'' At
the same time they must have laid the foundation for
many other congregations outside of Jerusalem. Every
preacher should hold meetings as often as possible; a
series of evangelistic meetings will warm his own heart

and lead him into "seasons of refreshing from the presence of the Lord." And the evangelist who preaches
every night must have lots of time to rest and pray
and study and meditate; like the apostles, he must be
"apart in the church."

### The Apostles Stand Apart in the World (vs. 17-42)

*The apostles stand apart in the world because they
were miraculously delivered from prison, almost worshiped by the church and undaunted in their witness for
Jesus and God* (17-32): "But the high priest rose up,
and all they that were with him (which is the sect of the
Sadducees), and they were filled with jealousy, and laid
hands on the apostles, and put them in public ward.
But an angel of the Lord by night opened the prison
doors, and brought them out, and said, Go ye, and stand
and speak in the temple to the people all the words of
this Life. And when they heard this, they entered into
the temple about daybreak, and taught. But the high
priest came, and they that were with him, and called
the council together, and all the senate of the children
of Israel, and sent to the prison-house to have them
brought. But the officers that came found them not in
the prison; and they returned, and told, saying, The
prison-house we found shut in all safety, and the keep-
ers standing at the doors: but when we had opened, we
found no man within. Now when the captain of the
temple and the chief priests heard these words, they
were much perplexed concerning them whereunto this
would grow. And there came one and told them, Behold,
the men whom ye put in the prison are in the temple
standing and teaching the people. Then went the captain with the officers, and brought them, but without
violence; for they feared the people, lest they should

be stoned. And when they had brought them, they set
them before the council. And the high priest asked
them, saying, We strictly charged you not to teach in
this name: and behold, ye have filled Jerusalem with
your teaching, and intend to bring this man's blood
upon us. But Peter and the apostles answered and said,
We must obey God rather than men. The God of our
fathers raised up Jesus, whom ye slew, hanging him on
a tree. Him did God exalt with his right hand to be
a Prince and a Saviour, to give repentance to Israel,
and remission of sins. And we are witnesses of these
things; and so is the Holy Spirit, whom God hath given
to them that obey him.'' The Jewish authorities were
badly mistaken in thinking that the crucifixion of Jesus
had silenced Him; they still had Him on their hands in
His apostles, who had His Spirit and His power, and
of whom they became as insanely jealous as they had
been of Him. Yea, the issue was more complicated than
ever; and the only way to settle it was obedience to the
gospel, which the apostles proclaimed to the ''council''
at every opportunity. These dupes of the devil were beginning to exert themselves to the utmost; but every move
they made only tapped new resources of heaven, and
they were constantly checkmated and outwitted. They
put the apostles in prison, but ''an angel of the Lord''
let them out; and the apostles went right on with their
work. Imagine the surprise and chagrin of ''the high
priest'' and his associates, when, on the next day, their
officers reported to their august assembly that the prison
was locked and guarded but empty! This ''council''
was dominated by sinners, perverse and incorrigible!
Instead of wondering how the Lord would punish them,
when they heard the words of their officers that the
apostles had vanished out of prison, ''they were much

perplexed concerning them whereunto this would grow.''
But "the captain with the officers" soon learned that
the apostles were in the temple "teaching the people,"
and arrested them, "but without violence; for they
feared the people, lest they should be stoned.'' Though
morally and spiritually obtuse themselves, yet these
officers sensed their own peril in this tense situation;
they may have observed stones in the hands of some of
the people and heard threats to throw them if the
apostles were abused. Anybody with discernment could
see the impropriety and the absurdity of rearresting
men who had been delivered from prison by "an angel
of the Lord.'' But the apostles were brought again into
the presence of the "council.'' The case was more definite against them than it had been originally. The
"high priest" accused them of violating the charge
"not to teach in the" name of Jesus, and of intending
to bring His blood upon them. But Peter and his brethren were absolutely undaunted, and pleaded guilty to
the accusation, because they had to obey God rather
than men; they also reminded their judges of their sin
in slaying Jesus, and preached to them the gospel of
repentance and remission of sins—the same gospel that
must be preached to all sinners. The sinner is always
active in his own "repentance," but the Lord gives the
opportunity to repent; and "remission of sins" is always
consequent on repentance and obedience. But for the
original mercy of the Lord in His plan of salvation, the
sinner might repent forever without forgiveness. The
apostles are the first witnesses of the cardinal facts of the
gospel; namely, the death and burial and resurrection and
appearance and ascension and glorification of the Lord
Jesus Christ, and the primary teachers of the practical
application of the gospel: "AND SO IS THE HOLY

SPIRIT, WHOM GOD HATH GIVEN TO THEM THAT OBEY HIM." The "gift of the Holy Spirit" in Acts 2:38 is *the Holy Spirit given*. "He that believeth on the Son of God hath the witness in him" (1 John 5:10). All who obey the gospel have the Holy Spirit in their hearts and lives, not to inspire a new message, but to enable them to understand the old message and to bless them in the Christian life.

*The apartness of the apostles in the world is likewise indicated by both the providential advice of Gamaliel and their joy in persecution and their prodigious industry in the service of the Lord Jesus Christ* (33-42): "But they, when they heard this, were cut to the heart, and were minded to slay them. But there stood up one in the council, a Pharisee, named Gamaliel, a doctor of the law, had in honor of all the people, and commanded to put the men forth a little while. And he said unto them, Ye men of Israel, take heed to yourselves as touching these men, what ye are about to do. For before these days rose up Theudas, giving himself out to be somebody; to whom a number of men, about four hundred, joined themselves: who was slain; and all, as many as obeyed him, were dispersed, and came to nought. After this man rose up Judas of Galilee in the days of the enrollment, and drew away some of the people after him: he also perished; and all, as many as obeyed him, were scattered abroad. And now I say unto you, Refrain from these men, and let them alone: for if this counsel or this work be of men, it will be overthrown: but if it is of God, ye will not be able to overthrow them; lest haply ye be found even to be fighting against God. And to him they agreed: and when they had called the apostles unto them, they beat them and charged them not to speak in the name of Jesus, and let them go. They therefore departed from the presence of the council, rejoicing that they were counted worthy to suffer dishonor for the name. And every day, in the temple and at home, they ceased not to teach and to preach Jesus as the Christ.'' Every time the apostles were brought before the Sanhedrin, Peter, their spokesman, hurled at their judges that they had shed innocent blood in murdering Jesus, whom God had made Lord and Christ; and they would have to answer to Him as the supreme Judge of all men. This so enraged the Sadducees that Gamaliel, with his sage advice, narrowly prevented them from turning the court into a mob to kill the apostles, which would have incriminated every member of this pretentious tribunal. This occasion reveals Gamaliel a big man among his associates, whose philosophy was that all mere human movements would come to nought of themselves; but he betrayed doubt that the apostles represented the plan of men, and we wonder why he did not line up with them. Gamaliel saved the council from slaying the apostles, but not from beating them. That they found joy in these blows, as suffering in the name of Jesus, rivals the miracles they wrought and stands them apart in the world forever. And that, in the face of this persecution, and in spite of all threats, ''every day, in the temple and at home, they ceased not to teach and to preach Jesus as the Christ,'' reveals the passionate industry of the Lord in them, and also glorifies their apartness in the world.

# VI

## THE HIGHEST ORGANISM

### (Acts 6)

*The church of the Lord Jesus Christ, being the highest form or expression of life in this world, is an organism, rather than an organization.* There are four kingdoms, which rise in ascending scale, as follows: Mineral, vegetable, animal and spiritual. And no member of a lower kingdom can project itself into any kingdom above it; but any higher realm has power to seize any object below it, and lift it into its own domain. The plant or the vegetable lays hold upon the mineral, and transmutes this inorganic substance into its own organic kingdom; and likewise the animal, feeding upon the vegetable, raises it into the realm of animal life. Natural man belongs to the animal kingdom; and the only way he can possibly enter into the spiritual kingdom above him is to "be born anew, or from above, of water and the Spirit," because "that which is *born* of the flesh *is* flesh; and that which is *born* of the Spirit *is* spirit" (John 3: 1-6). An organism is always alive, but an organization may be dead. A statue or a picture is visibly featured, but it has no life. A corpse is an organization, but the flown spirit has left it a heap of ruins; it is blind of eye and deaf of ear and paralyzed of hand and foot and speechless of tongue and thoughtless of brain and heedless of heart. The Lord Jesus Christ is the Head of the church, which is His body in this world (Eph. 1: 22, 23). Every animate body was

66

either created or born an organism properly related to its environment; the church is no exception to this rule. Life is itself the great organizer; both plants and animals and spirits are endowed for their proper function by the great Creator, the Lord Himself. The husbandman casts the seed and cultivates the plant, which resents any effort at organization as meddlesomeness with its growth. All the mere animal needs is food and exercise and air and rest. Indeed, all organisms reject artificial organization. The original church was not organized, for the simple reason that it was an organism. The church was created an organism in the twelve original apostles of the Lord Jesus Christ on the first Pentecost after His resurrection from the dead. Since that wonderful day, uninspired men have interfered seriously with this divine organism, and have almost destroyed the life and function of the church of Christ by their false teaching and un-Scriptural, presumptuous organization. Happily for us, the Holy Spirit through the apostles has thrust this question into our view in the sixth chapter of Acts of Apostles.

### The Church Is the Highest Organism (vs. 1-15)

*The church is the highest organism, because originally and fundamentally it met the problem of its own growth* (1-4): "Now in these days, when the number of the disciples was multiplying, there arose a murmuring of the Grecian Jews against the Hebrews, because their widows were neglected in the daily ministration. And the twelve called the multitude of the disciples unto them, and said, It is not fit that we should forsake the word of God, and serve tables. Look ye out therefore, brethren, from among you seven men of good report, full of the Spirit and of wisdom, whom we may appoint over this business. But we will continue stedfastly in prayer, and in the ministry of the word." The church, like every other organism, came into existence with its own organization as an inherence, which developed as occasion arose or necessity demanded. From the very beginning on Pentecost, the apostles themselves, in whom was every essential thing as the first Christians, constituted the norm of the church of the Lord Jesus Christ. At first, preaching and teaching met the whole demand of the church; and they must remain fundamental and comprehensive forever. In truth, neither the "murmuring of the Grecian Jews against the Hebrews, because their widows were neglected in the daily ministration," nor any other situation in the church, could deflect the apostles from the divine course and make them unfit by compelling them to "forsake the word of God." Woe to the congregation that forces its preacher to "forsake the word of God and serve tables," and direful the preacher that abides such inappropriate treatment! This kind of service is essential, of course, and whoever renders it should be "full of the Spirit and of wisdom." But there are other members of the church, besides the minister, who need something to do, upon whom this kind of work should be pressed. Let the servant or minister that preaches be free to "continue stedfastly in prayer, and in the ministry of the word"; and let the whole church pray with him. Verily, this is the norm of the apostolic church, departure from which in modern times has shorn the church of apostolic success. In all the history of the church, the apostles have never been equaled as preachers and teachers. Of course, they had the Holy Spirit in a degree in which no other preachers had or have Him. But the intensity and the singleness of their service must be considered

in accounting for their marvelous power. Quickly
under them the first church in Jerusalem became a great
multitude of believers, and the fire blazed all over the
world. All their lives, they did four things—they
preached and taught and prayed and healed. Really
they did one thing—they preached the gospel of the
Son of God, to which all their teaching and praying and
healing were made tributary.

*The church as an organism chooses its own servants*
(5, 6): "And the saying pleased the whole multitude:
and they chose Stephen, a man full of faith and of the
Holy Spirit, and Philip, and Prochorus, and Nicanor,
and Timon, and Parmenas, and Nicolaus a proselyte
of Antioch; whom they set before the apostles: and
when they had prayed, they laid their hands upon
them." While the office to which these brethren were
elected is not named, yet it is clearly indicated by what
they were chosen to do; namely, to be responsible for
the "daily *ministration*" of the common fund of the
church provided for the relief of indigent members,
and see that no "widows" or others in need "were
neglected." The Greek word from which we get the
word *ministration* here might be translated as *minister*
or *servant* or *deacon;* but each of these three English
words has acquired its own separate meaning. *Servant*
is a general term, applied to the Lord Himself or to the
apostles or to anybody that serves; *minister* describes
the preacher, and is a much better word for this purpose
than *pastor* or *elder* or *bishop;* but *deacon* describes the
office to which these seven brethren were elected by the
first church in Jerusalem. Luke does not particularize
just how the Jerusalem church chose these deacons;
every congregation should have some method of select-
ing its officers that will discover and express the choice

of its members. An organization may be complex, pre-sumptuous, impertinent, unwieldy, impractical, extra-Scriptural, impossible. And any such organization foisted on the church, from either outside or inside the local congregation, tends to confuse and distract the individual followers of the Lord Jesus Christ, and may manacle the church, derange its organism, pervert its function, quench its Spirit—the Holy Spirit. But the organism is always simple and practical. The organism of the church has only two functions or offices: (1) The eldership or bishopric or pastorate to look after the spir-itual interests, and provide gospel preaching and teach-ing for the local congregation. The preacher is also an elder or bishop or pastor, who should be called *minister;* every New Testament church had a plurality of pastors or bishops or elders. The apostles performed this duty in the first church in Jerusalem. (2) The diaconate to "serve tables," by easy transition, to serve the Lord's Table and look after the business affairs of the church. The qualifications of elders and deacons are practically the same: they must be "men of good report, full of the Spirit and of wisdom," and elders must be "apt to teach." Let no auxiliary or agency obscure the church in these two functions or in any other way. It is im-perative to have universal amenability to the Head of the church and harmony with the organism of the church, compatible with which was the tact of "the Hebrews" who chose the seven deacons (they all had Greek names) from "the Grecian Jews," to quiet their "murmuring" that threatened the unity of the first church in Jeru-salem; but there is no room in the church for the coarse, crass, political manipulator, or boss, which the so-called "organizer" may easily become, seeking his own way or "feathering his own nest."

*The church of Christ grows as an organism* (7):
"And the word of God increased; and the number of
the disciples multiplied in Jerusalem exceedingly; and
a great company of the priests were obedient to the
faith." The church of Christ, originally the creation of
the Holy Spirit, is fundamentally spiritual, and con-
cerned with the fleshly body and the material world only
incidentally. And, like every other organism, the church
was equipped and endowed from the very beginning of
its existence to fulfill the purpose of the great Creator.
Man in his conceit thinks he can *organize;* but an *organism* is a living being, and transcends all human knowledge or invention or creation. Every function of every
living thing, whether plant or animal, was created in
the beginning in the original organism, and lies latent
in the seed for reproduction; and this is equally and
emphatically true of the great spiritual creation, the
highest organism in this world, the church of the Lord
Jesus Christ. The seed that begets the Christian and
propagates the church is "the word of God," the preaching and teaching of which is the fundamental function
of the church. It was essential, therefore, that this
office of the church should be active immediately in the
apostles in whom the spiritual organism of the church
was originally created. However, the diaconate also
inhered in the original organism of the church, and was
merely called into action in the first congregation in
Jerusalem by "the murmuring of the Grecian Jews
against the Hebrews, because their widows were neglected in the daily ministration." After this, Luke shows
us the church functioning fully and perfectly, with
the result that "the word of God" reached more people,
and multiplied the members of the church beyond all
computation. Every congregation in the world would

obtain this same wonderful effect if it would be obedient
to Christ as the Head of the church, and keep Him as
the indwelling Guest of the church through the Holy
Spirit, quit meddling with the divine organism of the
church and eschew all human effort at organization.
The church of Christ, of course, though not even the
apostles saw this at first, was destined to supplant the
old Jewish economy under Moses; and that "a great
company of the priests were obedient to the faith"
meant progress in this direction. The Jewish dispensation really closed at the crucifixion of Christ, and the
Christian era actually began on Pentecost; but only time
could bring this change into general recognition. The
priests are the conservators of old forms, which go rapidly when the priests give way. To be "obedient to the
faith" is to be baptized; baptism is the very first act
of obedience in the path of the penitent believer.

*The organism of the church is potential in every
member of the church* (8-15) : "And Stephen, full of
grace and power, wrought great wonders and signs
among the people. But there arose certain of them that
were of the synagogue called the synagogue of the Freedmen, and of the Cyrenians, and of the Alexandrians, and
of them of Cilicia and Asia, disputing with Stephen.
And they were not able to withstand the wisdom and the
Spirit by which he spake. Then they suborned men,
who said, We have heard him speak blasphemous words
against Moses, and against God. And they stirred up
the people, and the elders, and the scribes, and came
upon him, and seized him, and brought him into the council, and set up false witnesses, who said, This man ceaseth
not to speak words against this holy place, and the law:
for we have heard him say, that this Jesus of Nazareth
shall destroy this place, and shall change the customs

which Moses delivered unto us. And all that sat in the
council, fastening their eyes on him, saw his face as it
had been the face of an angel.'' The organism of the
church lifted Stephen out of obscurity into the limelight,
and it has done the same thing for many humble Christians. Evidently, the apostles, in laying their hands on
Stephen, had imparted to him the miraculous power of
the Holy Spirit; so that he, being ''full of grace and
power, wrought great wonders and signs among the
people.'' And being himself a Hellenist, Stephen, before he became a Christian, must have been associated
with the other Hellenistic Jews ''in the synagogue of
the Freedmen.'' Here we have used the marginal ren-
dering, ''Freedmen,'' in preference to ''Libertines,'' because it is better understood. The ''Freedmen'' were
Jews that had been slaves and had obtained their freedom in some way and, from a natural desire to be together, they had their own synagogue in Jerusalem.
And Stephen's effort to convert his associates in this
synagogue to Christ brought on the persecution that
resulted in his death. This oppression was led by the
Pharisees, who secured lying witnesses and used the
same tactics they had employed in destroying the life of
Jesus. The organism of the church *inheres* in every
Christian, and should be not only *potential* but also
*potent*. Everybody that belongs to the church belongs
to every other member of the church and is obligated
to do his utmost for the welfare of all his brethren, and
should be able to serve in some measure either as elder
or deacon or minister or preacher. The organism of the
church relates the church to the lost also through the
individual Christian, who should have a passion to preach
or teach or explain the gospel to sinners at every opportunity, and thus ''beget'' them as Christians. Stephen,

whose face shone "as it had been the face of an angel,"
the diaconal comet, shot athwart the sky in brilliance
rivaling the glory of the apostolic stars. Certain qualifications are detailed for elders and deacons, because
they are the attributes of every Christian, to make them
exemplars both to the church and to the community.
All in whom the organism of the church is active are
useful and fruitful in the church, whether they are honored with any named office or not. The organism of the
church marries earth to heaven, weds time to eternity.

## VII

## THE ORIGIN OF MARTYRDOM

### (Acts 7)

*God is the Creator of all good; the devil is the origin of all evil.* Strike an *o* out of *good,* and you have written its source—God; prefix a *d* to *evil,* and you have named its *father*—devil. Sin did not originate in the human heart, but it came to man as a suggestion from Satan. Good is the goal of life; evil is the intrusion of the devil. All real authority inheres in God, who never underwrites sin. All wrong drifts without anchor or compass or hope, doomed to darkness and death and destruction and annihilation. Nothing runs to final issue in this temporary, disordered, unbalanced, insane world. The martyrdom of Stephen, like the crucifixion of Jesus, was the outburst of prejudice, the venom of hatred, the disdain of order, the scorn of law, the travesty of justice, the depravity of sin, the incorrigibility of the devil, the acme of wickedness. The good increase in righteousness, Christians grow in grace and knowledge; "but evil men and impostors shall wax worse and worse, deceiving and being deceived" (2 Tim. 3:13). No man, whether good or bad, is at a standstill; but he enlarges in the direction of his bent. This is true also of the generations. The crucifiers of Jesus and the martyrers of Stephen were the worst generation in the history of the world, whom Jesus described graphically: "Woe unto you, scribes and Pharisees, hypocrites! for ye build the sepulchres of the prophets, and garnish the tombs of the righteous, and say, If we had been in the days of our fathers, we should not have been partakers with them in the blood of the prophets. Wherefore ye witness to yourselves, that ye are sons of them that slew the prophets. Fill ye up then the measure of your fathers. Ye serpents, ye offspring of vipers, how shall ye escape the judgment of hell? Therefore, behold, I send unto you prophets, and wise men, and scribes: some of them shall ye kill and crucify; and some of them shall ye scourge in your synagogues, and persecute from city to city: that upon you may come all the righteous blood shed on the earth, from the blood of Abel the righteous unto the blood of Zachariah son of Barachiah, whom ye slew between the sanctuary and the altar. Verily, I say unto you, All these things shall come upon this generation'' (Matt. 23:29-36). There is double culpability here; whether the murderers of Jesus and Stephen were conscious of it or not, they were in league with the devil, as were their fathers also. The devil and his dupes, paralyzed in their hearts, are shut up to the weakness of the flesh, and can not operate at all in the realm of the strength of the Spirit; they can kill the body, as they often do, but not the soul. Being unable to resist the wisdom and the Spirit by which Stephen spoke, they simply killed his body.

## In His Defense, Stephen Outlined Hebrew History (vs. 1-50)

*Without disclosing his purpose, Stephen compelled attention by his interesting recital* (1-50): ''And the high priest said, Are these things so? And he said, Brethren and fathers, hearken: The God of glory appeared unto our father Abraham, when he was in Mesopotamia, before he dwelt in Haran, and said unto him, Get thee out of thy land, and from thy kindred, and

come into the land which I shall show thee. Then came
he out of the land of the Chaldeans, and dwelt in Haran:
and from thence, when his father was dead, God removed
him into this land, wherein ye now dwell: and he gave
him none inheritance in it, no, not so much as to set his
foot on: and he promised that he would give it to him
in possession, and to his seed after him, when as yet he
had no child. And God spake on this wise, that his seed
should sojourn in a strange land, and that they should
bring them into bondage, and treat them ill, four hundred years. And the nation to which they shall be in
bondage will I judge, said God: and after that shall they
come forth, and serve me in this place. And he gave
him the covenant of circumcision: and so Abraham begat
Isaac, and circumcised him on the eighth day; and Isaac
begat Jacob, and Jacob the twelve patriarchs. And the
patriarchs, moved with jealousy against Joseph, sold
him into Egypt: and God was with him, and delivered
him out of all his afflictions, and gave him favor and
wisdom before Pharaoh king of Egypt; and he made him
governor over Egypt and all his house. Now there came
a famine over all Egypt and Canaan, and great affliction:
and our fathers found no sustenance. But when Jacob
heard that there was grain in Egypt, he sent forth our
fathers the first time. And at the second time Joseph
was made known to his brethren; and Joseph's race became manifest unto Pharaoh. And Joseph sent, and
called to him Jacob, his father, and all his kindred, three
score and fifteen souls. And Jacob went down into
Egypt; and he died, himself and our fathers; and they
were carried over unto Shechem, and laid in the tomb
that Abraham bought for a price in silver of the sons
of Hamor in Shechem. But as the time of the promise
drew nigh which God vouchsafed unto Abraham, the

people grew and multiplied in Egypt, till there arose another king over Egypt, who knew not Joseph. The same dealt craftily with our race, and ill-treated our fathers, that they should cast out their babes to the end they might not live. At which season Moses was born, and was exceeding fair; and he was nourished three months in his father's house: and when he was cast out, Pharaoh's daughter took him up, and nourished him for her own son. And Moses was instructed in all the wisdom of the Egyptians; and he was mighty in his words and works. But when he was well-nigh forty years old, it came into his heart to visit his brethren the children of Israel. And seeing one of them suffer wrong, he defended him, and avenged him that was oppressed, smiting the Egyptian: and he supposed that his brethren understood that God by his hand was giving them deliverance; but they understood not. And the day following he appeared unto them as they strove, and would have set them at one again, saying, Sirs, ye are brethren; why do ye wrong one to another? But he that did his neighbor wrong thrust him away, saying, Who made thee a ruler and a judge over us? Wouldest thou kill me, as thou killedst the Egyptian yesterday? And Moses fled at this saying, and became a sojourner in the land of Midian, where he begat two sons. And when forty years were fulfilled, an angel appeared to him in the wilderness of Mount Sinai, in a flame of fire in a bush. And when Moses saw it, he wondered at the sight: and as he drew near to behold, there came a voice of the Lord, I am the God of thy fathers, the God of Abraham, and of Isaac, and of Jacob. And Moses trembled, and durst not behold. And the Lord said unto him, Loose the shoes from thy feet: for the place whereon thou standest is holy ground. I have surely seen the affliction of my people that is in Egypt, and have heard their groaning, and I am come down to deliver them: and now come, I will send thee into Egypt. This Moses whom they refused, saying, Who made thee a ruler and a judge? him hath God sent to be both a ruler and a deliverer with the hand of the angel that appeared to him in the bush. This man led them forth, having wrought wonders and signs in Egypt, and in the Red Sea, and in the wilderness forty years. This is that Moses, who said unto the children of Israel, A prophet shall God raise up unto you from among your brethren, like unto me. This is he that was in the congregation in the wilderness with the angel that spake to him in the mount Sinai, and with our fathers: who received living oracles to give unto us: to whom our fathers would not be obedient, but thrust him from them, and turned back in their hearts unto Egypt, saying unto Aaron, Make us gods that shall go before us: for as for this Moses, who led us forth out of the land of Egypt, we know not what is become of him. And they made a calf in those days, and brought a sacrifice unto the idol, and rejoiced in the works of their hands. But God turned, and gave them up to serve the host of heaven, as it is written in the book of the prophets,

"Did ye offer unto me slain beasts and sacrifices
Forty years in the wilderness, O house of Israel?
And ye took up the tabernacle of Moloch,
And the star of the god of Rephan,
The figures which ye made to worship them:
And I will carry you away beyond Babylon.

"Our fathers had the tabernacle of the testimony in the wilderness, even as he appointed who spake unto Moses, that he should make according to the figure that he had seen. Which also our fathers, in their turn, brought in with Joshua when they entered on the possession of the nations, that God thrust out before the face of our fathers, unto the days of David; who found favor in the sight of God, and asked to find a habitation for the God of Jacob. But Solomon built him a house. Howbeit the Most High dwelleth not in houses made with hands; as saith the prophet,

"The heaven is my throne,
  And the earth the footstool of my feet:
  What manner of house will ye build me? saith
    the Lord:
  Or what is the place of my rest?
  Did not my hand make all these things?"

Stephen must have known, while he was compressing this ancient history into small space so that now it is contained in one remarkable paragraph of fifty verses, the Sanhedrin and all his hearers were wondering how he was going to use this proud story of the origin and development of their Hebrew race in his defense against the charge of blasphemy which hung over him; but by Stephen's own design, they did not perceive his point till the beginning of the next paragraph, when it flashed or fell on them like a bolt of lightning. Though Stephen's statement was condensed and concentrated on his defense, yet we are indebted to him for three points of information; namely, (1) God's first appearance to Abraham "was in Mesopotamia, before he dwelt in Haran"; (2) "and Moses was instructed in all the wisdom of the Egyptians; and he was mighty in his words and works"; (3) God uses angels in visible, audible manifestations of Himself (30-34, 38). In verses 15 and 16, there are two errors, which must be clerical; it is inconceivable that any Jew with the intelligence of Stephen would make them. The first is easily corrected by supplying the ellipsis and remedying the punctuation, thus—"and he [Jacob] died; and our fathers died, and were carried over unto Shechem"; and the second mistake is eliminated by substituting the name of *Jacob* for that of *Abraham*. Abraham bought a burial ground, the cave of Machpelah, at Hebron; and Jacob was buried there. But the bones of Joseph were buried in Shechem (Josh. 24: 32); and Joseph's brethren, according to Stephen, who must have had access to some extra-Biblical source of information, were buried in Shechem also. The word rendered *church* in verse 38 is translated *congregation* in the margin, and so we have written it here: this same original word is usually translated *church* in the New Testament, but always *congregation* in the Old Testament; and uniformity requires that it be *congregation* here. *Church* is the New Testament name for the New Testament creation, the new creation, which flashed into existence, sprang into being on the first Pentecost following the resurrection of the Lord Jesus Christ from the dead; the Old Testament had a *congregation*, "the whole body of the Jewish people," called also "congregation of the Lord" (Webster), *but no church*.

## How Stephen Made His Application (vs. 51-60; 8: 1)

*Now, having discovered the likeness of his wicked judges in their stupid ancestors, Stephen disclosed his application in a great outburst of passion* (51-53): "Ye stiffnecked and uncircumcised in heart and ears, ye do always resist the Holy Spirit: as your fathers did, so do ye. Which of the prophets did not your fathers persecute? and they killed them that showed before of the

coming of the Righteous One; of whom ye have now
become betrayers and murderers; ye who received the
law as it was ordained by angels, and kept it not." The
first picture of you, shouted Stephen, is Joseph's brethren ignoring the lad's plea for mercy, and selling him
into slavery. And walk on through the halls of history,
continued Stephen, and see the reflection of your own
obtuseness in the brethren of Moses as they quenched
his enthusiastic spirit to save them from Egyptian bondage. But forty years later, God sent His angel to Moses
in Midian to overrule this rejection by his brethren,
and commission him to deliver His people from Egypt.
"This is that Moses, who said unto the children of
Israel, A prophet shall God raise up unto you from
among your brethren, like unto me." Stephen exhibited the portrait of Moses in Mount Sinai, receiving "living oracles"; and at the same time, this picture mirrored,
in the disobedience and idolatry of Moses' contemporaries, the depravity of the generation that crucified
Jesus and sought Stephen's own life. God made Moses
leader and deliverer, in spite of his faithless brethren;
all that the enemies of Jesus could do against Him did
not keep Him off the throne in heaven. The idolatry
of the Israelites sent them into captivity "beyond
Babylon"; the incorrigibility of the crucifiers of Jesus
and the martyrers of Stephen sent them into the eternal
world without hope. Stephen said, by the history he
recited and by the prophecy he quoted, "I am no blas-
phemer, I am telling you the truth; the tabernacle was
portable, and gave way for the temple as a more permanent building. The temple serves a temporary purpose,
and can not house our God, whose throne is heaven, and
whose footstool is the earth. And Moses must give way
for Christ, of whom he prophesied." Stephen poured

all the scorn of his race into his denouncement of the
court before whom he was being tried, when he called
them "stiffnecked and uncircumcised in heart and
ears"; as long as any man "resists the Holy Spirit,"
as these men and their fathers did, he is hopeless, open
to the devil and ready for any crime that comes along:
why, the ancestors of the Sanhedrin persecuted all the
prophets, and "killed them that showed before of the
coming of the Righteous One," whom this very supreme
council had betrayed and murdered in outrage of their
own law "ordained through angels by the hands of a
mediator."

*Stephen's deliberate, righteous, truthful, passionate
denunciation of his judges exploded their wickedness
with mob violence* (7:54-60; 8:1): "Now when they
heard these things, they were cut to the heart, and they
gnashed on him with their teeth.  But he, being full of
the Holy Spirit, looked up stedfastly into heaven, and
saw the glory of God, and Jesus standing on the right
hand of God, and said, Behold, I see the heavens
opened and the Son of man standing on the right
hand of God.  But they cried out with a loud voice,
and stopped their ears, and rushed upon him with one
accord; and they cast him out of the city, and stoned
him: and the witnesses laid down their garments at the
feet of a young man named Saul.  And they stoned
Stephen, calling upon the Lord, and saying, Lord Jesus,
receive my spirit.  And he kneeled down, and cried
with a loud voice, Lord, lay not this sin to their charge.
And when he had said this, he fell asleep.  And Saul
was consenting unto his death."  Stephen's enemies
were vastly inferior to him intellectually and spiritually;
and their endeavor to convict him of crime proved a
boomerang, rebounding on them, and exposing their own

ignorance and viciousness. He outwitted them in debate, and outshone them in character; he cut the ground from under their feet, and left them dangling in the air: yea, with righteous fury he lashed them back into the lair of the devil, the roaring, devouring wild beast (1 Pet. 5:8), their father, the creator of iniquity, the begetter of sinners, the originator and the instigator of persecution and crucifixion and martyrdom and every other vile act in all the brood of crime! And out of that brutish, hellish den, they paraded their unprotected victim, roaring, railing their rage to devour him. But let us be grateful forever that, before this mob beat his life out with stones, Stephen was able to witness what he saw: "But he, being full of the Holy Spirit, looked up stedfastly into heaven, and saw the glory of God, and Jesus standing on the right hand of God, and said, Behold, I see the heavens opened, and the Son of man standing on the right hand of God." With utter hypocrisy, the Sanhedrin had the witnesses against Stephen to begin the stoning (Deut. 17:7), as if they were abiding by the law of Moses! Here Luke mentions one witness of this appalling crime, on account of his subsequent prominence, no doubt, "a young man named Saul," at whose feet "the witnesses laid down their garments," so that they would be free to throw stones at Stephen; "and Saul was consenting unto his death." Just before Stephen "fell asleep," he prayed, "Lord Jesus, receive my spirit. And he kneeled down, and cried with a loud voice, Lord, lay not this sin to their charge": thus he manifested the Spirit of the Lord Jesus Christ, for whose cause he gave his life. (Here the chapter mark comes in the midst of a paragraph; the verse marked the first verse of chapter 8 really belongs to the seventh chapter, and we have classified it

so.)   Stephen was the product of faith and the Holy
Spirit; such combination insures co-operation with God,
and makes anybody great.   Stephen gripped history,
glimpsed its meaning, saw the present coming out of the
past and beheld the divine Purpose sweeping the ages!
As a soldier of the crucified, risen Lord, he was brave,
fearless, heroic, unconquerable.   Stephen was the first
Christian martyr; he lived amid superstition and ignorance and prejudice; he told his evil enemies in plain
words what they were; he fell into the hands of a devilish mob, which made him the victim of their insane,
furious hatred.   But the fortitude and faith and spirit
and vision in which he met the death of his body have
thrown a flood of light on the eternal destiny of the
Christian and accomplished more for the Lord than
his life.

# VIII

## PERSECUTION PRODUCING PREACHERS

### (Acts 8)

*There is wide difference between persecution and punishment.* Punishment is penalty for transgression; persecution, the oppression with which we are dealing here, was the unjust, wicked infliction of loss or pain or death on the members of the church of the Lord Jesus Christ by its ignorant, depraved enemies; punishment is personal, persecution is casual. The purpose of the persecutors of the church was to injure and destroy the cause represented by their victims. But persecution always falls far short of its object, because weakness and unfairness and unreasonableness and evil inhere in it. The Bible gives the only explanation of evil. Sin was originated in heaven by the devil and the other angels that he led, upon whom Michael and his angels made war, forcing them out of heaven, and casting them "down to the earth" (Rev. 12: 7-17). While we may not be able to understand or explain the mystery of evil, yet we can see that its very presence gives the church something to do. The enemies of the church, under the leadership of the Sadducees, had endeavored to forestall the growth of the church by threatening the apostles and imprisoning them and beating them; and, but for the tactful wisdom of Gamaliel, they might have inflicted upon the Twelve the same fate Stephen suffered. But the church continued to grow and prosper during all the Sadducean oppression; and

Stephen, with his brilliant mind and spiritual insight, forced the enemies of the church to meet him in open debate, and the cause went forward by leaps and bounds, when it seemed impossible to compute its numbers. Then the Pharisees took charge of the persecution, who evidently intended to keep their bloody work inside the forms of law; but Stephen's burning, passionate condemnation of them threw them into a frenzied, violent mob. Perhaps a dash of persecution or opposition might do the church good now. The members of the persecuted first church in Jerusalem had to suffer terribly, but they spread the truth everywhere. The leaders and pioneers in the modern movement to restore primitive Christianity were misunderstood and misrepresented and vilified and persecuted; but if all the generations following them had had the New Testament knowledge and zeal that this first generation of pioneers had, this greatest of all causes on earth would today be represented by many millions of Christians.

## Providence Makes Persecution Contributory to the Cause It Seeks to Destroy (vs. 1-13)

*Providence neutralized persecution and made it tributary to the cause it sought to destroy by glorifying its victim in death* (1-3): "And there arose on that day a great persecution against the church which was in Jerusalem; and they were all scattered abroad throughout the regions of Judea and Samaria, except the apostles. And devout men buried Stephen, and made great lamentation over him. But Saul laid waste the church, entering into every house, and dragging men and women committed them to prison." When Stephen met death as the first Christian martyr, the glory of heaven fell upon him, the ecstasy of happiness was in

his heart, the words of rapture were upon his lips, the
testimony of his triumph shall sound on the earth forever! No patriarch, no prophet ever died like Stephen.
Why should any Christian be alarmed at death, or fear
what is in the grave or beyond it, now? The enemies of
the Lord Jesus Christ were never vainer than when they
counted His crucifixion their victory. The only hope
for them was to acknowledge the devil as their leader
and inspirer, and throw themselves in the dust of penitence and humility at the feet of the Lord. Jesus did
not observe indifferently, helplessly when the life was
pounded out of His wonderful servant, Stephen, who
might have been classed with Paul if he had lived. But
God had something for His Son to do in His death
that could not be accomplished in any other way; and
He knew that the martyrdom of Stephen would cast
great shafts of light down through all time to come,
emboldening His followers to meet death in the exu-
berant joy of hope. And Stephen's stimulating, inspiring heroism had the immediate effect of strengthening
his brethren for the great storm of persecution that
began to break over their heads the very day of his
death. But the death of a good, great man, especially
when he has been murdered, as Stephen was, is always
an irreparable loss; and we do not wonder that "devout
men buried Stephen, and made great lamentation over
him." Perhaps the Sanhedrin felt that since "Saul
laid waste the church, entering into every house, and
dragging men and women committed them to prison,"
the apostles would be without audience and helpless in
Jerusalem; but all the other members of the church in
Jerusalem were driven into "the regions of Judæa and
Samaria"; and the Jewish authorities may have hesi-
tated to imprison the apostles again, since an angel of

the Lord had very mysteriously released them from prison the last time they had been deprived of their liberty.

*Persecution aroused and inspired the living to go "about preaching the word"* (4-8): "They therefore that were scattered abroad went about preaching the word. And Philip went down to the city of Samaria, and proclaimed unto them the Christ. And the multitudes gave heed with one accord unto the things that were spoken by Philip, when they heard, and saw the signs which he did. For from many of those that had unclean spirits, they came out, crying with a loud voice: and many that were palsied, and that were lame, were healed. And there was much joy in that city." Now we observe the first church in Jerusalem, whose members "were all scattered abroad throughout the regions of Judæa and Samaria, except the apostles," following the divine order of witnessing for Christ—"in Jerusalem, and in all Judæa and Samaria, and unto the uttermost part of the earth." Testimony had been borne in Jerusalem; and all the members of the church, except the apostles, or preachers, being driven from their homes by persecution, and finding themselves in Judea and Samaria, "went about preaching the word." They did not regret or weep or moan or mourn or despair; they picked themselves up in the devotion of the Lord, who had no home in this world, and preached Him to everybody they saw. Philip (not the apostle, but the deacon) captivated the multitudes in the city of Samaria by his signal miracles and dynamic message of the Christ: and unclean spirits, "crying with a loud voice," fled out of their unfortunate victims at Philip's approach, and many suffering from paralysis and lameness

were released from these diseases, and walked.  No wonder "there was much joy in that city."  These humble
Christians were inspired to forget any loss or pain the
persecutors had thrust upon them; they saw only the
opportunity straight ahead of them and all around them
to preach Christ to lost souls.  Why, the oppression that
the devil created in Jerusalem to destroy the church of
the Lord Jesus Christ, in His own dominant providence
merely dispersed His individual believers as firebrands
to kindle the fire of His love everywhere!  Through His
church, and absolutely in no other way, the Lord lifts
human feet out of the miry mud of sin and sets them
on His own rock of eternal truth and righteousness;
against His church, which is His creation, His dwelling, He will not suffer even the gates of hell to prevail,
for He makes it not only indomitable and indefeasible,
but invincible and inviolable.

*Philip supplanted Simon the sorcerer by preaching
the gospel and by showing the infinite superiority of the
real over the false and of the divine over the human*
(9-13) : "But there was a certain man, Simon by name,
who beforetime in the city used sorcery, and amazed
the people of Samaria, giving out that himself was some
great one: to whom they all gave heed, from the least
to the greatest, saying, This man is that power of God
which is called great.  And they gave heed to him,
because that of long time he had amazed them with
his sorceries.  But when they believed Philip preaching
good tidings concerning the kingdom of God and the
name of Jesus Christ, they were baptized, both men and
women.  And Simon also himself believed: and being
baptized, he continued with Philip; and beholding signs
and great miracles wrought, he was amazed."  While

the tricks of magic or sorcery or any sleight-of-hand
performance are inexplicable to the uninitiated, yet all
intelligent people know that their sole purpose is to
excite mere idle curiosity and entertain; and in no way
are these petty artifices to be classed with the real, genuine miracles wrought by the Lord Jesus Christ and
His apostles and others to whom these apostles imparted
the supernatural power of the Holy Spirit by laying
their hands upon them. Simon, the sorcerer, took advantage of the ignorance of the Samaritans, and had
amazed them with sorcery for a "long time"; but he
knew that he was deceiving them. And when Philip
came along, casting out devils and healing the sick and
preaching the gospel, he threw Simon into immediate
and permanent eclipse; Philip carried with him the air
of sincerity and reality, and the Samaritans became
conscious quickly that he met their most fundamental
need; namely, their salvation. The story of the conversion of the Samaritans is as simple and direct as the
Great Commission under which Philip preached: "He
that believeth and is baptized shall be saved." Luke
put this whole story in one sentence: "they believed,"
"were baptized"; their repentance and confession are
understood or included in their faith and baptism. Why,
Philip converted Simon, too; Simon "believed, and
being baptized, he continued with Philip." And
Simon's experience as a magician made him more susceptible to the amazement of the "signs and great miracles wrought" by Philip. Simon knew that his performance was false, but Philip's was real; and Philip
drove home to Simon's heart that the program of a
mere sorcerer was human, if not also diabolical, but
the plan of the Christian evangelist, such as Philip was,
is divine and saving of the lost.

### Philip the Projected Preacher of Persecution
### (vs. 14-40.)

*The apostles sent Peter and John to Samaria to guard and simplify the divine economy* (14-25): "Now when the apostles that were at Jerusalem heard that Samaria had received the word of God, they sent unto them Peter and John: who, when they were come down, prayed for them, that they might receive the Holy Spirit: for as yet it was fallen upon none of them: only they had been baptized into the name of the Lord Jesus. Then laid they their hands on them, and they received the Holy Spirit. Now when Simon saw that through the laying on of the apostles' hands the Holy Spirit was given, he offered them money, saying, Give me also this power, that on whomsoever I lay my hands, he may receive the Holy Spirit. But Peter said unto him, Thy silver perish with thee, because thou hast thought to obtain the gift of God with money. Thou hast neither part nor lot in this matter: for thy heart is not right before God. Repent therefore of this thy wickedness, and pray the Lord, if perhaps the thought of thy heart shall be forgiven thee. For I see that thou art in the gall of bitterness and in the bond of iniquity. And Simon answered and said, Pray ye for me to the Lord, that none of the things which ye have spoken come upon me. They, therefore, when they had testified and spoken the word of the Lord, returned to Jerusalem, and preached the gospel to many villages of the Samaritans." It is evident that Peter had no primacy in the apostolic group: he and John were amenable to their brethren, who sent them to Samaria, where a situation had arisen requiring apostolic supervision. Of course, the Samaritans, who had obeyed the gospel under

Philip's leadership, had "the gift of the Holy Spirit"; but that carried with it no miraculous power, which Philip had, but could not impart because he was not an apostle. It was necessary, therefore, that the apostles should visit the new church in Samaria, and set it in order by prayer and the impartation of the supernatural power of the Holy Spirit, that this congregation might be fully equipped and the divine economy guarded in it. At that time, there was no New Testament to guide the followers of the Lord Jesus Christ, and all the churches that sprang up were under the personal direction of the apostles; and all the churches in the world forever must be amenable to the apostles in the New Testament. Now Simon had obeyed the gospel, and he was a Christian; but he was "a babe in Christ." Simon shone before his conversion as a magician, and he thought he saw a chance to shine after his transformation, or new birth, if he could only have the spectacular power of the Holy Spirit and impart it by laying his hands on others as the apostles did. Of course, Simon did not understand this wonderful "matter"; but Peter's rebuke evidently set him right, and he began to grow in the Christian life. We have already discovered what an alien sinner is to do to be saved— hear, believe, repent, confess and be baptized; here we learn what an erring or sinning Christian must do— repent and pray for forgiveness.

*Philip proved the prominent preacher of the persecution* (26-40): "But an angel of the Lord spake unto Philip, saying, Arise, and go toward the south unto the way that goeth down from Jerusalem unto Gaza: the same is desert. And he arose and went; and behold, a man of Ethiopia, a eunuch of great authority under Candace, queen of the Ethiopians, who was over all her treasure, who had come to Jerusalem to worship; and he was returning and sitting in his chariot, and was reading the prophet Isaiah. And the Spirit said unto Philip, Go near, and join thyself to this chariot. And Philip ran to him, and heard him reading Isaiah the prophet, and said, Understandest thou what thou readest? And he said, How can I, except some one shall guide me? And he besought Philip to come up and sit with him. Now the passage of the Scripture which he was reading was this,

"He was led as a sheep to the slaughter;
 And as a lamb before his shearer is dumb,
 So he openeth not his mouth:
 In his humiliation his judgment was taken away:
 His generation who shall declare?
 For his life is taken from the earth.

"And the eunuch answered Philip, and said, I pray thee, of whom speaketh the prophet this? of himself, or of some other? And Philip opened his mouth, and beginning from this Scripture, preached unto him Jesus. And as they went on the way, they came unto a certain water; and the eunuch saith, Behold, here is water; what doth hinder me to be baptized? And Philip said, If thou believest with all thy heart, thou mayest. And he answered and said, I believe that Jesus Christ is the Son of God. And he commanded the chariot to stand still: and they both went down into the water, both Philip and the eunuch; and he baptized him. And when they came up out of the water, the Spirit of the Lord caught away Philip; and the eunuch saw him no more, for he went on his way rejoicing. But Philip was found at Azotus: and passing through he preached the gospel to all the cities, till he came to Cæsarea."

The Lord is infinitely resourceful; He did not take
Philip out of a populous section merely to minister to
one man. Philip's work in Samaria had run its course,
and reached its conclusion; and since Peter and John
as apostles had set the Samaritan congregation in order
and fortified it with the miraculous power of the Holy
Spirit, Philip was ready to prosecute his work as evangelist elsewhere. Evidently, it was not according to
the divine will that Philip should settle in Samaria
and give all his time to one church or group of believers:
there were too many people and too many communities
absolutely unevangelized to make that a wise or right
course for Philip to pursue. In truth, there now are
too many "pastors" and too few evangelists in the
world, while large sections are unreached and multitudes
are unsaved. Here is an important fundamental fact
that has been overlooked almost universally: The apostles trained and qualified the congregation to take care
of its own welfare, and released the minister or evangelist or preacher to reach and save the lost. This
could and should be done now; a strong church should
sustain a preacher, not merely as their "pastor" or
minister, but as their evangelist, thoroughly to evangelize every neglected community within their reach.
Here we have departed from the divine plan, and the
work lags. Of course, since the death of all the apostles,
and the decease of the last person to whom the apostles
imparted the miraculous power of the Holy Spirit by
the laying on of hands, this supernatural power is impossible to the church with or without a preacher; but
neither is it necessary, for we all have the complete
New Testament Scriptures, created by the Holy Spirit
through the apostles and some of their associates. The
prescience of the Lord is seen in the service of His

angel and Spirit in bringing Philip and the Ethiopian
eunuch together, each strange to the other, but both
known to Him. However, Philip and the eunuch soon
became acquainted for the purpose of their meeting;
Philip, hearing the eunuch reading a wonderful Messianic prophecy without understanding it, began "from
this scripture, and preached unto him Jesus." In
preaching Jesus, Philip must have explained baptism,
for the eunuch said, "Behold, here is water; what doth
hinder me to be baptized?" We have taken verse 37
out of the margin and put it in the body of the text,
where it should be; for it fits and is harmonious with
all the other New Testament Scriptures. The Lord
made it possible for Philip and the eunuch to meet
without any loss of time; neither did the meeting take
much time. Philip baptized the eunuch. "And when
they came up out of the water, the Spirit of the Lord
caught away Philip; and the eunuch saw him no more,
for he went on his way rejoicing." This suggests that
Philip was miraculously removed to "Azotus," where
he was later "found." And Philip preached the gospel
to all the cities he passed through, "till he came to
Cæsarea." As a preacher, Philip was amenable and
obedient to the angel and the Spirit of the Lord; and
his preaching was public and private and personal and
pointed and Scriptural and fundamental and central
and successful.

IX

## THE BORN APOSTLE

### (Acts 9)

*In the primary sense, only one apostle was born;
as we have already explained, the other apostles, the
original twelve, were created.* There are just two ways
for anything to begin or to come into existence: it must
be created or it must be born. And while these two
methods of origin or genesis differ, creation requiring
the miraculous power of God, and birth proceeding by
the operation of law, yet they both lead to the same
great reality of life. Creation does not necessarily mean
superiority, but it is from necessity; so far as we know,
the Lord creates only when birth is impossible. God
had to originate the human race, which He did by
creating one man and one woman, the first pair, from
whom every other human being has descended by birth;
and likewise, since His spiritual kingdom had no prior
existence or antecedent origin, the Lord created His
church on Pentecost in the original Twelve, miraculously
equipping them by the Holy Spirit to be at the same
time the first Christians and the first apostles and the
first preachers and the first fathers of all His believers
forever. Adam, the only created man, lived nine hundred and thirty years; but one of Adam's descendants,
Methuselah, who, of course, was born, lived nine hundred
and sixty-nine years. It may seem invidious to make
comparison among the apostles, who are equally great
in their common momentous office; yet Paul, the only

apostle that was born (1 Cor. 15:8), like all other
Christians, could trace himself back to the original
twelve apostles as his first fathers in the gospel. But
because Paul's enemies tried to discredit his apostleship,
he had the courage to tell the truth about himself, and
declared that he was "not a whit behind the very chief-
est apostles" (2 Cor. 11:5). However, on account of
their direct, immediate, personal association with Jesus
during His ministry in this world, the original twelve
apostles had precedence and priority over Paul; spiritually, they were Paul's fathers and he was their son.
And yet, as Methuselah surpassed Adam in the length
of his life, it seems that Paul exceeded the original
Twelve in the abundance of his labors, in the fruitfulness
of his service. At the time of his new birth, Paul was
known as "Saul"—"Saul of Tarsus." There is no
choice in the old birth of the flesh, which is the only
literal birth; but without choice there can be no new
birth, which is figurative but real. In the new birth
there is always a mingling of the natural and the supernatural; so remarkable was Saul's spiritual origin, that
we shall meet the circumstances of his transformation
often in Acts, pre-eminently the book of conversions.

### The First Story of Saul's Spiritual Birth (vs. 1-19)

*Jesus arrested Saul in his mad career* (1-9): "But
Saul, yet breathing threatening and slaughter against
the disciples of the Lord, went unto the high priest,
and asked of him letters to Damascus unto the synagogues, that if he found any that were of the way,
whether men or women, he might bring them bound to
Jerusalem. And as he journeyed, it came to pass that
he drew nigh unto Damascus: and suddenly there shone
round about him a light out of heaven: and he fell upon

the earth, and heard a voice saying unto him, Saul, Saul, why persecutest thou me? And he said, Who art thou, Lord? And he said, I am Jesus whom thou persecutest: but rise, and enter into the city, and it shall be told thee what thou must do. And the men that journeyed with him stood speechless, hearing the voice, but beholding no man. And Saul arose from the earth; and when his eyes were opened, he saw nothing; and they led him by the hand, and brought him into Damascus. And he was three days without sight, and did neither eat nor drink." "The disciples of the Lord" did well to be apprehensive of Saul, out of whom came "threatening and slaughter" like the breath of his nostrils; than whom the church never had a more determined enemy. When some Pharisees saw the followers of Jesus thriving and growing by leaps and bounds in spite of all the persecution that had been heaped upon them, they may have been discouraged; but not Saul of Tarsus, whose iron will only rose to new resolution. Arming himself with authority from "the high priest" in Jerusalem, and taking other men with him, he set out on foot for Damascus, one hundred and forty miles away, to persecute all the Christians he could find. It would be impossible for any man to be more against the Lord than Saul was the day he and his associates were approaching Damascus, when he was stricken to the earth, saw the Lord in the heavenly light that blinded him for three days, and heard His voice, asking why he persecuted Him, and disclosing Himself as Jesus whom he persecuted. Jesus did not tell Saul what to do to be saved, but sent him on into Damascus, where this question was to be answered by a believer, into whose hands the Lord placed it. The companions of Saul were dumbfounded: they heard "the

voice" without understanding the words spoken, and
saw "no man." Saul was led "by the hand into
Damascus," and went without food and drink during
the three days of his blindness. No man is right, merely
because he thinks he is right. Saul thought he was
right, but he was one of the greatest sinners in the world.
But he followed his own conscience, which was wrongly
educated; and that maintained his integrity and obtained him mercy. There is no hope for the sinner that
stabs his own conscience to death. Saul's suffering must
have been indescribably terrible, in which the Lord
allowed him to continue for three days. If Saul had
not accepted the new light Jesus gave him, he would
have been lost forever.

*The Lord sent Ananias as a gospel preacher to tell
Saul what to do to be saved* (10-19) : "Now there was
a certain disciple at Damascus, named Ananias; and
the Lord said unto him in a vision, Ananias. And he
said, Behold, I am here, Lord. And the Lord said
unto him, Arise, and go to the street which is called
Straight, and inquire in the house of Judas for one
named Saul, a man of Tarsus: for behold, he prayeth;
and he hath seen a man named Ananias coming in, and
laying his hands on him, that he might receive his sight.
But Ananias answered, Lord, I have heard from many
of this man, how much evil he did to thy saints at Jerusalem, and here he hath authority from the chief priests
to bind all that call upon thy name. But the Lord said
unto him, Go thy way: for he is a chosen vessel unto
me, to bear my name before the Gentiles and kings, and
the children of Israel: for I will show him how many
things he must suffer for my name's sake. And Ananias
departed, and entered into the house; and laying his
hands on him said, Brother Saul, the Lord, even Jesus,

who appeared unto thee in the way which thou camest,
hath sent me, that thou mayest receive thy sight, and
be filled with the Holy Spirit. And straightway there
fell from his eyes as it were scales, and he received
his sight; and he arose and was baptized; and he took
food and was strengthened." The authenticity of
Luke's story is indicated by his specific statements of
particular people at definite locations: *Straight Street*,
where *Judas* lived, and where *Ananias,* a certain disciple, found Saul, can still be located in Damascus.
Ananias was probably not official among his brethren;
but the organism of the church was active in him, and it
was perfectly proper for him to preach the gospel to
Saul and baptize him. However, having heard of his
persecuting proclivities toward the "saints at Jerusalem," Ananias was afraid of Saul, and wanted to argue
with the Lord that he should not go to him at all; but
the Lord commanded Ananias, "Go thy way." Jesus
Christ, foreseeing what course Saul would take, had
already chosen him as His witness before Gentiles and
Jews and kings, and as a great sufferer for His "name's
sake." For three days before Ananias came to him,
Saul was in deep distress and penitence and prayer on
account of his sins. Before Ananias actually came,
Saul saw him in a vision "laying his hands on him,
that he might receive his sight." When he received his
sight, Ananias baptized him, and he received "the gift
of the Holy Spirit." "And he took food and was
strengthened." Jesus preached Himself to Saul; but
He did not tell him what to do to be saved, because He
had given that into the hands of men. Baptism in
water was not essential to the creation of the Twelve,
but it was necessary to Saul's new birth, as it is indis-
pensable to every new birth; and when he arose from

the water of his baptism, he knew that his sins were forgiven. Saul or Paul complied fully with the gospel he pressed on all sinners—he heard the gospel, believed on Christ, repented of his sins, confessed Christ before men, was baptized and lived faithful till death. In order to qualify Saul (Paul) to be an apostle, the Lord Jesus Christ appeared to him; and after he was baptized and received "the gift of the Holy Spirit," which all baptized believers receive, the Lord must have given him directly the miraculous power of the Holy Spirit, which neither Ananias nor anybody but the apostles could impart.

### Saul Was Genuine in His Conversion (vs. 19-30)

*Saul was genuine in his conversion, because he began immediately to preach, and rose above persecution* (19-25) : "And he was certain days with the disciples that were at Damascus. And straightway in the synagogues he proclaimed Jesus, that He is the Son of God. And all that heard him were amazed, and said, Is not this he that in Jerusalem made havoc of them that called on this name? and he had come hither for this intent, that he might bring them bound before the chief priests. But Saul increased the more in strength, and confounded the Jews that dwelt at Damascus, proving that this is the Christ. And when many days were fulfilled, the Jews took counsel together to kill him: but their plot became known to Saul. And they watched the gates also day and night that they might kill him: but his disciples took him by night, and let him down through the wall, lowering him in a basket." When later Saul, as Paul the apostle, declared the gospel the divine power unto the salvation of all that believe, he spoke out of his own experience, though it was exceptional in some

respects: the Lord's appearance in His resurrection body
in heavenly light equipped Saul to be an apostle, and
his three-day physical blindness evinced the reality of
this vision, eliminating any mere illusion. Naturally,
in his preaching in the synagogues, Saul sought to convince his fellow Jews in Damascus that "Jesus is the
Son of God," whom he "confounded," if he could not
persuade them. But his Jewish brethren in their deep-
seated enmity were against him, and not susceptible to
any of his arguments; and they attempted to force on
him the same kind of suffering he had inflicted on other
believers in the Lord. However, the Lord in His providence revealed to Saul the plot of the Jews to kill him;
and by the help of "his disciples," he escaped his enemies, thus rising above their persecution. But nobody
knew better than Saul that, in answering the call of the
risen Lord, he had everything to lose from a worldly
standpoint; but he counted his loss mere "refuse" that
he might gain Christ. Luke's "many days" include
the time that Saul spent in Damascus after his conversion to Christ, and also the time he was in Arabia, before
his return to Jerusalem; but that he would employ three
years in Arabia or anywhere else in mere meditation is
incompatible with his fiery temperament and restless
energy. Saul must have preached in Arabia, as he did
wherever he went; and the attempt on his life in
Damascus was subsequent to his journey into Arabia.
At first when the unbelieving Jews heard Saul in
Damascus, they were amazed that he would preach
Jesus at all, whose followers he had persecuted unto
death; then they were confounded, and finally they
sought his life.

*Saul's sincerity in his salvation is seen in the*
*fellowship accorded him by the other apostles and dis-*

*ciples in Jerusalem* (26-30) : "And when he was come
to Jerusalem, he assayed to join himself to the disciples:
and they were all afraid of him, not believing that he
was a disciple. But Barnabas took him, and brought
him to the apostles, and declared unto them how he
had seen the Lord in the way, and that He had spoken
to him, and how at Damascus he had preached boldly in
the name of Jesus. And he was with them going in
and going out at Jerusalem, preaching boldly in the
name of the Lord: and he spake and disputed against
the Grecian Jews; but they were seeking to kill him.
And when the brethren knew it, they brought him down
to Cæsarea, and sent him forth to Tarsus." So radical
had been the change in Saul in the few years he had
been away from Jerusalem, that the disciples of that
important city could not believe him in sympathy with
their great cause at all; he had formerly been their most
resourceful enemy, and naturally they suspected that
he sought the upper hand of them to persecute them.
But through the mediation of generous Barnabas, Saul's
brethren in Jerusalem learned that he was as completely
identified with the church of Christ as any human being
could be; and all the time he was with them, his preaching "in the name of the Lord" equaled in boldness and
clarity any advocacy of the divine message ever heard
in that populous center. During this visit in Jerusalem,
Saul was Peter's guest for fifteen days. However, Saul's
clash with "the Grecian Jews" must have reminded him
keenly and painfully of Stephen, the first Christian martyr, whose death was on Saul's hands till Jesus cleansed
them in His own blood. These foreign sons of Abraham
discovered in Saul of Tarsus a contestant whose mettle
was more superior to their steel than even Stephen's
temper was; and in seeking to kill Saul, they paid him

the same compliment that they had conferred on Stephen. No doubt Saul's brethren in Jerusalem were glad to make amends for their former suspicion of him by taking him to a place of safety in Cæsarea. From there he returned to his native home in Tarsus a fugitive from persecution for Christ's sake from two great cities, Damascus and Jerusalem. But we learn later from Saul himself that he wanted to stay in Jerusalem; yet the Lord warned him in a trance to depart, and told him He would send him "forth far hence to the Gentiles." A short voyage from Cæsarea on the Mediterranean Sea and up the Cydnus River brought Saul to his old home. Here Luke dropped Saul out of sight for a while, but not into inactivity; because he went "into the regions of Syria and Cilicia," where he preached and suffered much, was himself stoned to death, and was "caught up even to the third heaven" and "into paradise," after which his life was restored miraculously to finish his work in this world. Saul, as a great sinner, according to his own spiritual analysis, "obtained mercy" for two reasons: (1) Because he sinned "ignorantly in unbelief"; (2) because the Lord wanted to demonstrate that in saving Saul He could and would save any sinner and all sinners that would accept Him. The gospel saves wicked adults as well as children.

## The Church Grew After Saul's New Birth (vs. 31-43)

*Outlining this period of prosperity, Luke made easy transition from Paul to Peter* (31-35): "So the church throughout all Judæa and Galilee and Samaria had peace, being edified; and, walking in the fear of the Lord, and in the comfort of the Holy Spirit, was multiplied. And it came to pass, as Peter went throughout all parts, he came down also to the saints that dwelt at Lydda. And there he found a certain man, named Æneas, who had kept his bed eight years; for he was palsied. And Peter said unto him, Æneas, Jesus Christ healeth thee: arise, and make thy bed. And straightway he arose. And all that dwelt at Lydda and in Sharon saw him, and they turned to the Lord." At first the church grew most rapidly in "Judæa and Galilee and Samaria," where the Lord had spent the time of His personal ministry; the elements conducive to this prosperity of the cause of Christ were peace, edification, "the fear of the Lord and the comfort of the Holy Spirit." Formerly, this divine kingdom had progressed in spite of persecution, rather than on account of it; the conversion of Saul from bitter enmity to staunch support and heroic service of the gospel, though it enraged his associates in persecution so they sought to slay him, must have been the main cause of the peace and success of the church at this particular time. And Peter, taking advantage of this fine opportunity to visit the congregations in "all parts" of these provinces, "came down also to the saints that dwelt at Lydda," where he performed one of the most remarkable miracles on record. Evidently Jesus did not heal everybody, neither did His apostles; but both the Lord and His apostles cured whom *He chose*. Peter was so dominated by the Holy Spirit that he knew Jesus had chosen to restore Æneas' health, and said to him, "Æneas, Jesus Christ healeth thee: arise, and make thy bed." Neither Peter nor any other apostle nor anybody else who received the miraculous power of the Holy Spirit through the body of any apostle could work a sign by his own power, but only by the power and in the name of the Lord Jesus Christ. But the most distinguishing thing about the cure of Æneas' malady, which had confined him to his bed for eight long years, was its spiritual effect—"And all that dwelt at Lydda and in Sharon saw him, and they turned to the Lord." These people living in the city of Lydda and in the plain of Sharon, being acquainted with Æneas, knew that there could be no question about his healing; and no doubt many other influences had played on their hearts, wooing them for Christ.

*Peter also raised Tabitha or Dorcas or Gazelle from the dead* (36-43): "Now there was at Joppa a certain disciple named Tabitha, which by interpretation is called Dorcas [or Gazelle]: this woman was full of good works and almsdeeds which she did. And it came to pass in those days, that she fell sick, and died: and when they had washed her, they laid her in an upper chamber. And as Lydda was nigh unto Joppa, the disciples, hearing that Peter was there, sent two men unto him, entreating him, Delay not to come on unto us. And Peter arose and went with them. And when he was come, they brought him into the upper chamber: and all the widows stood by him weeping, and showing the coats and garments which Dorcas made, while she was with them. But Peter put them all forth, and kneeled down, and prayed; and turning to the body, he said, Tabitha, arise. And she opened her eyes; and when she saw Peter, she sat up. And he gave her his hand, and raised her up; and calling the saints and widows, he presented her alive. And it became known throughout all Joppa: and many believed on the Lord. And it came to pass, that he abode many days in Joppa with one Simon, a tanner." Acts of Apostles, like the rest of the New Testament, and the Old Testament, too, for that matter, is specific and matter-of-fact in its narration, adapting itself to the speech and language of man, and basing itself in common experience, so that truth inheres in its story and finds the heart of every honest reader or every sincere hearer. Luke had no literary pride, he made no effort at fine writing; and yet everything from his pen is classic. He gave the name of the subject of this paragraph in two languages, which should be translated in our language as *Gazelle;* she was a *certain* disciple, and lived in Joppa. It would be utterly impossible to improve, or even to approach, Luke's graphic description here. Jesus did not resuscitate all the dead, neither did His apostles, nor anybody else to whom He gave that power; nobody was ever revived from the dead except for some divine purpose, which must have obtained in the case of Gazelle. All modern preachers, when the death of the body comes, are shut up to preaching a funeral sermon and expressions of sympathy for the bereaved; but Peter raised the dead! So far as we know, Jesus never preached a funeral sermon; He called the dead back to life, which He could do any time He chose. Out of the restoration of Gazelle's body came the salvation of many souls, and the opportunity for Peter to do much good by abiding "many days in Joppa with one Simon, a tanner." It is noteworthy that Luke made no effort to describe the scene when Peter called "the saints and widows," and presented Gazelle, whom they admired and loved and praised, alive from the dead; that striking exhibition was impossible even for Luke's gifted, inspired pen to delineate.

# X

## GOD GIVING THE GOSPEL TO THE GENTILES

### (Acts 10)

*The order of the application of the gospel, "to the Jew first, and also to the Greek," was by no means haphazard but inevitable.* In the providence of God, Abraham originated the Hebrews, who were also called Israelites after Jacob or Israel, and Jews for Judah, to provide the world a Saviour in the Lord Jesus Christ. Jesus was a Hebrew or an Israelite or a Jew; and on account of all that went before Him, He limited His personal ministry to His own people. The law of Moses, which the world generally did not have or recognize, became the tutor to bring this chosen race to Christ; and while multitudes failed utterly in this school, yet choice souls graduated with high honors, in whom the Lord began His spiritual kingdom, His church. Many of His own people, in spite of the glory of their training by the law and the prophets, stumbled over the simple teaching of Jesus, and it would have been impossible for Him to get adequate audience among the great Gentile populations. And so for a while the gospel was preached only to the Jews. The members of the great first church in Jerusalem, and of all the other congregations up to the time of the tenth chapter of Acts, which we are now studying, were Jews or proselytes to the Jewish religion; and for a good while after this, every church among the Greeks or Gentiles seemed to have a Hebrew nucleus. But it was the divine purpose from

the beginning to extend the gospel to the whole wide
world. The rejection of Jesus and His church by the
rulers and the vast majority of His race, the tragedy
of tragedies, was foreseen by the prophets and by the
Lord Himself, the greatest of all the seers. Acts of
Apostles, like all the other books of the Bible, is of
necessity mostly in outline; but at times, on occasions,
as in the chapter we are now studying, its particularity
is remarkable. The Lord left nothing to chance or accident; He specified the tabernacle in the wilderness; He
has detailed His church in the New Testament, and we
must follow the divine plan; He chose Cornelius to be
the first Gentile to receive the gospel, and He made
Peter the first preacher to the Jews on Pentecost, and
first in extending the gospel to the Gentiles at the house
of Cornelius.

### God Brought Cornelius and Peter Together (vs. 1-33)

*God sent an angel to Cornelius* (1-8): "Now there
was a certain man in Cæsarea, Cornelius by name, a
centurion of the band called the Italian band, a devout
man, and one that feared God with all his house, who
gave much alms to the people, and prayed to God always.
He saw in a vision openly, as it were about the ninth
hour of the day, an angel of God coming in unto him,
and saying to him, Cornelius. And he, fastening his
eyes upon him, and being affrighted, said, What is it,
Lord? And he said unto him, Thy prayers and thine
alms are gone up for a memorial before God. And
now send men to Joppa, and fetch one Simon, who is
surnamed Peter: he lodgeth with one Simon, a tanner,
whose house is by the sea side. And when the angel
that spake unto him was departed, he called two of his
household servants, and a devout soldier of them that

waited on him continually; and having rehearsed all things unto them, he sent them to Joppa.'' Cornelius was a Gentile; but it is evident that his excellent character had been formed and developed under the influence of the Jewish faith, the only true religion in the world before the Lord Jesus Christ created His church. Even now the almost universal verdict would be that Cornelius was so eminently righteous that he needed nothing; when will men learn that no human being is saved merely because he is ''good''! ''Salvation is of Jehovah,'' prayed Jonah ''out of the fish's belly.'' Humanity was led into sin, but neither conceived nor wrought redemption. Only the Lord can read the heart, and dictate what it must do to be made whole. It was a signal honor for Cornelius to be chosen of God to represent the whole Gentile world in coming into Christ; but he never would have received new light if he had not maintained his integrity by living in the light he already had. Luke passed over some details without mention or implication; but here he put them all in with special emphasis, because at this point the story became universal, typical, crucial! Evidently, Cornelius and Peter had no former acquaintance, but God knew them both; let us read the narrative carefully, and note how He brought them together for a great purpose. The ''devout soldier'' whom Cornelius sent with ''two of his household servants'' to Joppa for Peter, represented the Roman Government for the protection of the messengers. God sent His angel to Cornelius, not to tell him what to do to be saved, but to enable him to get in touch with Peter as one of His preachers; in every case of conversion in the Book of Acts, some Christian preached the gospel to the lost.

*The Lord opened the heaven to Peter in a vision, and
the Spirit announced to him the arrival of the three
messengers* (9-23): "Now on the morrow, as they were
on their journey, and drew nigh unto the city, Peter
went up upon the housetop to pray, about the sixth hour:
and he became hungry, and desired to eat: but while
they made ready, he fell into a trance; and he beholdeth
the heaven opened, and a certain vessel descending, as it
were a great sheet, let down by four corners upon the
earth: wherein were all manner of fourfooted beasts
and creeping things of the earth and birds of the heaven.
And there came a voice to him, Rise, Peter; kill and
eat. But Peter said, Not so, Lord; for I have never
eaten anything that is common and unclean. And a
voice came unto him again the second time, What God
hath cleansed, make not thou common. And this was
done thrice: and straightway the vessel was received
up into heaven. Now while Peter was much perplexed
in himself what the vision which he had seen might
mean, behold, the men that were sent by Cornelius,
having made inquiry for Simon's house, stood before
the gate, and called and asked whether Simon, who was
surnamed Peter, were lodging there. And while Peter
thought on the vision, the Spirit said unto him, Behold,
three men seek thee. But arise, and get thee down,
and go with them, nothing doubting: for I have sent
them. And Peter went down to the men, and said,
Behold, I am he whom ye seek: what is the cause wherefore ye are come? And they said, Cornelius a centurion, a righteous man and one that feareth God,
and well reported of by all the nation of the Jews,
was warned of God by a holy angel to send for thee
into his house, and to hear words from thee.. So he
called them in and lodged them." As in the case of

Philip and the Ethiopian eunuch, we note with what exactness the heavenly clock works: the preparation of Peter to receive the messengers of Cornelius was timed perfectly with their arrival. The Lord Himself knew that for Peter to go into the house of an uncircumcised Gentile, and preach the gospel, meant nothing short of a revolution of Peter in conception, sentiment, outlook, character, life; and that is the reason why "the heaven opened" to Peter with the most remarkable and the most radical vision ever given to any man. Peter knew that to eat the unclean animals he saw in the heavenly vessel or sheet would violate the law of Moses, under which he had lived all his life; and with his character-istic impetuosity he instantly and hotly refused to do it, even daring to take issue with heaven itself! And this fiery declination flashed out of Peter at the very time when his heart was softened by prayer and his appetite sharpened by hunger. But when the heavenly Voice rebuked Peter, warning him, "What God hath cleansed, make not thou common," and this startling vision was emphasized by repetition, before "the vessel was received up into heaven" finally, Peter came down off the top of Simon the tanner's house, where he had gone to pray, a changed man, obeying the command of the Spirit, who was in him as an apostle, to receive the messengers of Cornelius, who "stood before the gate of Simon's house." Peter must have seen that God had repealed the law of Moses as to the kind of animals to eat, which He had the right to do, because He was the Giver of that law and of all real regulation of human conduct. It is certain, however, that Peter did not understand at once the fullness of the meaning of this vision: God had not only abrogated the statute defining animals as clean and unclean, but He had actually abolished the whole Mosaic system of law and religion, and had already ushered in a new age by the creation of the church of Christ on Pentecost; and since the skins or bottles or vessels of the Old Testament could not hold the new wine of the Lord Jesus Christ, the New Testament had to supersede the Old Testament.

*Peter and Cornelius came together* (23-33) : ''And on the morrow he arose and went forth with them, and certain of the brethren from Joppa accompanied him. And on the morrow they entered into Cæsarea. And Cornelius was waiting for them, having called together his kinsmen and his near friends. And when it came to pass that Peter entered, Cornelius met him, and fell down at his feet, and worshipped him. But Peter raised him up, saying, Stand up; I myself also am a man. And as he talked with him, he went in, and findeth many come together: and he said unto them, Ye yourselves know how it is an unlawful thing for a man that is a Jew to join himself or come unto one of another nation; and yet unto me hath God showed that I should not call any man common or unclean: wherefore also I came without gainsaying, when I was sent for. I ask therefore with what intent ye sent for me. And Cornelius said, Four days ago, until this hour, I was keeping the ninth hour of prayer in my house; and behold, a man stood before me in bright apparel, and saith, Cornelius, thy prayer is heard, and thine alms are had in remembrance in the sight of God. Send therefore to Joppa, and call unto thee Simon, who is surnamed Peter; he lodgeth in the house of Simon, a tanner, by the sea side. Forthwith therefore I sent to thee; and thou hast well done that thou art come. Now therefore we are all here present in the sight of God, to hear all things that have been commanded thee of the Lord." This acquaintance of Peter and Cornelius was the most significant meeting of any two men in the history of the human race: it saved the church of Christ from being a mere Jewish institution, and set it in the direction of the conquest and the salvation and the unity of the world: though it did not rise to the heights of the Pentecostal creation, still it became the most pregnant occasion in all the record of Christianity. While it must have taken time for Peter's vision to break the force of his racial separateness and prejudice, which it could do only as he realized in his own heart the depth of its meaning, yet he knew a momentous experience was just ahead of him, and thoughtfully took with him "certain of the brethren from Joppa," when he set out to visit Cornelius at the call of the Lord. Ordinarily the Gentile messengers of Cornelius would not have been accepted as the guests of Simon Peter or Simon, the tanner, because of their strong Jewish conceit, which had been disintegrated by Peter's vision and the report of the angelic warning to Cornelius. Luke spent no time, gave no space to what may have happened en route; but he wrote all the details after Peter and his party walked into the house of Cornelius, who "was waiting for them." With his distinguishing humility, Peter refused to allow Cornelius to worship him. Cornelius was a man of distinction, and probably lived in a large house, where Peter found "many come together"; and this audience, the first Gentile assembly to whom Peter preached, was by no means promiscuous, but picked, for Cornelius had "called together his kinsmen and his near friends," to hear seriously what Peter had to say to them as the messenger of the Lord. Peter said God had showed him not to "call any man common or unclean"; lower animals, beasts of the field or of the jungle, birds of the heaven, fish of the sea, may be ordinary, but man is extraordinary. Cornelius rehearsed what the angel had said to him, and announced to Peter that he and his kinsmen and friends were ready "in the sight of God, to hear all things that have been commanded thee of the Lord."

## God Gave the Gospel to the Gentiles Through Peter (vs. 34-48)

*Peter preached to the house of Cornelius as representatives of all the Gentiles* (34-43): "And Peter opened his mouth, and said, Of a truth I perceive that God is no respecter of persons: but in every nation he that feareth him, and worketh righteousness, is acceptable to him. The word which he sent unto the children of Israel, preaching good tidings of peace by Jesus Christ (he is Lord of all)—that saying ye yourselves know, which was published throughout all Judæa, beginning from Galilee, after the baptism which John preached; even Jesus of Nazareth, how God anointed him with the Holy Spirit and with power: who went about doing good, and healing all that were oppressed of the devil; for God was with him. And we are witnesses of all things which he did both in the country of the Jews, and in Jerusalem; whom also they slew, hanging him on a tree. Him God raised up the third day, and gave him to be made manifest, not to all the people, but unto witnesses that were chosen before of God, even to us, who ate and drank with him after he rose from the dead. And he charged us to preach unto the people, and to testify that this is he who is ordained of God to be the Judge of the living and the dead. To him bear all the prophets witness, that through his name every one that believeth on him shall receive

remission of sins." There is no finality even in the
knowledge of an inspired apostle: Peter introduced this
sermon by proclaiming the absolute impartiality of God
toward the persons of all men, which was brand-new to
him, and to all his Jewish brethren. In truth, the misconception of the divinely chosen race that Jehovah
had called them as His pets or favorites, merely for
their own sake, blinded them to the truth that they
were to be missionaries to save the world through the
leadership of their Messiah, the Lord Jesus Christ, and
set them adrift, and made their very name a byword
among the nations forever. And Peter, his eyes opened,
reminded his Gentile audience of the "good tidings of
peace by Jesus Christ, as Lord of all," of which they
had heard, and which he was about to offer them. There
is only one gospel, which can never be duplicated; and
Peter, having declared this gospel to the Jews, proclaimed it to the Gentiles also. Peter preached the life
and the death and the resurrection and the appearance of
the Lord Jesus Christ, and offered Cornelius and his associates the testimony of Jesus' chosen witnesses, "who ate
and drank with him after he rose from the dead." Originally, the Man called Jesus was in the form of God, or
the form of the Spirit; and He was born into this world
in the form of the flesh: and when He was in one form,
He could change at will into the other form. Evidently,
He changed from the flesh form to the Spirit form at
Nazareth when He vanished from His enemies who were
about to kill Him, and again on the mountain when
He was transfigured: after "he rose from the dead,"
He was in the Spirit form, and changed Himself back
to the flesh form when He appeared to His selected
witnesses and ate with them. The Hebrew prophets,
being inspired, rose above the fatal misunderstanding

of the divine purpose in their people; and when Peter preached to the uncircumcised Gentiles in the house of Cornelius, ''To him bear all the prophets witness, that through his name every one that believeth on him shall receive remission of sins,'' he threw the door of the church of Christ open to all believing, penitent, obedient sinners every-where and every-when.

*And right at that very point, the Holy Spirit interrupted Peter to emphasize and magnify what he had said, and make the gospel universal in its application* (44-48): ''While Peter yet spake these words, the Holy Spirit fell on all them that heard the word. And they of the circumcision that believed were amazed, as many as came with Peter, because that on the Gentiles also was poured out the gift of the Holy Spirit. For they heard them speak with tongues, and magnify God. Then answered Peter, Can any man forbid the water, that these should not be baptized, who have received the Holy Spirit as well as we? And he commanded them to be baptized in the name of Jesus Christ. Then prayed they him to tarry certain days.'' The purpose of the outpouring of the Holy Spirit on Pentecost was to create the church of Christ in the twelve original apostles; the reason why ''that on the Gentiles also was poured out the gift of the Holy Spirit,'' was to show the Jews and the Gentiles and everybody forever two things: (1) That God, or the Lord, being ''no respecter of persons,'' would do everything for the Gentiles that He did for the Jews; (2) that every Gentile (as well as every Jew) that believed in Christ and repented of his sins and confessed Christ before men should embody his faith and evince his penitence and glorify his confession and complete his primary obedience by being ''baptized in the name of Jesus Christ.'' Pentecost

was never repeated, because, after the church was originally created in the apostles, everybody that wanted to
become a Christian could be spiritually born; the miracle
of the Holy Spirit at the house of Cornelius never happened again, for it settled the question once for all time
to come. The Holy Spirit caused no confusion by
breaking in on Peter's preaching, but rather re-enforced
Peter at the very point when he had reached the climactic act of Christian baptism. When the Gentiles at
the house of Cornelius had been baptized, they, just
like everybody else who completes the process of the
new birth in this pictorial deed, received "the gift of
the Holy Spirit," which is the Holy Spirit Himself,
and more to be desired than any spectacular power He
might confer. In only two ways could anybody receive
the miraculous power of the Holy Spirit—it must come
directly from heaven or be imparted through the body of
an apostle. It was given through the apostles by the
guidance of the Lord. It came directly on Pentecost, to
Paul to make him an apostle, and to Cornelius' house to
prove Gentiles should be baptized and saved.

## XI

## THE "NEW NAME"

### (Acts 11)

*Evidently, Christian or Christians is the "new name" by which Isaiah prophesied the people of Jehovah should be called* (Isa. 62:2): *indeed, it is the only name peculiar to the New Testament.* The most common appellation applied in Acts to the followers of the Lord Jesus Christ is *disciples,* which lacks the exactness and the glory of *Christians.* Paul rebuked the Corinthians for calling themselves Apollosites or Cephasites or Paulites, thus manifesting their contention and carnality; and urged them to give Christ all their devotion, and Peter pronounced the name *Christian* the glorification of God. *Disciple* is a wonderful word; but it is easily possible for one to be a *disciple* without being a *Christian* at all. The twelve original apostles were disciples—disciples of John the Baptist and disciples of Jesus of Nazareth— but they were not, and could not be, Christians prior to their spiritual creation on the first Pentecost after the resurrection of Jesus from the dead. A disciple is a learner; a Christian is a learner who has actually entered into covenant relation with the Lord Jesus Christ by believing on Him as the Son of God, and by repenting of sin and by confessing His name before men and by being baptized into Him. Every Christian should be an obedient disciple of the Lord all the days of His life, but not every disciple may be a Christian in every respect. A druggist, who sold Bibles on the side but who thought he was smart and superior because he did not believe the Bible, bristling with argument and challenge and scorn, threw an open Bible on his counter, put his finger on a statute in the law of Moses, and sneered, "That thing would not be tolerated in our city; was Moses a Christian?" He expected me to answer, "Yes"; and on the basis of this positive response, he intended to vent his spleen against the Book of God. But I exclaimed, "No," which amazed him, and took all the wind out of his sails. Moses was "the man of God"; but he could not have been a Christian, because he lived and died hundreds and thousands of years before the Lord Jesus Christ, the great Exemplar for the Christian to follow, to copy, had been born into this world. God has always had believers who lived in the light they had; but it was impossible for any patriarch or Jew or prophet or anybody else prior to the life of Jesus and Pentecost to be a Christian! On Pentecost, the new creation, which is spiritual, just as the old creation was physical, flashed into existence, sprang into being by the fiat of the great God; the church of Christ is the new creation, and *Christian* is the "new name" for the fundamental unit of the church. Christ is the anointed One; Christians are anointed ones to represent Christ in the world.

### The Gentiles Were Entitled to Salvation in Christ (vs. 1-30)

*God forced the Jews to recognize this fundamental right of the Gentiles* (1-18): "Now the apostles and the brethren that were in Judæa heard that the Gentiles also had received the word of God. And when Peter was come up to Jerusalem, they that were of the circumcision contended with him, saying, Thou wentest in to men uncircumcised, and didst eat with them. But Peter began, and expounded the matter unto them in order, saying, I was in the city of Joppa praying: and in a trance I saw a vision, a certain vessel descending, as it were a great sheet let down from heaven by four corners; and it came even unto me: upon which when I had fastened mine eyes, I considered, and saw the four-footed beasts of the earth and wild beasts and creeping things and birds of the heaven. And I heard also a voice saying unto me, Rise, Peter; kill and eat. But I said, Not so, Lord: for nothing common or unclean hath ever entered into my mouth. But a voice answered the second time out of heaven, What God hath cleansed, make not thou common. And this was done thrice: and all were drawn up again into heaven. And behold, forthwith three men stood before the house in which we were, having been sent from Cæsarea unto me. And the Spirit bade me go with them, making no distinction. And these six brethren also accompanied me; and we entered into the man's house: and he told us how he had seen the angel standing in his house, saying, Send to Joppa, and fetch Simon, whose surname is Peter; who shall speak unto thee words, whereby thou shalt be saved, thou and all thy house. And as I began to speak, the Holy Spirit fell on them, even as on us at the beginning. And I remembered the word of the Lord, how he said, John indeed baptized with water; but ye shall be baptized in the Holy Spirit. If then God gave unto them the like gift as he did also unto us, when we believed on the Lord Jesus Christ, who was I, that I could withstand God? And when they heard these things, they held their peace, and glorified God, saying, Then to the Gentiles also hath God granted repentance unto life.'' Of course, the Lord is infinitely resourceful; He could

have inspired the mind of Peter inwardly and directly
to preach the gospel to Cornelius and his relatives and
friends and baptize them, but He chose to prepare both
Peter and Cornelius objectively for their meeting, reaching their hearts through the testimony of their eyes
and ears. This made it possible for Peter, by merely
rehearsing his experience, to clear the whole matter up
to the other "apostles and the brethren that were in
Judæa." In a similar manner today, the Holy Spirit
appeals to men to convince them and indoctrinate them
in the way of the Lord, by the Word of God. Peter
must have foreseen that his associates in Jerusalem would
question his acceptance of uncircumcised Gentiles; and
so he took six of the Joppa brethren with him to the
house of Cornelius, and also to Jerusalem when he returned home, as witnesses to what occurred in Cæsarea.
And "they that were of the circumcision" were not
bigoted, as they have sometimes been dubbed; but they
were amenable to the Spirit of the Lord, "and when
they heard these things, they held their peace, and
glorified God, saying, Then to the Gentiles also hath
God granted repentance unto life." Human nature
is conservative; and it required time and education for
these first Jewish Christians to see that circumcision,
preserving the identity of the Hebrews till Christ came
of them to the world, had served its purpose as a separating rite, no longer had religious significance and
should be given up for the sake of the Gentiles.

*Indeed, the "new name" Christian was originated
in a great Gentile or Greek center* (19-26): "They therefore that were scattered abroad upon the tribulation
that arose about Stephen traveled as far as Phœnicia,
and Cyprus, and Antioch, speaking the word to none
save only to Jews. But there were some of them, men

of Cyprus and Cyrene, who, when they were come to
Antioch, spake unto the Greeks also, preaching the
Lord Jesus. And the hand of the Lord was with them:
and a great number that believed turned unto the Lord.
And the report concerning them came to the ears of
the church which was in Jerusalem: and they sent forth
Barnabas as far as Antioch: who, when he was come,
and had seen the grace of God, was glad; and he exhorted them all, that with purpose of heart they would
cleave unto the Lord: for he was a good man, and full
of the Holy Spirit and of faith: and much people was
added unto the Lord. And he went forth to Tarsus to
seek for Saul: and when he had found him, he brought
him unto Antioch. And it came to pass, that even for
a whole year they were gathered together with the
church, and taught much people; and that the disciples
were called Christians first in Antioch.'' Having traced
the preaching of Philip in Samaria to the Ethiopian
eunuch and to all the cities between Azotus and Cæsarea,
having narrated the new birth of Saul of Tarsus and
outlined his work in Damascus and referred to his ex-
cursion into Arabia and followed him back to Jerusalem
and to Cæsarea and to his native home in Tarsus, and
having sketched Peter's work in the provinces of Judea
and Galilee and Samaria, Luke turns back to the martyrdom of Stephen to recount other lines of activity
among the servants of the Lord Jesus Christ, whose
names are not given, but who preached ''the word to
none save only to Jews'' in ''Phœnicia and Cyprus and
Antioch.'' But later, evidently after Peter extended
the gospel to the Gentiles in Cæsarea, ''men of Cyprus
and Cyrene'' visited Antioch and preached ''the Lord
Jesus'' ''unto the Greeks also.'' With Jerusalem as the
center, the apostles surveyed the whole field of action,

and kept in touch with the preachers everywhere, sending them aid or advice as it was necessary. Peter's brethren in Jerusalem were about to rebuke him for accepting uncircumcised Gentiles; and no other preacher at Antioch or at any other point would have dared to do that, without the precedent and authority of Peter's course at the house of Cornelius. Simon, who bore the cross of Christ when He broke down under the load, may have been one of the Cyrenians that preached the gospel for the first time to the uncircumcised Greeks in Antioch. Peter's work in Cæsarea opened the way to the Gentiles, but the preaching in Antioch turned out to be the first extensive invasion of Greek territory, where "a great number that believed turned to the Lord." Christian baptism is the turning act, and this really means, "a great number that believed were baptized." To Antioch came Barnabas from Jerusalem, with his famous gift of exhortation to reinforce the young Christians in that populous city, where he also won many new recruits to the divine army. But Barnabas had not been in Antioch very long till he saw the need of efficient help in this rapidly growing work, which he sought and found in his friend and brother, Saul of Tarsus, who combined happily and powerfully with Barnabas in a double, fruitful ministry for a solid year in Antioch. When we consider the size and importance of Antioch at this time, called "the queen of the East, and the third metropolis of the world," with half a million inhabitants, we are not surprised that, under the leadership of such preachers as Saul and Barnabas, Antioch soon became the second capital of the Christian world, subordinate only to Jerusalem. It is significant also that the "new name" "*Christians*," the most appropriate, the most descriptive, the happiest,

the most beautiful, the most glorious name ever on
human tongue or applied to mortal man, was created
in Antioch, and thus articulated with the rising tide
of the Gentiles: for this reveals that the gospel is
neither racial nor national nor classific, but fundamentally and inherently world-wide and time-long. The
conversion of Cornelius coupled the cause of Christ to
the whole Gentile world, but God had to take the initia-
tive and force the issue.

*And Jews and Greeks or Gentiles were knit together
in the Lord Jesus Christ* (27-30): ''Now in these days
there came down prophets from Jerusalem unto Antioch.
And there stood up one of them named Agabus, and
signified by the Spirit that there should be a great
famine over all the world: which came to pass in the
days of Claudius. And the disciples, every man according to his ability, determined to send relief unto the
brethren that dwelt in Judæa: which also they did, sending it to the elders by the hand of Barnabas and Saul.''
In this paragraph, Luke makes his first reference to
prophets among the Christians, whose gift must have
already brought them into prominence; for his brethren
accepted with implicit faith Agabus' prediction of a
universal famine, deciding to raise a fund to relieve the
poorer members of the church in Judea. Here we see
the love of the Lord Jesus Christ dissolving the strong
prejudice between the Jews and the Greeks or Gentiles,
and knitting their hearts and lives together in unity—
the same kind of unity that prevailed in the great first
church in the city of Jerusalem among the Jews themselves. And these Greek Christians actually carried
their good resolution into effect, and sent their offering
''to the elders by the hand of Barnabas and Saul'';
incidentally, this mission gave Saul and Barnabas a

vacation from their strenuous labor in the city of Antioch, and at the same time furnished them useful, profitable employment of a different kind. Apparently this Christian beneficence on the part of the Greeks in Antioch required no exhortation from Saul or Barnabas, but it was spontaneous; no doubt the givers were actuated by their gratitude for the great spiritual blessing of salvation in the Lord Jesus Christ, which had come to them through their Hebrew brethren. And these generous, grateful Antiochans did not wait to see how severe this predicted dearth might be among themselves or with their near neighbors, but they responded first to the poverty of populous Judea, where they knew the famine would cause more suffering than in their own fair city of Antioch, which was greatly enriched by foreign trade. In fact, they saw the benevolence, or practical love, of the first church in Jerusalem, not as the irrational manifestation of communistic zealots, but as an authorized example, which they followed at their very first opportunity. Now we can not let this paragraph go without calling attention again to the organism of the church, of which we are reminded by Luke's mention of "the elders" in Judea, to whom Barnabas and Saul delivered the gifts of the Greek Christians in Antioch. Luke has put no emphasis on the "organization" of the church, because the church was created as an organism in the apostles in whom its "organization" inhered: the apostles functioned at first as elders, and guided the inherent office of the diaconate, so that seven qualified brethren took charge as deacons in the historic first church in Jerusalem. Of course, every congregation had elders and deacons, though Luke has not bothered to tell us about them; neither has he named or listed the churches or congregations themselves, save in a few representative cases. In all his history, Luke sticks to fundamental facts and primary principles, and puts them plainly. Of course, ''the elders'' were the proper persons to receive the contributions Barnabas and Saul took from the Greek Christians in Antioch to relieve their distressed brethren in Judea.

# XII

## ASTOUNDING ACTS OF AN ANGEL

### (Acts 12)

*Like the rest of the New Testament and the whole Bible, for that matter, Acts of Apostles is perfectly consistent.* Whoever seeks to eliminate the miraculous from Christianity bars his own heart against the Lord Jesus Christ, whether he is conscious of it or not; if one rejects the supernaturalism of the Bible, he throws the entire Book away. Indeed, if the Scriptures did not transcend nature and include the Creator, they could not, as they do, give the most satisfactory explanation of nature itself. Even the heathen or pagan or savage or barbarian or idolater blindly insists on the mysterious in his religion. The Christian religion uses the supernatural intelligently, conservatively, purposefully, to accomplish what is otherwise impossible, that the light of the Lord may shine upon the earth; it reveals to us the great God and prayer and angels and heaven, through the Lord Jesus Christ. God is independent and self-existent and eternal; no man ever knew His mind to whom He did not reveal it, and He never had a counselor. God answers prayer, but He does it in His own way; none can dictate to Him or force Him. The Lord follows His own counsel: He let Herod cut off the head of James, and delivered Peter from prison. If any man takes issue with the divine will, he is forced to turn to the devil and suffer the doom of the damned. Angels are, Sadducees, ancient and modern, to the contrary, notwithstanding. The angels of the Lord's "little ones" always behold God; and they are "ministering spirits, sent forth to do service for the sake of them that shall inherit salvation." Once when a north-bound passenger train hit a truck, carelessly left obliquely across the platform where I had the right to walk, and knocked the truck against me, and hurled me into the path of a south-bound freight train, I almost heard the whir of an angel's wings as I summoned instantly all my power to get off the track and save my life. A lady on a train that stopped on the brink of a drawbridge, on leaving this train, went directly to prayer-meeting to thank the Lord for saving her life; doubtless He had saved her life many times without her consciousness or thanksgiving. However, God does not always protect His believers from misfortune, because, in His perfect vision, He sees that calamity will discipline them and contribute to their spiritual good. After all, the best of men are poor and weak and blind and helpless; how beautiful, how comforting is the doctrine, buttressed by the Bible, that every Christian has his guardian angel all along the way through this world! Heaven notes the falling bird, and marks the minutest detail in man; the light of the day and the darkness of the night are the same to the Lord, who beholds all things all the time.

### Peter's Deliverance from Prison Was Astounding (vs. 1-17)

*Peter's deliverance from prison was astounding, because Herod had made it humanly impossible* (1-6): "Now about that time Herod the king put forth his hands to afflict certain of the church. And he killed James, the brother of John, with the sword. And when

he saw that it pleased the Jews, he proceeded to seize
Peter also.  And those were the days of unleavened
bread.  And when he had taken him, he put him in
prison, and delivered him to four quaternions of soldiers to guard him; intending after the Passover to
bring him forth to the people.  Peter therefore was kept
in the prison: but prayer was made earnestly of the
church unto God for him.  And when Herod was about
to bring him forth, the same night Peter was sleeping
between two soldiers, bound with two chains: and guards
before the door kept the prison.''  Previous persecutions of the apostles and the church had been instigated
by the Jews as religious bigots, who closed their eyes
and stopped their ears and hardened their hearts against
the revelation of the Lord Jesus Christ, apparently
without any help from the rulers of the land; but now
''Herod the king,'' grandson of the Herod who slew the
infants of Bethlehem in an effort to kill the child Jesus,
and a nephew of the ruler of the same name who beheaded John the Baptist, came forward and took charge
of this oppression. One can easily imagine this profligate,
dissolute prince, this wicked king, challenging the Jewish
Sanhedrin and the priests and the captain of the temple,
''You fellows had the apostles in prison, and let them
get out; now watch me make it impossible for Peter to
escape.''  Herod had the daring and the depravity of
the devil, of which he had already given proof by be-
heading ''James the brother of John''; why the Lord
permitted the death of James and saved Peter's life
miraculously is a divine secret into which we can not
pry.  Like the Pharisees before him, Herod aimed to
destroy the church in Jerusalem, and probably boasted,
''The way to crush this movement is to kill its leaders'';
but he failed utterly.  To make doubly sure that Peter

could not flee from his terrible fate, Herod placed him in a prison protected by a great iron gate, and guarded him by sixteen soldiers, to two of whom he was chained in his cell, the others being at two places between the cell and the gate and in front of the gate. Peter's brethren prayed for him while he was in jail, not that he might be delivered, which they did not expect, but probably that he might be saved from his former fickleness in this imminent peril. Every man, whether good or bad, is influenced by his fellows: if Herod had had any conscience at all, his murder of James would have made him a coward, which he was without knowing it; but "when he saw that it pleased the Jews, he proceeded to seize Peter also." Herod had bad blood; he had inherited the viciousness of his ancestors.

*When the angel delivered Peter from prison, the guards knew not what happened, neither did Peter himself know at the time* (7-11): "And behold, an angel of the Lord stood by him, and a light shined in the cell: and he smote Peter on the side, and awoke him, saying, Rise up quickly. And his chains fell off from his hands. And the angel said unto him, Gird thyself, and bind on thy sandals. And he did so. And he saith unto him, Cast thy garment about thee, and follow me. And he went out, and followed; and he knew not that it was true which was done by the angel, but thought he saw a vision. And when they were past the first and the second guard, they came unto the iron gate that leadeth into the city; which opened to them of its own accord: and they went out, and passed on through one street; and straightway the angel departed from him. And when Peter was come to himself, he said, Now I know of a truth, that the Lord hath sent forth his angel and delivered me out of the hand of Herod, and from all the expectation of the people of the Jews." Spirit transcends matter; heaven rises above mind, and has power over all material things, whether animate or inanimate. It is not written that an angel came down out of heaven to where Peter was in prison, but that "an angel of the Lord stood by him"; and evidently the light that shone in Peter's cell flashed from the angel's own person. The angel did not have to touch the chains that manacled Peter to the soldiers between whom he was sleeping, for "his chains fell off from his hands" of their own accord. It was likewise wonderful that the angel partially awoke Peter and told him to dress himself, without disturbing in the slightest degree the soldier-guards to whom he was fettered: and this celestial messenger, with perfect control over Peter through his subjective mind, by the light of his own spirit form guided Peter out of the cell, right by "the first and the second guard" without their knowing it in any respect, and through "the iron gate that leadeth into the city," which opened to them and swung shut again "of its own accord," without any noise or the use of any key at all or any injury to the lock whatsoever. Afterwards, the angel and Peter "passed on through one street; and straightway the angel departed from" Peter. And by that time, Peter had completely recovered his objective mind, and realized that he had not merely seen a vision, but that the angel of the Lord had gloriously delivered him from the wicked king Herod "and from all the expectation of the people of the Jews." Surely this is one of the most remarkable, one of the most complex and one of the most unexpected miracles recorded in all the Word of God, or ever injected into the years of time! Nothing is impossible to the Lord that thus took Peter out of the very jaws of death, discomfited his villainous

persecutor and filled his old-time enemies, the infidel
Jews, with bitter disappointment.

*The angel's astounding salvation of Peter from the
murderous king Herod overcame the brethren with
amazement and joy* (12-17) : "And when he had considered the thing, he came to the house of Mary the mother
of John whose surname was Mark; where many were
gathered together and were praying. And when he
knocked at the door of the gate, a maid came to answer,
named Rhoda. And when she knew Peter's voice, she
opened not the gate for joy, but ran in, and told that
Peter stood before the gate. And they said unto her,
Thou art mad. But she confidently affirmed that it was
even so. And they said, It is his angel. But Peter continued knocking: and when they had opened, they saw
him, and were amazed. But he, beckoning unto them
with the hand to hold their peace, declared unto them
how the Lord had brought him forth out of the prison.
And he said, Tell these things unto James, and to the
brethren. And he departed, and went to another place."
When Peter realized the astounding reality of his triumphant delivery from the complicated jail in which
the depraved King Herod had bound him, his original
quick wit came upon him in renewed vigor; and he
decided instantly what course to take. The home of
Mary, the mother of John Mark, Peter's son in the
gospel, was easy of access; and thither Peter hastened
in the darkness of the night. In that house, as in many
another residence in Jerusalem, there was a remarkable
prayer meeting that night; and nobody was ever more
surprised than the maid, Rhoda, who, hearing a rap "at
the door of the gate," answered that call, and, recogniz-
ing "Peter's voice," "opened not the gate for joy, but
ran in, and told that Peter stood before the gate"; and

no group was ever more amazed than Mary and her guests, who thought Rhoda had lost her sanity or had heard Peter's guardian angel, when, on account of Peter's "continued knocking," the door was opened, and Peter stood before them. But the impetuous Peter proceeded with due caution; he knew that if his new freedom became known to the enemy, the astounding miracle of the angel in delivering him from prison would have been wrought in vain: and he signaled for peace, and told the wonderful story of his release from jail; he also commanded the company in Mary's house, "Tell these things unto James, and to the brethren," and the shadows of that night swallowed him up out of their sight. Where Peter went, nobody knew; he kept his own counsel. But Peter wanted all his associate apostles and fellow Christians to know that the Lord had saved his life, for their own happiness. The "James" to whom Peter referred was probably the brother of the Lord Jesus Christ. Two of the original twelve apostles were named "James"—James, the brother of John, or the son of Zebedee, whom Herod beheaded, and James, the son of Alphæus. After the death of James, John's brother, and in the absence of Peter, the Lord's brother James seemed to be the leader of the church in the city of Jerusalem.

## Herod's Death Was Another Astounding Act of an Angel (vs. 18-25)

*"An angel of the Lord smote"* Herod, *because, with hellish wickedness and presumptuous depravity and overweening vanity and devilish pride, he would usurp the glory of God* (18-23) : "Now as soon as it was day, there was no small stir among the soldiers, what was become of Peter. And when Herod had sought for

him, and found him not, he examined the guards, and commanded that they should be put to death. And he went down from Judæa to Cæsarea, and tarried there. Now he was highly displeased with them of Tyre and Sidon: and they came with one accord to him, and, having made Blastus the king's chamberlain their friend, they asked for peace, because their country was fed from the king's country. And upon a set day Herod arrayed himself in royal apparel, and sat on the throne, and made an oration unto them. And the people shouted, saying, The voice of a god, and not of a man. And immediately an angel of the Lord smote him, because he gave not God the glory: and he was eaten of worms, and gave up the spirit.'' Psychologically, man has two minds—the objective mind and the subjective mind—both of which the Lord can control. In this material world, the objective is dominant, and the subjective is mostly below the threshold of consciousness; but the death of the body destroys the objective mind when the subjective mind, as the soul or the spirit, comes into complete and permanent consciousness. Peter's deliverance from prison was both objective and subjective, but his objective mind was below consciousness and his subjective mind was in control; which is evinced by the fact that he thought he saw a vision, till, when the angel left him, he became objectively conscious again as his body awoke fully from sleep and he perceived the reality of his release from prison. Only the objective mind sleeps; the subjective mind, which must be the soul or the spirit, dreams and sees visions and never sleeps. Of course, the sixteen soldiers detailed to guard Peter and keep him in jail were excited when he could not be found, because they knew that their lives were at stake; of course, also, the

Lord so controlled their minds both objectively and subjectively that they had no consciousness of the angel releasing Peter from their grip. And Herod must have seen clearly, when "he examined the guards," that they were all innocent, for heaven had intervened to save Peter by a stupendous miracle; but this king was so monstrously mean that he inflicted the death penalty on all these blameless men, rather than acknowledge his own impotence. We do not wonder that the bloody wretch left the scene of his crime and established his capital in Cæsarea, where, according to Josephus, he delivered an oration in a silver suit, accepted seriously the adulation of his silly subjects, and suffered death at the hand of an angel, "because he gave not God the glory: and he was eaten of worms, and gave up the spirit."

*And again "the word of God" won over the forces of evil* (24, 25): "But the word of God grew and multiplied. And Barnabas and Saul returned from Jerusalem, when they had fulfilled their ministration, taking with them John whose surname was Mark." The miraculous is woven into the warp and woof of the Word of God as the fabric of divine revelation; the Bible not only reports what the Lord *said*, but it likewise pictures His *action*, to make the vehicle of His will satisfactory and complete. If mere words are easy and weak for men, how much more so with God! "The heavens declare the glory of God; and the firmament showeth his handiwork." The book we are now studying is happily called, "Acts [not mere words] of Apostles." Luke has informed us with much repetition what the Lord Jesus Christ *said* through the apostles and some of their associates; and in every chapter he has graphically described what the Lord *did*, directly or through angels or men as His servants. There is never anything stiff or strained or affected or far-fetched or false in the miracles of the Word of God, with whom the supernatural is as simple and common as the natural is with man; of course, God can and does operate in the realm high above man; otherwise He would not, He could not, be God at all. It imposed no impossible tax on the Lord to work a miracle by the power that inhered in Him as the Son of God, or by the strength He delegated to the apostles or through them to others; He released Peter from prison with the grace by which He lights the world every day, and slew Herod as easily as He envelops the earth in darkness every night. And when the Lord lifted Peter out of the slimy presence and power of Herod, and struck Herod down in miserable, shameful death, "the word of God grew and multiplied," as it had done as the result of every other persecution. Herod's sins went "before unto judgment," that he might be an example unto other men; let no wicked man vainly imagine he is safe because he does not suffer the spectacular fate of Herod, for he can not hide his evident sins, which shall "follow after," unless he obeys the gospel and receives the forgiveness of the Lord Jesus Christ (1 Tim. 5:24, 25). Now, having given us the account of the death of James, the imprisonment of Peter and the death of Herod, which evidently happened between the time Barnabas and Saul left Antioch on their benevolent mission to the poor Christians in Judea and the time of their return from Jerusalem to Antioch, Luke referred again to Barnabas and Saul, mentioning that they "fulfilled their ministration," and took John Mark with them when they went back to Antioch. Saul and Barnabas may have stayed out of Jerusalem, on account of possible danger to themselves, till Herod had established himself in Cæsarea. Of course, Saul and Barnabas must have carried to the brethren in Antioch the great news of the death of James, the deliverance of Peter and the death of Herod.

## XIII

## PAUL LOOMING INTO PROMINENCE

### (Acts 13)

*Nature's greatest achievement is a man or a woman.*
Sam Jones said, "It takes time to make a man; no man
should go out by himself till he is thirty years old, and
a woman never." Some humorist declared, "It is a
good thing that some men do claim to be self-made, for
they relieve the Lord of responsibility for a mighty bad
job." Testified the psalmist (Ps. 8: 3-9),

"When I consider thy heavens, the work of thy
      fingers,
The moon and the stars, which thou hast ordained;
What is man, that thou art mindful of him?
And the son of man, that thou visitest him?
For thou hast made him but little lower than God,
And crownest him with glory and honor.
Thou makest him to have dominion over the works
      of thy hands;
Thou hast put all things under his feet:
All sheep and oxen,
Yea, and the beasts of the field,
The birds of the heavens, and the fish of the sea,
Whatsoever passeth through the paths of the seas.
O Jehovah, our Lord,
How excellent is thy name in all the earth!"

Paul himself explained (1 Cor. 11: 7), "Forasmuch
as he [man] is the image and glory of God: but the

woman is the glory of the man." Jesus taught that
man is "of more value than many sparrows" (Matt.
10:31), and "how much then is a man of more value
than a sheep!" (Matt. 12:12). Man is infinitely more
than the lower animals or the starry heavens; man is
the connecting link between the Creator and creation;
man has capacity for citizenship in two worlds—on earth
and in heaven—for both of which he was made. Yea,
the great God has lavished His highest and best gifts,
even His own glory, on man as His favorite creature.
And all the great men that ever lived were produced
by the Lord Jesus Christ, either in the promise and
hope of His coming, or by the power of the operation
of His glorious gospel. Jesus, like the sun, shines in
His own original light; but men, like the moon, glow
with borrowed light in the luminosity of the Lord. Now
of all the men that ever lived, or perhaps that shall ever
walk the earth, save the Lord Himself only, Paul the
Apostle is the greatest. In the first twelve chapters of
Acts, Peter looms large; and Saul is rather obscure.
But beginning with the thirteenth chapter of Acts,
Saul's name is changed to Paul, and he is in the center
of the stage; indeed, from now on to the close of Luke's
record, we shall find a biography of Paul. But Paul's
coming into prominence is neither accidental emphasis
nor unfair favoritism; Paul made himself famous and
eminent by the reality of his faith and the comprehen-
sion of his doctrine and the energy of his life. After
his conversion, Paul kept his back on the devil and his
face toward the Lord; his faith never wavered and his
enthusiasm never abated and his zeal never lagged till
the day of his death. Any difference in what the Lord
does for men depends on the individual man, rather than
on the Lord Himself, who is without respect of persons.

### The Holy Spirit Selecting and Sending Missionaries (vs. 1-15)

*At first Saul's name was last in the list* (1-3) : "Now there were at Antioch, in the church that was there, prophets and teachers, Barnabas, and Symeon that was called Niger, and Lucius of Cyrene, and Manaen the foster-brother of Herod the tetrarch, and Saul. And as they ministered to the Lord, and fasted, the Holy Spirit said, Separate me Barnabas and Saul for the work whereunto I have called them. Then, when they had fasted and prayed and laid their hands on them, they sent them away." A prophet is defined as "one who delivers divine messages or interprets the divine will," also as "one who foretells the future." The New Testament does not make a sharp distinction between prophets and teachers; the men named in this paragraph were both prophets *and* teachers, and that qualified them to be missionaries for the Lord Jesus Christ. Indeed, every Christian is not only *missionary,* but he is *a* missionary. The Holy Spirit chose Barnabas and Saul to represent Christ in parts distant from Antioch, but Symeon and Lucius and Manaen and all the other members of the church in Antioch were no less His messengers where they were. A halo no more attaches to the so-called "foreign missionary" than to the humble, faithful Christian that remains at home all the days of his life. Great calls come to men in the atmosphere of service and self-denial and worship, the environment in which Barnabas and Saul were divinely selected from among their associates for a great special enterprise. In a sense, the church in Antioch elected Barnabas and Saul to represent their brethren in the evangelization of waste places; but behind that call, as should always be the case in every similar summons, was the Holy Spirit and the Lord Jesus Christ. Of course, the Antiochan congregation of believers must have provided for the physical support of their representatives in that great original work, but not a word is said or written about this matter. Neither were Barnabas and Saul in any way hampered by their human sustainers: verily every missionary of the Lord Jesus Christ should be free under Him. The simple ceremony of fasting and prayer and the laying on Barnabas and Saul of the hands of their brethren, in sending "them away" on their mission, was born of the blessed influence under which they were originally called by the command of the Holy Spirit. Neither their work nor their maintenance was general, but it was specific: they were "living links" of the church in Antioch, who knew them and whom they knew, *personally;* which should always be the case if possible. Now, it is refreshing to observe Saul's happy fitness for this kind of service, which brought him quickly to the front, placing his name at the head of the list, and making him the greatest apostle and missionary in the history of Christianity. His genius was surpassing, his gifts superb, his education broad, his training complete, his service heroic, his influence world-wide and time-long!

*Saul, whose name was changed to Paul, discovered and punished "a false prophet"* (4-12) : "So they, being sent forth by the Holy Spirit, went down to Seleucia; and from thence they sailed to Cyprus. And when they were at Salamis, they proclaimed the word of God in the synagogues of the Jews: and they had also John as their attendant. And when they had gone through the whole island unto Paphos, they found a certain sorcerer, a false prophet, a Jew, whose name was Bar-Jesus; who was with the proconsul, Sergius Paulus, a man of understanding. The same called unto him Barnabas and Saul, and sought to hear the word of God. But Elymas the sorcerer (for so is his name by interpretation) withstood them, seeking to turn aside the proconsul from the faith. But Saul, who is also called Paul, filled with the Holy Spirit, fastened his eyes on him and said, O full of all guile and all villany, thou son of the devil, thou enemy of all righteousness, wilt thou not cease to pervert the right ways of the Lord? And now, behold, the hand of the Lord is upon thee, and thou shalt be blind, not seeing the sun for a season. And immediately there fell on him a mist and a darkness; and he went about seeking some to lead him by the hand. Then the proconsul, when he saw what was done, believed, being astonished at the teaching of the Lord." Here Luke has recorded one of the most startling incidents in his narrative: Paul was about to get the attention of a very important personage, "the proconsul, Sergius Paulus, a man of understanding," to the gospel, when "Elymas the sorcerer," "full of all guile and all villany, the son of the devil, the enemy of all righteousness," stood in the way, seeking "to pervert the right ways of the Lord"; and the Holy Spirit filled Paul, and his anger flashed in righteous indignation. And through Paul the Lord arrested Elymas in his perverse wickedness and hellish madness by smiting him with blindness: this eliminated Elymas; and "the proconsul, when he saw what was done, *believed,* being astonished at the teaching of the Lord." Acts of Apostles, always dominated by the maxim of brevity, found space for this exhibition of miraculous power, which marked the authority of Paul as the apostle. The apostolic office fundamen-

tally in Paul or any other man would be impossible
without the definite selection and the visible, tangible
approval of the Lord Jesus Christ. Nothing could be
more primary in the practical application of Christianity than this doctrine. Evidently, Luke, to conserve
space, compressed the salvation of Sergius Paulus, or
his acceptance of the divine remedy for sin, into the
one word *"believed"*: *faith* always includes *repentance*
and *confession* and *baptism* in every account of conversion in Acts where they are not particularized. We can
not disassociate Saul's new name of *Paul* from *Sergius
Paulus,* whom Paul converted, as the first proconsul to
accept the Lord Jesus Christ as his Saviour. Paul had
to work injury to the person of Elymas to show him
a mere sorcerer pretending to be a prophet, and save
the proconsul from his devilish deceit.

*Paul and his company prosecuted with power their
work as missionaries* (13-15): "Now Paul and his
company set sail from Paphos, and came to Perga in
Pamphylia: and John departed from them and returned to Jerusalem. But they, passing through Perga,
came to Antioch of Pisidia; and they went into the
synagogue on the sabbath day, and sat down. And
after the reading of the law and the prophets, the
rulers of the synagogue sent unto them, saying, Brethren, if ye have any word of exhortation for the people,
say on." Of course, it was inevitable that Paul, with
the miraculous power of the Holy Spirit, as manifested
in the previous paragraph, added to his inborn initia-
tive and wide knowledge, should be the leader of his
associates; after this, neither Barnabas nor John Mark,
nor any one else that worked with Paul questioned his
authority to lead. Paul's work was always full of
movement; it was probably due to his influence that

his party hurried through Cyprus to Perga and on "to Antioch of Pisidia," where they sought opportunity to do effective preaching in execution of the wonderful mission upon which they were sent. Paul never waited for invitation from strangers, but with his characteristic hardihood he humbly pressed himself upon their attention for the sake of the message he had to deliver: that is the reason he and Barnabas "went into the synagogue on the sabbath day, and sat down." Here we learn incidentally the order of service in an ancient Jewish synagogue: (1) A section of the law was read; (2) a selection was read from prophecy; (3) exhortations followed, based on the Scriptures read. No doubt Paul and Barnabas had introduced themselves to the rulers of the synagogue and asked the privilege of speaking in the synagogue, where they sat modestly among the worshipers. John, who had set out with Paul and Barnabas at Antioch, as "their attendant," left them at Perga "and returned to Jerusalem"; Luke at this point in his story gives no hint why John Mark forsook the party or whether his apparent faithlessness displeased either of the senior associates in the company. We shall see later that Paul was highly disappointed. John Mark may have been afraid of the robbers that infested the Pisidian mountains, through which he would have had to travel if he had gone farther with Paul and Barnabas. Paul and Barnabas had the respect and confidence of "the rulers of the synagogue"; who called them "Brethren," and threw the meeting wide open to them, inviting them to deliver "any word of exhortation for the people" that they had. Thus there came to Paul the favorable occasion he earnestly sought to preach the gospel in "Antioch of Pisidia," which had many Jews and Gentiles, and

had become a commercial center; and we shall see with
what tact and effect Paul entered this open door in the
wonderful sermon that follows.

## The First Written Report of a Sermon by Paul
## (vs. 16-52)

*With masterly skill, Paul introduced his message by
happy reference to proud Jewish history* (16-22) : "And
Paul stood up, and beckoning with the hand said, Men
of Israel, and ye that fear God, hearken: The God of
this people Israel chose our fathers, and exalted the
people when they sojourned in the land of Egypt, and
with a high arm led he them forth out of it.  And for
about the time of forty years as a nursing-father bare
he them in the wilderness.  And when he had destroyed
seven nations in the land of Canaan, he gave them their
land for an inheritance, for about four hundred and
fifty years: and after these things he gave them judges
until Samuel the prophet.  And afterward they asked
for a king: and God gave them Saul the son of Kish,
a man of the tribe of Benjamin, for the space of forty
years.  And when he had removed him, he raised up
David to be their king; to whom also he bare witness
and said, I have found David the son of Jesse, a man
after my heart, who shall do all my will."  Without
any hard and fast rules of homiletics, every preacher
should learn much from Paul, who was a great sermon-
izer.  Every preacher has his own peculiar mannerisms;
Paul's characteristic gesture was "beckoning with the
hand," which won attention and indicated his sincerity.
When Paul arose, and looked at his audience, he saw
two classes of people before him, Jews and Gentiles,
whom he described as "men of Israel, and ye that
fear God," the latter description being of Gentiles who

had accepted the religion of the Israelites. Dr. Jefferson, evidently impatient of modern, tiresome formality, says in his "Quiet Hints to Growing Preachers," "Have no introduction and have no conclusion; begin and quit, pitch in and pitch out." However, an introduction must introduce and be pertinent. Paul's introduction here sought and secured sympathetic audience for his main theme. Like Stephen, whom he heard but did not copy, Paul won the attention of his Jewish hearers by recounting their original heroic history: Stephen seized a bundle of ancient misdeeds and threw them at his wicked contemporaries to show his enemies that they were like their evil ancestors; Paul outlined events from Abraham to David, of whom Christ came. "For about four hundred and fifty years," from the time God called Abraham into Canaan to David's complete victory over the Canaanites or Philistines, God was giving Palestine to the Hebrews or Israelites or Jews as their "inheritance." Since the Old Testament does not mention the length of king Saul's reign, Paul must have had extra-Biblical information that this sovereign ruled forty years. Stubborn Saul sought his own way; contrariwise, humble David had a godlike heart and did the divine will. This does not mean that God approved the unfortunate, sinful things David did, but describes his character when he was chosen to take Saul's place as king; where Saul failed, David succeeded.

*Jesus, Saviour, Slain, Risen, was the theme of Paul's sermon* (23-41): "Of this man's seed hath God according to promise brought unto Israel a Saviour, Jesus; when John had first preached before his coming the baptism of repentance to all the people of Israel. And as John was fulfilling his course, he said, What suppose ye that I am? I am not he. But behold, there cometh

one after me the shoes of whose feet I am not worthy
to unloose.  Brethren, children of the stock of Abraham,
and those among you that fear God, to us is the word
of this salvation sent forth.  For they that dwell in
Jerusalem, and their rulers, because they knew him not,
nor the voices of the prophets which are read every
sabbath, fulfilled them by condemning him.  And
though they found no cause of death in him, yet asked
they of Pilate that he should be slain.  And when they
had fulfilled all things that were written of him, they
took him down from the tree, and laid him in a tomb.
But God raised him from the dead: and he was seen
for many days of them that came up with him from
Galilee to Jerusalem, who are now his witnesses unto
the people.  And we bring you good tidings of the
promise made unto the fathers, that God hath fulfilled
the same unto our children, in that he raised up Jesus;
as also it is written in the second psalm, Thou art my
Son, this day have I begotten thee.  And as concerning
that he raised him up from the dead, now no more to
return to corruption, he hath spoken on this wise, I
will give you the holy and sure blessings of David.
Because he saith also in another psalm, Thou wilt not
give thy Holy One to see corruption.  For David, after
he had in his own generation served the counsel of God,
fell asleep, and was laid unto his fathers, and saw corruption: but he whom God raised up saw no corruption.
Be it known unto you therefore, brethren, that through
this man is proclaimed unto you remission of sins: and
by him every one that believeth is justified from all
things, from which ye could not be justified by the law
of Moses.  Beware, therefore, lest that come upon you
which is spoken in the prophets:

"Behold, ye despisers, and wonder, and perish;
    For I work a work in your days,
    A work which ye shall in no wise believe, if one
        declare it unto you."

In order to convince his audience, which was pre-
dominantly Jewish, Paul used the law of Moses and the
prophets of Israel as the background of his marvelous
message; indeed, he read easily and confidently a new,
wonderful meaning in these sacred Scriptures, which,
prior to his conversion to Christ only a short time before,
though he was trained at the feet of Gamaliel, was absolutely foreign to his own heart.    It is passing strange
to us now that, not only the common people, but the
great Jewish specialists and leaders, failed to see the
Lord Jesus Christ when He came and compelled His
death.    But still more remarkable is it that all that the
devils in hell and sinners on earth could do was to fulfill
the Scriptures and accomplish the divine will.    Paul
knew that, unlike Peter on Pentecost, who had a great
harvest to reap, the newness and strangeness of his first
sermon in "Antioch of Pisidia" inhibited immediate
fruit and gave no invitation.    Nevertheless, out of this
occasion came great results, as we shall see.

*Out of this sermon came power, stirring the whole
city, angering the Jews, gladdening the Gentiles, spread-
ing the Word of God "throughout all the region (42-
52):* "And as they went out, they besought that these
words might be spoken to them the next sabbath.    Now
when the synagogue broke up, many of the Jews and of
the devout proselytes followed Paul and Barnabas;
who, speaking to them, urged them to continue in the
grace of God.    And the next sabbath almost the whole
city was gathered together to hear the word of God.
But when the Jews saw the multitudes, they were

filled with jealousy, and contradicted the things which were spoken by Paul, and blasphemed. And Paul and Barnabas spake out boldly, and said, It was necessary that the word of God should first be spoken to you. Seeing ye thrust it from you, and judge yourselves unworthy of eternal life, lo, we turn to the Gentiles. For so hath the Lord commanded us, saying,

"I have set thee for a light to the Gentiles,
    That thou shouldest be for salvation unto the
        uttermost part of the earth.
"And as the Gentiles heard this, they were glad, and glorified the word of God: and as many as were ordained to eternal life believed. And the word of the Lord was spread abroad through all the region. But the Jews urged on the devout women of honorable estate, and the chief men of the city, and stirred up a persecution against Paul and Barnabas, and cast them out of their borders. But they shook off the dust of their feet against them, and came unto Iconium. And the disciples were filled with joy and with the Holy Spirit." We have here in the attitude of those who had just heard Paul preach, and were still under the spell of his personal magnetism, convincing evidence that he was master of the art of public speaking and in the front rank as an orator, with conquering, subjective power. While they may not have understood Paul's eloquent speech, yet they were so thrilled by the speaker that they wanted to hear him say the same words the very "next sabbath." Once a mature man, fascinated by a student of the University of Tennessee, heard this young man preach one of his first sermons, and spontaneously paid him a high compliment, by storming the audience with the announcement, "This same sermon will be preached here tomorrow night." But privately

this older man said to the embarrassed young preacher, "That is the greatest sermon I ever heard; of course, I knew you would not repeat it, but I wanted the church full tomorrow night again." Moreover, when the meeting in the synagogue "broke up," "many of the Jews and of the devout proselytes followed Paul and Barnabas" to their lodging, being drawn to them personally; of course, these Jews and Gentiles were "in the grace of God," in the sense that they sought the truth in which Paul and Barnabas "urged them to continue." But "the next sabbath almost the whole city" came to hear Paul preach; and this supreme success embittered the Jews with jealousy against Paul and Barnabas, who heroically met the challenge of their own people, and "turned to the Gentiles." Of course, this gladdened the Gentiles; but the word *"ordained"* in verse 48 is a wrong translation: the meaning is, "as many as were *determined* for eternal life *believed.*" The only way to seek or to have eternal life is to *believe;* no Jew, no Gentile, can enjoy eternal life without faith and its consequents of repentance and confession and baptism. Most of the Jews rejected this divine plan; many of the Gentiles accepted it. The work of the Lord went right on. "The disciples were filled with joy and with the Holy Spirit," in "Antioch of Pisidia," in the absence of Paul and Barnabas, who went "unto Iconium."

## XIV

## PREACHING THE GOSPEL THE WORK OF THE MISSIONARY

### (Acts 14)

*Every Christian, every missionary, should be a gospel preacher.* Neither education nor training is the first requisite for any man's being a proclaimer of the fundamental truth of the Lord Jesus Christ, but it is his own salvation from sin. All the intellectual development in all the schools on the face of the earth will avail absolutely nothing along this line unless one has been himself born again, "born anew," "born of water and the Spirit," and thus saved from his own past sins. And surely every sinner who has so entered into the new life should be moved by common gratitude to bear witness to the lost world; and, with much instruction or little or none, he will find a way to bring others to the Lord who has saved him. If the professed followers of Christ would make available to Him every friendly relationship they sustain among their acquaintances, vast multitudes would troop to Him before they were devoured by the monster of death. But this phenomenal harvest can not be forced by any process known to mortal man; verily, it comes neither by the cultivation of the natural powers nor by the inculcation of mere human exemplars: it is born of prayer, real, genuine prayer, of which this superficial, flippant, indifferent, worldly generation seems to be incapable; it comes with spontaneity out of the new life, it springs out of our "first love," the joy of our salvation in the Lord Jesus Christ. The New Testament church is without class or rank or any other distinction among its members; it has neither "clergy" nor "laity," but all are on a common footing before the Lord; some serve as apostles or evangelists or preachers or ministers or elders or deacons, but all are priests and kings and brethren and disciples and Christians. Every official capacity exists for the whole church, every member of which should be normally and potentially and potently and patently a missionary and a preacher of the gospel of the Son of God. We are not saying that every Christian can be a formal preacher; it may be impossible for every member of the church to master the art or technique of public speaking. But if anyone who claims to be a Christian is never instrumental in the hands of the Lord of the harvest to save other lost souls, it may be reasonably questioned that he has ever been born again himself and saved from his own sins. Andrew brought his brother Peter to Jesus, and thus gave evidence of his own live interest in the great Teacher; Andrew was not equal to Peter as a technical preacher, but he was back of Peter, in whose wonderful harvest he shared: Andrew surpassed Peter in his knowledge of details, and met as great a need as Peter in the service of Jesus of Nazareth; indeed, the kind of preacher Andrew was should be more numerous in the church today than the kind of preacher Peter was.

## As Missionaries, Paul and Barnabas "Preached the Gospel" (vs. 1-28)

*Their preaching created faith* (1-7): "And it came to pass in Iconium that they entered together into the synagogue of the Jews, and so spake that a great mul-

titude both of Jews and of Greeks believed. But the
Jews that were disobedient stirred up the souls of the
Gentiles, and made them evil affected against the
brethren. Long time therefore they tarried there speaking boldly in the Lord, who bare witness unto the word
of his grace, granting signs and wonders to be done
by their hands. But the multitude of the city was
divided; and part held with the Jews, and part with
the apostles. And when there was made an onset both
of the Gentiles and of the Jews with their rulers, to
treat them shamefully and to stone them, they became
aware of it, and fled unto the cities of Lycaonia, Lystra
and Derbe, and the region round about: and there they
preached the gospel.'' Here Paul demonstrated the
doctrine he subsequently stated; namely, ''So belief
cometh of hearing, and hearing by the word of Christ''
(Rom. 10:17). The reason the missionary must preach
or publish the gospel is, that without hearing or reading
the Word of God absolutely nobody can believe at all;
and all men who do not or will not or can not believe,
are lost forever. The Lord in His Great Commission
has laid on the church the responsibility of preaching
Him to the lost world; neglect or failure here is dangerous and might prove fatal. Of course, not all that
heard Paul and Barnabas in Iconium believed, but ''a
great multitude'' did. The preacher is never commanded to ''save'' anybody; he who tells the story
clears his own skirts. Whoever hears the gospel is
solely responsible himself for what he does about it.
The very act of declaring the Word of God, as in
Iconium, always sets the bad against the good, and
provokes a conflict between them. Paul and Barnabas
''so spake that a great multitude both of Jews and of
Greeks believed,'' but disobedient Jews poisoned the

minds of unbelieving Gentiles against these missionaries. However, Paul and Barnabas continued this fight aggressively for a "long time," upon whom the Lord put the stamp of His approval miraculously, in spite of the fact that Iconium was cleaved in twain, and these heroic preachers barely escaped death at the hands of a mob of their enemies. Man's connection with the Lord has priority and precedence over all other relationships, and He deliberately draws His line through the home and the family and the community and the world. In truth, the Lord Jesus Christ compels all who hear the story of His life and death and resurrection to accept Him or go with the devil; there is no other alternative. Whether in Iconium or "the cities of Lycaonia, Lystra and Derbe, and the region round about," wherever Paul and Barnabas went, "there they preached the gospel"; their antagonists and the enemies of the truth compelled them to change location, but could not silence them or hinder their testimony that Jesus is the Son of God and the Saviour of sinners.

*Paul healed a natal impotent cripple at Lystra, where he and Barnabas narrowly escaped being worshiped by the heathen as idol gods* (8-18): "And at Lystra there sat a certain man, impotent in his feet, a cripple from his mother's womb, who never had walked. The same heard Paul speaking: who, fastening his eyes upon him, and seeing that he had faith to be made whole, said with a loud voice, Stand upright on thy feet. And he leaped up and walked. And when the multitude saw what Paul had done, they lifted up their voice, saying in the speech of Lycaonia, The gods are come down to us in the likeness of men. And they called Barnabas, Jupiter; and Paul, Mercury, because he was the chief speaker. And the priest of Jupiter whose temple was before the city, brought oxen and garlands unto the gates, and would have done sacrifice with the multitudes. But when the apostles, Barnabas and Paul, heard of it, they rent their garments, and sprang forth among the multitude, crying out and saying, Sirs, why do ye these things? We also are men of like passions with you, and bring you good tidings, that ye should turn from these vain things unto a living God, who made the heaven and the earth and the sea, and all that in them is: who in the generations gone by suffered all the nations to walk in their own ways. And yet he left not himself without witness, in that he did good and gave you from heaven rains and fruitful seasons, filling your hearts with food and gladness. And with these sayings scarce restrained they the multitudes from doing sacrifice unto them.'' Of course, Luke has merely sketched Paul's miraculously healing the cripple at Lystra, ''who never had walked,'' ''who heard Paul speaking''; it is probable he heard Paul refer to some of the miracles of Jesus, and to his own miracles of healing, when Paul, seeing the sufferer believed he could make him whole, shouted, ''Stand upright on thy feet.'' Nothing could have been more startling to Paul's heathen audience, who, in their tense excitement, reverted to their native tongue, in which they pronounced Barnabas Jupiter and Paul Mercury, their own idol gods, and were about to worship them as such. Without the law of Moses and the prophecy of Israel, these Gentiles looked for the explanation of the strange phenomenon they had just witnessed, in their own pagan philosophy. Paul and Barnabas were horrified at the prospect of being themselves the objects of blind, godless sacrifice and worship, and made it the

occasion to preach the "living God, who made the
heaven and the earth and the sea, and all that in them
is." Here we have the outline of a wonderful sermon
designed to reach the Gentiles, to whom it was delivered.
Barnabas was an apostle in the sense of being a zealous
advocate of the gospel, but he is not to be classed as an
apostle with the original twelve and Paul, whose apostolate is special to the Gentiles. Evidently the climax
of this paragraph sprang out of the heart of Paul, who
always sought to convince the Jews by the law and
prophecy, and the Gentiles out of nature and providence. The Word of God always proclaims Him as the
Creator, but never offers explanation of the necessarily
mysterious, inscrutable process of creation. Some men,
however, are presumptuous enough to think they can
make plain what God has never elucidated. But to
discard the Bible, and follow these so-called scientists
in the senseless theory of extreme evolution is wicked
folly.

*Paul, stoned to death, was miraculously restored, so
that he and Barnabas revisited the churches and returned
to Antioch, where they had been commissioned* (19-28):
"But there came Jews thither from Antioch and
Iconium: and having persuaded the multitudes, they
stoned Paul, and dragged him out of the city, supposing
that he was dead. But as the disciples stood round
about him, he rose up, and entered into the city: and
on the morrow he went forth with Barnabas to Derbe.
And when they had preached the gospel to that city,
and had made many disciples, they returned to Lystra,
and to Iconium, and to Antioch, confirming the souls
of the disciples, exhorting them to continue in the faith,
and that through many tribulations we must enter into
the kingdom of God. And when they had appointed for

them elders in every church, and had prayed with fasting, they commended them to the Lord, on whom they had believed. And they passed through Pisidia, and came to Pamphylia. And when they had spoken the word in Perga, they went down to Attalia; and thence they sailed to Antioch, from whence they had been committed to the grace of God for the work which they had fulfilled. And when they were come, and had gathered the church together, they rehearsed all things that God had done with them, and that he had opened a door of faith unto the Gentiles. And they tarried no little time with the disciples." There is just one adequate explanation of what happened to Paul at Lystra: *he was stoned to death, and the life of his body was miraculously restored.* Even if one lets his imagination run riot, and sees Paul all through the night in the home of Lois, Timothy's grandmother, with Timothy, as a fifteen-year-old boy, weeping over him, and the disciples dressing his wounds and ministering to him, he must admit with McGarvey, that the mystery of Paul's speedy recovery is only "in part explained." The incorrigibly wicked Jews from Antioch and Iconium came to Lystra to *kill* Paul, and they *did kill him;* when they dragged him out of the city, they supposed he was dead, and *he was dead.* "The disciples that stood round about him" did not pick him up and carry him; but "he rose up, and entered into the city: and on the morrow he went forth with Barnabas to Derbe." For a while Paul's body was actually dead at Lystra, but his spirit neither died nor lost consciousness, but actually (see 2 Corinthians 12) was "caught up even to the third heaven . . . into Paradise, and heard unspeakable words, which it is not lawful for a man to utter." It is only man's spirit that is conscious; the body of flesh is always unconscious, whether dead or alive.   Paul's spirit persisted in conscious existence after he left his body of flesh; this is true of every human being.   The Lord restored Paul's body without the use of medicine or the intervention of a doctor or a nurse, and he went right on with his work, with no loss of time.   He and Barnabas went immediately to Derbe, where they "preached the gospel . . . and made many disciples." Then they retraced the whole course of their missionary journey, revisited every church they had established, for whom they appointed elders, whom "they commend-ed to the Lord, on whom they had believed."   Finally they reached Antioch, from which they had been sent, and to whom they made their report, in which loomed large this item: "God had opened a door of faith unto the Gentiles."   And we are not surprised that "they tarried no little time with the disciples" in Antioch.

## XV

## CONTROVERSY IN THE CHURCH OF CHRIST

### (Acts 15)

*Debate, inevitable in this world, should always promote and elevate the truth.*  Without careful thought and thorough investigation, one may not even know the truth of any question into the knowledge of which disputation with other sincere persons may lead him. To scorn a plain, simple, truthful statement from any source whatsoever is not a sign of sincerity, or intellectual or spiritual honesty, but of prejudice and stubbornness and bigotry.  In order to be a disciple or a learner all the days of one's life, one must maintain the curiosity and the docility and the humility of one's own childhood.  Discussion should be sober and earnest and dignified; but even if it descend to *contention,* it is still good when it turns on the light.  In truth, *contention* or contempt is the only attitude the Christian can have toward the falsehood of the devil and his dupes, but he must never assume to be the judge.  "But Michael, the archangel, when *contending* with the devil, he disputed about the body of Moses, durst not bring against him a railing judgment, but said, The Lord rebuke thee" (Jude 9).  Michael knew the truth about Moses' body; but the devil, conformable to the falsity of his character as the originator of deception, deliberately lied.  Paul rejoiced that Christ was preached even in *strife* or *contention* (Phil. 1:15-18), or when the gospel was spoken in conflict (1 Thess. 2:1, 2).

Moreover, Jude's exhortation is also pertinent here: "Beloved, while I was giving all diligence to write unto you of our common salvation, I was constrained to write unto you exhorting you to *contend* earnestly for the faith which was once for all delivered unto the saints." The faith that Jesus of Nazareth is the Christ and the Son of the living God and the Saviour of all sinners that believe on Him and obey Him and turn away from the sinful life is the most glorious thing, the most valuable possession within the reach of our lost race, of any mortal man! And it is legitimate and proper and wise and imperative, and with the Holy Spirit of whom we are born into the new life, it is unavoidable, to fight, to argue, to testify, to debate, to reason, to exhort, to discuss, to preach the Word of God, to pray, to work, to contend—in short, to say and do everything in our power—for this triumphant faith that saves us from our distress and death and gives us this intrinsic wealth that shall be in our hands and hearts and lives forever! And not thus to be aggressive in the grandest, noblest cause on the face of the earth or among the sons and daughters of men, and help the Lord Jesus Christ save the world for whom He died, and rose again, marks us as spiritually poor, weak, sick Christians, if indeed it does not cast us adrift from Him, hardening our hearts till we crucify Him again, and sinking us in incorrigible wickedness and hopeless impenitence, amid the dark, angry, rolling, roaring waves of the appalling sea of hell!

## That Baptized Gentiles Should Be Circumcised Agitated the Church (vs. 1-35)

*This question was affirmed by Pharisees, and denied by Paul and Barnabas and Peter and James* (1-21):

"And certain men came down from Judæa and taught the brethren, saying, Except ye be circumcised after the custom of Moses, ye cannot be saved. And when Paul and Barnabas had no small dissension and questioning with them, the brethren *determined* (this word is preferable to *appointed* here) that Paul and Barnabas, and certain other of them, should go up to Jerusalem unto the apostles and elders about this question. They, therefore, being brought on their way by the church, passed through both Phœnicia and Samaria, declaring the conversion of the Gentiles: and they caused great joy unto all the brethren. And when they were come to Jerusalem, they were received of the church and the apostles and the elders, and they rehearsed all things that God had done with them. But there rose up certain of the sect of the Pharisees who believed, saying, It is needful to circumcise them, and to charge them to keep the law of Moses. And the apostles and the elders were gathered together to consider of this matter. And when there had been much questioning, Peter rose up, and said unto them, Brethren, ye know that a good while ago God made choice among you, that by my mouth the Gentiles should hear the word of the gospel, and believe. And God, who knoweth the heart, bare them witness, giving them the Holy Spirit, even as he did unto us; and he made no distinction between us and them, cleansing their hearts by faith. Now therefore why make ye trial of God, that ye should put a yoke upon the neck of the disciples which neither our fathers nor we were able to bear? But we believe that we shall be saved through the grace of the Lord Jesus, in like manner as they. And all the multitude kept silence; and they hearkened unto Barnabas and Paul rehearsing what signs and wonders God had wrought among the

Gentiles through them. And after they had held their peace, James answered, saying, Brethren, hearken unto me: Symeon hath rehearsed how first God visited the Gentiles, to take out of them a people for his name. And to this agree the words of the prophets; as it is written,

"After these things I will return,
And I will build again the tabernacle of David,
    which is fallen;
And I will build again the ruins thereof,
And I will set it up:
That the residue of men may seek after the
    Lord,
And all the Gentiles, upon whom my Name is
    called,
Saith the Lord, who maketh these things known
    from of old.

"Wherefore my judgment is, that we trouble not them that from among the Gentiles turn to God; but that we write unto them, that they abstain from the pollutions of idols, and from fornication, and from what is strangled, and from blood. For Moses from generations of old hath in every city them that preach him, being read in the synagogues every sabbath." We treat this text as a unit and as one paragraph germane to the subject, which also saves space. Luke wrote of the Pharisees who, without any basis of argument whatsoever, espoused circumcision as a condition of salvation, that they "believed"; but it would seem that their faith did not go deep enough to change their chronic formalism, and later Paul called them spies to destroy liberty in Christ by foisting the bondage of the law of Moses on Christians. Indeed, they pleaded

for circumcision as a definite pledge by baptized Gentiles
to keep the whole Mosaic law, which no Jew had ever
been able to do.  Peter, at the house of Cornelius, had
already settled once for all that any Gentile that believed on Christ as the Son of God and repented of
his sins and confessed his faith in Christ, should be
baptized without being circumcised at all; these Pharisees acknowledged that, but took the unreasonable, untenable position that they must be circumcised and live
according to the law of Moses, or they could not be
saved.  Verily, this would have made the church of
Christ a mere Jewish sect; but, thank the Lord, it was
settled, in the light of the inspired teaching of the
apostles of the Lord Jesus Christ, in the negative.  And
yet the Pharisee is still with us, saying that baptism is
"in the room of circumcision," and sprinkling both
babies and adults.  Paul and Barnabas, who had gone
forward among the Gentiles in the light of the revelation given originally to Peter, stated again and again
their knowledge which was both revealed and empirical,
that this new doctrine worked gloriously.  Peter, who
had also preached the gospel on Pentecost to the Jews
for the first time it was ever heard on earth in its
fullness, rehearsed briefly his experience in opening the
door of the divine kingdom to the Gentiles, and commanded that God should not be tried by the church's
placing on the Gentiles the yoke of the law, which no
Hebrew or Israelite or Jew had ever been "able to
bear"; for the only way any human being, Jew or
Gentile, could be saved at all was "through the grace
of the Lord Jesus."  Then James, introducing his conclusion by brief reference to the original extension of
the gospel to the Gentiles through Simon Peter, and
buttressing it with pertinent citation of prophecy, an-

nounced that the Gentiles who "turn to God" should
not be expected to keep the law, but simply urged to
"abstain from the pollutions of idols, and from fornication, and from what is strangled, and from blood."
Circumcision, given originally to Abraham, was designed
as a separating rite to keep his descendants distinct
from other people; now it has no religious significance
at all. Circumcision is one thing, baptism is an entirely
different thing; circumcision is of the Old Testament,
baptism is of the New Testament; one is Jewish, the
other is Christian, and there can be no likeness, no
comparison, no similarity, no similitude, between them.
Whatever was peculiar to the patriarchal or the Jewish
dispensation has been done away in Christ.

*And thus this controversy over circumcision in the
church occasioned the first epistle, or written document,
of the New Testament, later incorporated in Acts*
(22-35): "Then it seemed good to the apostles and
the elders, with the whole church, to choose men out of
their company, and send them to Antioch with Paul and
Barnabas; namely, Judas called Barsabbas, and Silas,
chief men among the brethren: and they wrote thus by
them, The apostles and the elders, brethren, unto the
brethren who are of the Gentiles in Antioch and Syria
and Cilicia, greeting: Forasmuch as we have heard
that certain who went out from us have troubled you
with words, subverting your souls; to whom we gave
no commandment; it seemed good unto us, having come
to one accord, to choose out men and send them unto
you with our beloved Barnabas and Paul, men that
have hazarded their lives for the name of our Lord Jesus
Christ. We have sent therefore Judas and Silas, who
themselves also shall tell you the same things by word
of mouth. For it seemed good to the Holy Spirit, and

to us, to lay upon you no greater burden than these
necessary things: that ye abstain from things sacrificed
to idols, and from blood, and from things strangled,
and from fornication; from which if ye keep yourselves, it shall be well with you. Fare ye well. So
they, when they were dismissed, came down to Antioch;
and having gathered the multitude together, they delivered the epistle. And when they had read it, they
rejoiced for the consolation. And Judas and Silas,
being themselves also prophets, exhorted the brethren
with many words, and confirmed them. And after they
had spent some time there, they were dismissed in
peace from the brethren unto those that had sent them
forth. But Paul and Barnabas tarried in Antioch,
teaching and preaching the word of the Lord, with
many others also.'' That this meeting in Jerusalem
can not legitimately be counted as a precedent for
ecclesiastical courts or so-called church councils or delegated conventions is evinced by the fact that it was
merely the appeal of one church, the congregation in
Antioch, to another church, the congregation in Jerusalem, for authoritative teaching to settle a question
of fundamental doctrine in the salvation of souls; and
while ''the elders, with the whole church,'' were in
''one accord'' with the apostles in the decision not to
inflict Jewish circumcision on Gentile Christians, yet
this appeal was really to the apostles and their associates as the only inspired teachers and preachers the
church has ever had. Verily, it is impossible to over-
emphasize this point: the church of the Lord Jesus
Christ in all lands and in all time must go to these
men through whom the Holy Spirit has created the
New Testament, for its faith and practice, or be false
to its Creator, and wander in the vagaries and foolish-

ness of men, and lose itself in the deception of the devil;
there is absolutely no other alternative. In the main,
the religion of the New Testament is positive rather than
negative. The ''burden'' the apostles laid on Gentile
Christians to ''abstain from things sacrificed to idols,
and from blood, and from things strangled, and from
fornication'' rose above the law of Moses, of which
circumcision became the symbol, both in antecedence
and subsequence. It can not be classified as an expe-
dient, rising above circumstances, but, rather, grounds
itself in the eternal, unchangeable truth of God.

## Even Paul and Barnabas Had "a Sharp Contention" (vs. 36-41)

*But this difference in personal judgment resulted in
two missionary parties, where there had been only one
before* (36-41): ''And after some days Paul said unto
Barnabas, Let us return now and visit the brethren in
every city wherein we proclaimed the word of the Lord,
and see how they fare. And Barnabas was minded to
take with them John also, who was called Mark. But
Paul thought not good to take with them him who
withdrew from them from Pamphylia, and went not
with them to the work. And there arose a sharp contention, so that they parted asunder one from the other,
and Barnabas took Mark with him, and sailed away unto
Cyprus: but Paul chose Silas, and went forth, being
commended by the brethren to the grace of the Lord.
And he went through Syria and Cilicia, confirming
the churches.'' The gospel reveals the Lord Jesus
Christ as the only object of faith, and the Holy Spirit
has inspired fundamental doctrine through the New
Testament. Verily the Lord has imparted to the New
Testament Scriptures His own eternal significance, and

made them the most glorious possession in the hands
of all the generations.   But the gospel is neither
a method nor a custom nor a circumstance; the gospel
is fundamentally and eternally a message.   The gospel
does not concern itself with methods and plans of work;
here there must of necessity be liberty and tolerance
and forbearance.   Paul and Barnabas had ''a sharp
contention'' over the mere circumstance of taking John
Mark with them on the second missionary journey.
Evidently Paul was afraid Mark would not be faithful,
because he had left him and Barnabas on their former
journey; but, naturally Barnabas was in sympathy with
Mark, his cousin.   And  so two successful missionary
parties came  immediately  into  existence—Paul  and
Silas, and Barnabas and John Mark.   It is good to
know, from subsequent reference Paul made to Barnabas
and Mark, that he believed in their integrity and no
strain was put upon their essential brotherhood.   Indeed, it seems providential that they separated, because
the missionary work to which they were devoted pros-
pered over a wider area.   However, we do not read of
Barnabas any more in Acts.   Still it is by no means
essential that one's work find record in this world; the
thing that counts is that it be known in heaven, and
that one become a citizen of that eternal realm.   It is
hopeful in these modern days to note the rising tide
of emphasis on unity.   But the only place where unity
is possible or even desirable is in FAITH: and before
it can ever be realized, faith must be differentiated from
circumstances, methods, customs or the temperaments
of men, and human productions discarded as authoritative, and the fundamental food of the New Testament
must be eaten.

# XVI

## THE ETERNAL EXECUTIVE

### (Acts 16)

*Each of the three departments of government—executive, legislative and judicial—centers in the Lord.* Isaiah wrote (9:6, 7). "For unto us a child is born, unto us a son is given; and the government shall be upon his shoulder: and his name shall be called Wonderful, Counsellor, Mighty God, Everlasting Father, Prince of Peace. Of the increase of his government and of peace there shall be no end, upon the throne of David, and upon his kingdom, to establish it, and to uphold it with justice and with righteousness from henceforth even for ever. The zeal of Jehovah of hosts will perform this." Back of all the nations and of all the peoples is the great God, who makes the law and interprets the law and enforces the law. God turns the key on the past and moves it out of view; He holds the future in His hands till it is upon us in the present. The devil sought the defeat of the divine purpose by poisoning the antediluvian world against God, who cleansed the earth of the incorrigibly wicked and made a new beginning. Many rebellious nations have arisen and been blown out of existence; and only the Lord knows how many more are bound for a similar fate. When will men learn that without the Lord human life is utterly vain! It is infinitely better never to be born than to ignore the great eternal God, who has revealed Himself in His Word, and supremely through His Son, the Lord Jesus Christ. Said the Bard of Avon, "There is a divinity that shapes our ends, rough hew them how we will." One of the interesting sidelights in the study of the Word of God is the dominance of Providence in the lives of both saints and sinners: finally the Lord has His way with men, whether they will or not. Either one accepts the Lord and enters into the joy of His salvation, or he suffers the doom of the lost; not even the devils in hell can conjure any other alternative. But it often seems to the saints that the Lord allows many things to get in their way; perhaps He does,

"For whom the Lord loveth he chasteneth,
And scourgeth every son whom he receiveth"
(Heb. 12:6).

It is impossible to live in this lost world without suffering; sometimes the good and the innocent seem to experience more pain than the bad and the guilty. The only absolutely good and perfect Man that ever lived was at the same time the greatest sufferer the world ever saw! Neither the patriarchs nor the prophets nor the apostles nor the primitive church exhausted the providence of God; the Christian that lives now must be blind if he can not glimpse in his own life and experience the hands of the eternal Executive. But whether we can understand the untoward in our lives today or not, we continue the journey in faith that the Lord will untangle and unwind the skein at last.

### The Lord Is the Eternal Executive (vs. 1-18)

*The Lord brought Paul and Silas and Timothy and Luke together, but would not permit them "to speak the word in Asia" or "to go into Bithynia" (1-10):* "And he came also to Derbe and to Lystra: and behold, a certain disciple was there, named Timothy, the son of a Jewess that believed; but his father was a Greek. The same was well reported of by the brethren that were at Lystra and Iconium. Him would Paul have to go forth with him; and he took and circumcised him because of the Jews that were in those parts: for they all knew that his father was a Greek. And as they went on their way through the cities, they delivered them the decrees to keep which had been ordained of the apostles and elders that were at Jerusalem. So the churches were strengthened in the faith, and increased in number daily. And they went through the region of Phrygia and Galatia, having been forbidden of the Holy Spirit to speak the word in Asia; and when they were come over against Mysia, they assayed to go into Bithynia; and the Spirit of Jesus suffered them not; and passing by Mysia, they came down to Troas. And a vision appeared to Paul in the night: There was a man of Macedonia standing, beseeching him, and saying, Come over into Macedonia, and help us. And when he had seen the vision, straightway we sought to go forth into Macedonia, concluding that God had called us to preach the gospel unto them.'' The God that knows the minutest detail in all His creation and notes the falling sparrow took a determining hand in the selection and the direction of this missionary party, perhaps the greatest in the history of the church of Christ. The choice of such heroic spirits as Paul and Silas and Timothy and Luke in one body must of itself be regarded as an outstanding act of Providence. The Lord observes the whole scene of action, and sees the end from the beginning; but man is circumscribed in view and local in interest. Even these great and wonderful men were about to go in the wrong direction and preach

in the wrong place. We are not saying that there is
any abode of man where the story of Jesus should not
be told; we are declaring that the eternal Executive
strategically led His missionaries out of Asia, where
the evangel had already been heard, into Europe, where
the story of the Lord Jesus Christ had never been
preached, and into which the populous East was beginning to pour its inhabitants. And thus the Lord
leavened with His own gospel the ever increasing tide
of migration from the East to the West, through Paul
and his associates, to whom we in America can trace
ourselves as Christians. Xerxes crossed the Hellespont
on a pontoon bridge with an army of 2,000,000, which
required seven days and seven nights to pass, with no
appreciable effect on history; when Paul crossed the
Dardanelles, with only three companions, he carried the
destiny of the western world beneath his cloak.

*Through Paul, the Lord opened the heart of Lydia,
and cast "a spirit of divination" out of a maid, who was
a slave* (11-18): "Setting sail therefore from Troas,
we made a straight course to Samothrace, and the day
following to Neapolis; and from thence to Philippi,
which is a city of Macedonia, the first of the district,
a Roman colony: and we were in this city tarrying
certain days. And on the sabbath day we went forth
without the gate by a river side, where we supposed
there was a place of prayer; and we sat down, and
spake unto the women that were come together. And
a certain woman named Lydia, a seller of purple, of
the city of Thyatira, one that worshipped God, heard
us: whose heart the Lord opened to give heed unto
the things which were spoken by Paul. And when
she was baptized, and her household, she besought us,
saying, If ye have judged me to be faithful to the Lord,

come into my house, and abide there. And she constrained us. And it came to pass, as we were going to the place of prayer, that a certain maid having a spirit of divination met us, who brought her masters much gain by soothsaying. The same following after Paul and us cried out, saying, These men are servants of the Most High God, who proclaim unto you the way of salvation. And this she did for many days. But Paul, being sore troubled, turned and said to the spirit, I charge thee in the name of Jesus Christ to come out of her. And it came out that very hour." Paul's nocturnal vision in Troas cleared up the perplexity of him and his party as to where they should go and preach; and though the "man of Macedonia," whom Paul saw in this dream, was conspicuous for his apparent absence in Philippi, yet subsequent events soon disclosed that Paul had not seen a mere apparition, but had received an inspired revelation. The "man" of Macedonia that called Paul into Europe was the Lord Himself, as the eternal Executive, articulating and interpreting the deep need and profound yearning, conscious or unconscious, of the teeming millions flowing into Europe and on to America, creating the Occident or the West. Of all the conversions recorded in Acts, that of Lydia is the only one of which Luke wrote that "the Lord opened" her heart; He did this in no miraculous way, but through Paul, who simply preached the gospel to her. Indeed, the immediate purpose of the eternal Executive in sending Paul and his company to Philippi was to answer the prayers of Lydia and her group of women that worshiped God on the Sabbath day by a riverside. She and her household were baptized, and "she constrained" the missionaries to be her guests. Another striking thing the eternal Executive did through

Paul at Philippi was to expose the fraudulent practice
of soothsaying by the masters of a certain maid, by
casting "a spirit of divination" out of her. The object
of this pretense, which must have been supported by
the devil, was mercenary. Through Paul, the Lord
Jesus Christ here manifested His power by executing
"that very hour" Paul's "charge" or command for
this evil spirit to come out of the maid.

### The Eternal Executive Foils Suffering With Joy
### (vs. 19-40)

*The persecution of Paul and Silas was overshadowed
by the salvation of the jailer and his household* (19-34):
"But when her masters saw that the hope of their gain
was gone, they laid hold on Paul and Silas, and dragged
them into the marketplace before the rulers, and when
they had brought them unto the magistrates, they said,
These men, being Jews, do exceedingly trouble our city,
and set forth customs which it is not lawful for us to
receive, or to observe, being Romans. And the multitude rose up together against them: and the magistrates
rent their garments off them, and commanded to beat
them with rods. And when they had laid many stripes
upon them, they cast them into prison, charging the
jailor to keep them safely: who, having received such
a charge, cast them into the inner prison, and made
their feet fast in the stocks. But about midnight Paul
and Silas were praying and singing hymns unto God,
and the prisoners were listening to them; and suddenly
there was a great earthquake, so that the foundations
of the prisonhouse were shaken: and immediately all
the doors were opened: and every one's bands were
loosed. And the jailor, being roused out of sleep and
seeing the prison doors open, drew his sword and was

about to kill himself, supposing that the prisoners had
escaped. But Paul cried with a loud voice, saying, Do
thyself no harm: for we are all here. And he called
for lights and sprang in, and, trembling for fear, fell
down before Paul and Silas, and brought them out
and said, Sirs, what must I do to be saved? And they
said, Believe on the Lord Jesus, and thou shalt be
saved, thou, and thy house. And they spake the word
of the Lord unto him, with all that were in his house.
And he took them the same hour of the night, and
washed their stripes; and was baptized, he and all his,
immediately. And he brought them up into his house,
and set food before them, and rejoiced greatly, with
all his house, having believed in God." It was easy
for the masters of this slave girl to make out their case
against Paul and Silas, honeycombed with lies as it
was; and the terrible treatment inflicted on them in
persecution remains a shame to Philippi and a disgrace
to humanity. Yet this all serves as the background of
the whole picture to bring out the glorious light of
the conversion of the Philippian jailer with the members of his house, and the signal success of Paul and
Silas as gospel preachers. That this jailer and his
associates were raw heathens compelled Paul and Silas,
in answering his question as to what he should do to
be saved, to speak in the most ultimate primary terms:
"Believe on the Lord Jesus, and thou shalt be saved,
thou and thy house." Of course, they explained that
faith produces repentance and causes the confession of
Jesus as the Christ and impels baptism into Him; and
they must have also made their answer PERSONAL
IN APPLICATION TO EACH INDIVIDUAL, for in
no other way can the gospel be applied at all. This
eliminates infants in the jailer's house; each one in that

house was old enough to believe, and did believe, for himself. Being saved from sin is like eating food—each one must eat for himself, and each sinner must obey the gospel for himself.

*In the delicately balanced divine scale, the Lord leaves room for justice* (35-40): "But when it was day, the magistrates sent the serjeants, saying, Let those men go. And the jailor reported the words to Paul, saying, The magistrates have sent to let you go: now therefore come forth, and go in peace. But Paul said unto them, They have beaten us publicly, uncondemned, men that are Romans, and have cast us into prison; and do they now cast us out privily? nay verily; but let them come themselves and bring us out. And the serjeants reported these words unto the magistrates: and they feared when they heard that they were Romans; and they came and besought them; and when they had brought them out, they asked them to go away from the city. And they went out of the prison, and entered into the house of Lydia: and when they had seen the brethren, they comforted them, and departed." Paul and Silas preached the gospel to the jailer and his household, and baptized them, at night; and the next day, when the word came that the rulers had released Paul and Silas, they had taken their places in the jail as prisoners, to whom the jailer was naturally grateful as his greatest benefactors, and happily announced to them their freedom. But immediately the genius of Paul detected the incongruity and the injustice that the magistrates should beat him and Silas before the people and liberate them from jail secretly, and he flatly and scornfully refused a proffer so cowardly. Moreover, Paul amazed these local rulers, and struck terror to them by the charge that, in their mad persecution of him and Silas, they had really made an attack, vicious and outrageous, on uncondemned Roman citizens. Then the tables turned instantly; and these persecutors, fearful that they might be called to account for their crime by their superiors in office, made obeisance to Paul and Silas, and implored them to leave the city of Philippi. And thus victorious, but without outward show, these fruitful, resourceful missionaries, and great servants of the Lord, after visiting in their headquarters in Lydia's house, and seeing and comforting their brethren, sought new fields of conquest. It remained for this man Paul, the greatest of all the apostles, to give in his letter to this very church in Philippi, the keenest, the completest analysis on record of the scale or the standard of the Lord Jesus Christ, in the following wonderful words: ''Finally, brethren, whatsoever things are *true,* whatsoever things are *honorable,* whatsoever things are *just,* whatsoever things are *pure,* whatsoever things are *lovely,* whatsoever things are of *good report;* if there be any *virtue,* and if there be any *praise, think on these things.* The things which ye both learned and received and heard and saw in me, these things do: and the God of peace shall be with you'' (Phil. 4: 8, 9).

# XVII

## TURNING THE WORLD UPSIDE DOWN

### (Acts 17)

*The world is disordered, with the downside up, and, to be righted, must be turned upside down.* While the enemies of Paul and Silas sought to injure them, giving credit to these gospel preachers for the mob spirit, which they themselves inspired and fostered by accusing them of turning the world upside down, yet unwittingly they gave a proper description, morally and spiritually, of these great missionaries. Talk about evolution! The change, the growth, the development of the gospel of the Son of God in the hearts and lives of men and women of the communities and states and nations of the world is destined to pale into utter insignificance all other evolutionary movements in the history of the race, and, by the power and leadership of the risen Lord, shall never stop short of the completest, most glorious revolution in all the universe of God! Man has two component elements, he is made of two things—matter and mind, body and spirit—in point of time, the body is natural and comes first; but as to significance and capacity, the spirit rises infinitely above the body. The body of flesh soon comes to its zenith, and then begins to recede; the intellect, however, may grow as long as the body can serve it, and the spirit may become what it will. Physically, man is limited to a few fleeting years of time, but spiritually he has eternity before him. The first man, Adam, who had to be created because he

had no antecedents, as the physical type elevated the
body above the spirit, lost the battle in sin and brought
death into the world; but the Lord Jesus Christ, as "the
last Adam, became a lifegiving Spirit," conquered death
by resuming life in His resurrection body, which is
the spiritual body, and won the fight over wickedness
forever. Physical man and his descendants turned the
world downside up by giving the flesh priority and
precedence over the spirit; but the Lord Jesus Christ,
as the great eternal spiritual Man, has inaugurated His
campaign through His gospel to turn the world upside
down, by giving back to the spirit its infinite superiority, and rehabilitating it in a spiritual body, a body
of its own kind and glory. Both Jesus and Paul and
all the apostles strove to avoid the war and violence
and destruction of revolution, and bring the radical
change they preached by the quiet, peaceable, reasonable
methods of evolution; but it will amount to the greatest
of all alterations when it comes in the fullness of the
Lord. In truth, when the whole wide world has been
thus completely turned upside down, it shall have been
transformed into the image of the Lord Jesus Christ;
and the misery and death of the body of flesh shall have
vanished forever, and life, the life of God, eternal life,
shall flow in perfection through the cycles and eons of
heaven forever and forever.

### Paul Turned the World Upside Down (vs. 1-15)

*Paul preached that Jesus proved Himself the Christ
by suffering death and arising from the dead* (1-9):
"Now when they had passed through Amphipolis and
Apollonia, they came to Thessalonica, where there was
a synagogue of the Jews: and Paul, as his custom was,
went in unto them, and for three sabbath days reasoned

with them from the scriptures, opening and alleging that
it behooved the Christ to suffer, and to rise again from
the dead; and that this Jesus, whom, said he, I proclaim
unto you, is the Christ. And some of them were persuaded, and consorted with Paul and Silas; and of the
devout Greeks a great multitude, and of the chief women
not a few. But the Jews, being moved with jealousy,
took unto them certain vile fellows of the rabble, and
gathering a crowd, set the city on an uproar; and
assaulting the house of Jason, they sought to bring them
forth to the people. And when they found them not,
they dragged Jason and certain brethren before the
rulers of the city, crying, These that have turned the
world upside down are come hither also; whom Jason
hath received: and these all act contrary to the decrees
of Cæsar, saying that there is another king, one Jesus.
And they troubled the multitude and the rulers of the
city, when they heard these things. And when they had
taken security from Jason and the rest, they let them
go." After all, every man proves, reveals, shows himself; especially did this law hold true with the Son of
God. There was no coercion forcing Jesus to the slaughter; He suffered death, because it "behooved" Him, it
became Him, it was like Him, it revealed Him, to die
that His believers might live. Moreover, He died to get
His hands of power on death as the stronghold of the
devil and crash it in a heap of ruins at His feet forever,
which He did in His resurrection. No wonder the
angels and the prophets were agog at the glorious prospect of the gospel; and in the gray light of the new
day, the first day of the week, when the angel rolled
the stone away that sealed His grave, and the Lord
of glory, leaving the earthly raiment in the tomb forever, appeared in the habiliment of heaven, the universe

shook with the greatest and best news of the whole creation! Verily, it was this transcendently great preaching
that gave Paul more power than Xerxes' army of
2,000,000 soldiers, and left the glory of God in his
wake wherever he went. And let the Jews or the
Gentiles, all the enemies of Jesus in all the world and
all time, say what they will, "THERE IS ANOTHER
KING, ONE JESUS," the unique Jesus, the only Lord,
the absolute Christ, whom the wicked can never depose
nor even approach. Assuredly, this dominant, dogmatic
message solves the mystery that one man, Paul the
apostle, turned the world upside down; and without
this positive preaching, no propaganda will ever reach
far or last long on the earth.

*But the disordered lost world struck back at Paul*
(10-15) : "And the brethren immediately sent away Paul
and Silas by night unto Berœa: who when they were
come hither went into the synagogue of the Jews. Now
these were more noble than those in Thessalonica, in
that they received the word with all readiness of mind,
examining the scriptures daily, whether these things
were so. Many of them therefore believed; also of the
Greek women of honorable estate, and of men, not a
few. But when the Jews of Thessalonica had knowledge
that the word of God was proclaimed of Paul at Berœa
also, they came thither likewise, stirring up and trou-
bling the multitudes. And then immediately the brethren sent forth Paul to go as far as to the sea: and Silas
and Timothy abode there still. But they that conducted
Paul brought him as far as Athens: and receiving a
commandment unto Silas and Timothy that they should
come to him with all speed, they departed." The same
evil forces that opposed Jesus and encompassed His
death, set themselves with all their power against Paul

as the greatest apostle and exponent of the Lord. Previously they had sought Paul and Silas in the spirit of
a mob, at the house of Jason in Thessalonica, with the
evident purpose of slaying them; and hearing Paul was
preaching in Berœa also, they hastened thither in the
same threatening, dangerous mood. Paul's brethren
knew that it would imperil his life to remain in Berœa,
and provided him escort to Athens. Persecution was
no new experience for Paul: these same low-lived enemies had dogged his steps all through his ministry,
and once they actually killed him, whose life the Lord
restored because his work was not finished. This struggle between good and evil was precipitated by the devil,
who brought sin into the world, into whose penalty
Jehovah God compressed history into a single sentence:
"And I will put enmity between thee and the woman,
and between thy seed and her seed: he shall bruise
thy head, and thou shalt bruise his heel" (Gen. 3:15).
Here is what Paul wrote about this time-long conflict:
"Finally, be strong in the Lord, and in the strength of
his might. Put on the whole armor of God, that ye may
be able to stand against the wiles of the devil. For our
wrestling is not against flesh and blood, but against
the principalities, against the powers, against the world-
rulers of this darkness, against the spiritual hosts of
wickedness in the heavenly places. Wherefore take
up the whole armor of God, that ye may be able to
withstand in the evil day, and, having done all, to stand"
(Eph. 6:10-13). Of course, there are both good spirits
and bad spirits; but our arch enemy, the devil, has
intrenched himself in this world in the flesh, and turned
the world downside up by making the body more important than the spirit. There were two Pauls, Paul
the spirit and Paul the flesh, with constant conflict

between them: sin has thrust this duality of existence
upon every human being. Every man's biggest job is
to turn the world upside down in himself, and keep it
that way.

## The Body Doomed; Spirit Ultimate Reality (vs. 16-34)

*Heathen curiosity may spawn idols and abstract
theories, but recoils on itself in pitiable helplessness*
(16-21): "Now while Paul waited for them at Athens,
his spirit was provoked within him as he beheld the
city full of idols. So he reasoned in the synagogue
with the Jews and the devout persons, and in the marketplace every day with them that met him. And certain also of the Epicurean and Stoic philosophers en-
countered him. And some said, What would this babbler
say? others, He seemeth to be a setter forth of strange
gods: because he preached Jesus and the resurrection.
And they took hold of him and brought him unto the
Areopagus, saying, May we know what this new teaching is, which is spoken by thee? For thou bringest
certain strange things to our ears: we would know therefore what these things mean. (Now all the Athenians
and the strangers sojourning there spent their time in
nothing else, but either to tell or to hear some new
thing.)" The gospel is neither discovery nor invention
nor imagination nor dream nor vision nor myth nor
figment nor ratiocination; the gospel is the actual creation and real revelation of Jesus of Nazareth, who strode
across the horizon in plain view of the world, with the
gospel in His heart and life and on His face and in
His hands and under His feet and entwined about His
form, like the halo of God. The gospel was preached
to Abraham and born of his faith; but it is smashing
to heathen idolatry and intolerant of pagan philosophy.

Paul was never idle; he could always find something to do. While he was waiting for Silas and Timothy to join him in Athens, he was "provoked" at the multiplicity of idols the benighted minds of the heathen had created all over the city; here he found opportunity in the synagogue to teach the Jews and the devout, and others who met him in the marketplace. The Epicureans said that pleasure is the chief good, and all they wanted, all they looked for, was something, anything, to make them happy at the moment; but the Stoics declared that they had no emotions—neither pain nor pleasure excited them, and they endured without complaint or expression whatever came along. However, neither one of these opposite kinds of philosophers told the truth about themselves, whose pitiable plight Paul could not but see. It evinces the superficiality of the Athenians that they called Paul a "babbler" and "a setter forth of strange gods." Luke's parenthesis here that "Now all the Athenians and the strangers sojourning there spent their time in nothing else, but either to tell or to hear some new thing," throws a flood of light on their character; perhaps many of them were retired, and came to Athens to increase their knowledge. But they needed the gospel, which Paul pressed on their attention. If curiosity and religiousness and philosophy could save folk (to use Sam Jones' phrase), "the Athenians would have had their wings, and gone to heaven," before Paul came to Athens.

*There is no eternal life, no ultimate reality, in mere intellectual development* (22-34): "And Paul stood in the midst of the Areopagus, and said, Ye men of Athens, in all things I perceive that ye are very religious. For as I passed along, and observed the objects of your worship, I found also an altar with this inscrip-

tion, TO AN UNKNOWN GOD. What therefore ye
worship in ignorance, this I set forth unto you. The
God that made the world and all things therein, he,
being Lord of heaven and earth, dwelleth not in temples
made with hands; neither is he served by men's hands,
as though he needed anything, seeing he himself giveth
to all life, and breath, and all things; and he made of
one every nation of men to dwell on all the face of
the earth, having determined their appointed seasons,
and the bounds of their habitation; that they should
seek God, if haply they might feel after him and find
him, though he is not far from each one of us: for in
him we live, and move, and have our being; as certain
even of your own poets have said, For we are also his
offspring. Being then the offspring of God, we ought
not to think that the Godhead is like unto gold, or silver,
or stone, graven by art and device of man. The times
of ignorance therefore God overlooked; but now he
commandeth men that they should all everywhere repent: inasmuch as he hath appointed a day in which
he will judge the world in righteousness by the man
whom he hath ordained; whereof he hath given assurance unto all men, in that he hath raised him from the
dead. Now when they heard of the resurrection of the
dead, some mocked; but others said, We will hear thee
concerning this yet again. Thus Paul went out from
among them. But certain men clave unto him, and
believed: among whom also was Dionysius the Areopa-
gite, and a woman named Damaris, and others with
them.'' It is proverbial that the ancient Greeks gave
much attention to the development of the body and to
the training of the mind; but they were much farther
from the ultimate reality of spirit than the Hebrews,
who were led into faith by Abraham and Isaac and

Jacob and trained by Moses and the prophets. But while these leading Gentiles were steeped in idolatry, yet their very altar inscription, "TO AN UNKNOWN GOD," which Paul used to introduce his sermon on the hill of the Areopagus, is suggestive of the vacancy of their minds, and of the yearning of the spirits of the Athenians for the true and only God, which Paul proceeded immediately to preach to them through the things that He had made or created and given to the sons of men everywhere. Indeed, this altar, obscured by the numerous altars to idol gods, and slight in recognition and worship of Jehovah, was the only hope Paul had of reaching his auditors in Athens; but he entered the door of this hope with tact and power, declaring that God through Jesus had made ignorance impossible and repentance and judgment inevitable, by His resurrection from the dead. "Some mocked," but others were interested and believed, two of whom Luke mentions by name, one man and one woman. Paul could not appeal to raw Gentiles by the Scriptures, but he reached them by the program of nature and by the providence of God in their own lives. Verily, it requires the same power to run the world that it demanded to create it in the first place. How can men of any insight at all walk in the light of the day and grope in the darkness of the night and live through the seasons as they come and go, beholding the new life of spring, the strength of summer, the fruit of fall and the white and artistry of winter, without believing in the great God, who is the very atmosphere of human life!

## XVIII

## THE COMPULSION OF THE WORD OF GOD

### (Acts 18)

*The Word of God has adequate power.* What the Lord has said is to His institution, the church of Christ, and to His work what steam is to the railway engine, what gasoline is to the automobile, what food is to the body; namely, the power that makes it go. However, Jesus went beyond this metaphor when He said in explanation of the parable of the sower (Luke 8:11), "Now the parable is this: *The seed is the word of God.*" Steam and gasoline and meat produce motion, yet exhaust themselves in doing it; but the divine Word has the power of propagation and creation. Yea, the Word of God is the very seed from which the Christian originates and grows: herein lies the safety of the church. Neither the lie of the devil nor the mere word of man is as deadly dangerous as one might at first fear, because it is sterile: while the sterility of this false teaching can not save any who accepts it, yet it can never make anything out of him but a deceived sinner or a dupe of the devil. Besides, it is always possible to uproot error, and replace it with the truth of the Word of God, for which there is absolutely no substitute in this world. Read Heb. 6:4-8: "For as touching those who were once enlightened and tasted of the heavenly gift, and were made partakers of the Holy Spirit, *and tasted the good word of God,* and the powers of the age to come, and *then* fell away, it is impossible to renew them

188

again unto repentance; seeing they crucify to themselves the Son of God afresh, and put him to an open
shame. For the land which hath drunk the rain that
cometh oft upon it, and bringeth forth herbs meet for
them for whose sake it is also tilled, receiveth blessing
from God: but if it beareth thorns and thistles, it is
rejected and nigh unto a curse; whose end is to be
burned.'' Verily, the Lord has given to His Word
His own attributes: hear Paul again in Heb. 4:12, 13:
''For the word of God is living and active, and sharper
than any two-edged sword, and piercing even to the
dividing of soul and spirit, of both joints and marrow,
and quick to discern the thoughts and intents of the
heart. And there is no creature that is not manifest
in his sight: but all things are naked and laid open
before the eyes of him with whom we have to do.''
Most certainly, the divine Word is the very power by
which believing, penitent, obedient sinners are born
Christians, and the spiritual bread by which the saints
attain maturity in the Lord Jesus Christ. The Word
of God is not mere cake or candy or ice cream, but bread,
the very sustenance of spiritual life, upon which our
spirits must feed to give up the sinful life and live
righteously and triumphantly in this wicked world. God
has *spoken* all things into existence, and He can annihilate them by the power of His Word, to which He has
given His own infinitude.

## The Word of God Compels or Constrains Men (vs. 1-28)

*''Paul was constrained by the word''* to preach Jesus
as the Christ to all he met or saw, both Jews and Greeks
(1-11): ''After these things he departed from Athens,
and came to Corinth. And he found a certain Jew
named Aquila, a man of Pontus by race, lately come

from Italy, with his wife Priscilla, because Claudius had commanded all the Jews to depart from Rome: and he came unto them; and because he was of the same trade, he abode with them, and they wrought; for by their trade they were tentmakers. And he reasoned in the synagogue every sabbath, and persuaded Jews and Greeks. But when Silas and Timothy came down from Macedonia, Paul was constrained by the word, testifying to the Jews that Jesus was the Christ. And when they opposed themselves and blasphemed, he shook out his raiment and said unto them, Your blood be upon your own heads; I am clean: from henceforth I will go unto the Gentiles. And he departed thence, and went into the house of a certain man named Titus Justus, one that worshipped God, whose house joined hard to the synagogue. And Crispus, the ruler of the synagogue, believed in the Lord with all his house; and many of the Corinthians hearing believed, and were baptized. And the Lord said unto Paul in the night by a vision, Be not afraid, but speak and hold not thy peace: for I am with thee, and no man shall set on thee to harm thee: for I have much people in this city. And he dwelt there a year and six months, teaching the word of God among them.'' Neither all the general education of all the schools of this world nor any special training among men can possibly equip a human being to preach the gospel of the Son of God, who is not susceptible to the compulsion or the constraint of the Word of God, which is the one essential qualification of serving the Lord Jesus Christ and the great God Himself in the highest capacity. Indeed, this truth finds illustration in Paul himself, who had the best education the world of his day could give, about which much has been said; but all this human learning made small, if any, contribution

to his apostolate, because it was shown false and thrown
into eclipse and made useless and rubbish by the great
revelation that came to him through the Word of the
Lord. Now, of course, we are not arguing against education or training of the right kind; but we are saying
that if any man does not believe with all his heart that
the Bible is the Word of God, he should vacate the sacred
desk till faith conquers him. Verily, it was this deep-
seated conviction that drove Paul into "the synagogue
every sabbath," where he "persuaded Jews and Greeks,"
and incidentally found him fellowship with Aquila and
Priscilla; and when his old associates, Silas and Timothy,
stood by his side again in Corinth, this impulse or passion seemed to come upon him with greater force. The
Lord was with Paul, and nothing could stop him; when
the Jews rejected with blasphemy his testimony of the
Messiahship of Jesus, he was not discouraged, but turned
to the Gentiles. Titus Justus gave Paul recognition and
hospitality and protection; "and Crispus, the ruler of
the synagogue, believed in the Lord with all his house;
and many of the Corinthians hearing believed, and were
baptized." Neither the atheist nor the infidel nor the
skeptic can turn a wheel toward human redemption;
but the preacher who believes the Word of God can
beget the church of Christ any place where men live.

*The Word of God became a passion with Paul, sus-
taining him in persecution and impelling him both to
beget churches and establish them* (12-23): "But when
Gallio was pro-consul of Achaia, the Jews with one
accord rose up against Paul and brought him before
the judgment seat, saying, This man persuadeth men
to worship God contrary to the law. But when Paul
was about to open his mouth, Gallio said unto the Jews,
If indeed it were a matter of wrong or of wicked villany,

O ye Jews, reason would that I should bear with you: but if they are questions about words and names and your own law, look to it yourselves; I am not minded to be a judge of these matters. And he drove them from the judgment seat. And they all laid hold on Sosthenes, the ruler of the synagogue, and beat him before the judgment seat. And Gallio cared for none of these things. And Paul, having tarried after this yet many days, took his leave of the brethren, and sailed thence for Syria, and with him Priscilla and Aquila: having shorn his head in Cenchreæ; for he had a vow. And they came to Ephesus, and he left them there: but he himself entered into the synagogue, and reasoned with the Jews. And when they asked him to abide a longer time, he consented not; but taking his leave of them, and saying, I will return again unto you if God will, he set sail from Ephesus. And when he had landed at Cæsarea, he went up and saluted the church, and went down to Antioch. And having spent some time there, he departed, and went through the region of Galatia, and Phrygia, in order, establishing all the disciples.'' Without purpose and passion, life sags sour and insipid and flavorless and flattens in failure; man has no certain balance or ballast or compass or anchor in himself. The secret of Paul's towering success, which elevated him above his contemporaries and rings the world with his fame is that he married himself indissolubly to the Lord Jesus Christ by the purpose and passion and power of His Word. When all the atheists and infidels and agnostics and skeptics and presumptuous philosophers and self-centered modernists and unbelievers have vanished in eternal darkness, Paul will continue to shine as a star of the first magnitude. For a year and six months Paul taught the Word of God

to the Corinthians in the face of dangerous persecution
that threatened his life; but he had the assurance of
the Lord: "I am with thee, and no man shall set on
thee to harm thee: for I have much people in this city."
It is interesting to note how the Lord protected Paul
providentially through the superior human wisdom of
Gallio, the pro-consul of Achaia at that time: if all the
rulers before whom the ancient saints, and even the
Lord Jesus Himself, were dragged in persecution that
still disgraces the human race, had had the good sense
and hardihood of Gallio, this hellish oppression might
have reacted on its instigators, as it did in this case "on
Sosthenes, the ruler of the synagogue." But the same
potent divine Word that compelled Paul to go among
the lost to preach the gospel primarily to them, also
sent him on from Corinth and Ephesus and Cæsarea
and Antioch, "through the region of Galatia, and
Phrygia, in order, *establishing all the disciples*" *in the
faith*. Shame on anybody that tries to belittle this man
Paul! But this attitude in nowise depreciates Paul; it
is only a commentary on the smallness of those that
affect it! Here is the fullness of Paul's stature: His
spirit, the Spirit of the risen Lord, who was in him,
yearned to evangelize the human race and minister to
all the churches everywhere; yea, he carried the world
on his heart.

*Apollos was also "fervent in spirit" and controlled
by the Word of the Lord* (24-28): "Now a certain Jew
named Apollos, an Alexandrian by race, an eloquent
man, came to Ephesus; and he was mighty in the scriptures. This man had been instructed in the way of the
Lord; and being fervent in spirit, he spake and taught
accurately the things concerning Jesus, knowing only
the baptism of John: and he began to speak boldly in

the synagogue. But when Priscilla and Aquila heard him, they took him unto them, and expounded unto him the way of God more accurately. And when he was minded to pass over into Achaia, the brethren encouraged him, and wrote to the disciples to receive him: and when he was come, he helped them much that had believed through grace; for he powerfully confuted the Jews, and that publicly, showing by the scriptures that Jesus was the Christ." Really fervency of spirit and amenability to the Scriptures are synonymous terms; no man can be warm in his heart toward the Lord who does not bow in humble recognition and submission to the final authority of His Word. Apollos was not only sound in his attitude toward the divine Word, but "he was mighty in the scriptures"; his knowledge was "accurate," but it was not complete because he knew "only the baptism of John." When Priscilla and Aquila discovered this defect in the teaching and preaching of Apollos, they acted with due discretion and delicacy of feeling: they risked no public reproof, but took Apollos into the sacred secrecy of their own presence, "and expounded unto him the way of God more accurately." And that Apollos evidently accepted this correction in a spirit of humble gratitude, and went forward in the light of it, marks him as a big man. John's baptism was of divine origin, and in order when it was practiced, to which Jesus Himself submitted; but it was introductory and temporary, like John's mission itself, and associated with no name save that of John himself, being only to the Jews as "the baptism of repentance unto the remission of sins." However, the baptism of the Great Commission, the baptism that Jesus Himself commanded, is entirely different, being addressed to every believing, penitent sinner in the world

forever, whether of the Jews or of the Gentiles, and
always solemnized by the great triune name of the
Deity, "the name of the Father and of the Son and
of the Holy Spirit." The brethren in Corinth were so
delighted with the remarkable work of Apollos among
them that they gladly recommended him to the churches
of Achaia, among whom he was "minded" to go, where
his success was as distinguished as it had been in Corinth.
There are many types of mind in the world, if not in
every community, to some of which one preacher might
make a more apt appeal than another preacher. No
doubt Apollos was different from Paul; but he was like
him also, because "he helped them much that had believed through grace; for he powerfully confuted the
Jews, and that publicly, showing by the scriptures that
Jesus was the Christ."

# XIX

## "THE WAY"

### (Acts 19)

*"The Way" is both doctrinal and practical.* Of
course, "The Way" is the product or the creation of
Him who said, "I am the way, and the truth, and the
life," and therefore triune: in this trinity, "the truth"
is the doctrine or the definition, and "the life" is the
object and the inspiration of "The Way": without the
truth or the doctrine or the teaching or the revelation
of the Word of the Lord Jesus Christ, we could not find
"The Way," which could take us nowhere. In this
world there are two ways described by the Lord Jesus
Christ: "Enter ye in by the narrow gate: for wide is
the gate, and broad is the way, that leadeth to destruction, and many are they that enter in thereby. For
narrow is the gate, and straitened the way, that leadeth
unto life, and few are they that find it" (Matt. 7:13,
14). Some resent the severity of this doctrine, and
refuse to walk in "The Way." Well, everybody must
of necessity look life in the face, select what he wants
and choose the way in which he will travel through this
world. None can have everything, or journey on both
roads, which lead in opposite directions, at the same
time; one can not cater to the flesh and have the full
sway of the Spirit in himself; neither can one walk in
the mud or sit in the dirt or roll in the dust and be
clean and pure; nor can he hold the false, momentary
delights of sin like a sweet morsel in his mouth and

have the elixir of life and the buoyancy of hope. The devil is not particular, whose gate is wide and whose way is broad, and any can go to hell in it who wants to; the Lord, however, has a definite standard, whose gate is narrow and whose way is straitened, and all can go to heaven in His way who give up sin and accept Him as Saviour and Lord. Only the Deity can define "The Way" of life, which has been done repeatedly in the Word of God, in the New Testament, particularly and primarily in Acts of Apostles, which we are now analyzing, which it is the height of presumption for any uninspired man to try to modify in the slightest degree fundamentally. It is tragic and fatal to stumble over any exaction of "The Way," without ever seeing the glorious reward of eternal life to which it leads. Let us see the whole truth. Sometimes we are advised by affected superior wisdom that Christianity is not a system of doctrine, but a way of life: now that is only a half-truth, and a half-truth is false. The gospel is *both* a system of doctrine *and* "The Way" of life; if we did not have the divine teaching, we could know absolutely nothing about "The Way"; let there be no distortion of the truth or false emphasis here or elsewhere. We can not deceive the Lord, and we must not delude ourselves or impose on others. The alien sinner must do everything the Lord has commanded him to do, and set his feet in "The Way," in which he must travel faithfully to the end to receive immortality and eternal happiness.

## "The Way, and the Truth, and the Life" (vs. 1-41)

*"The Way" is doctrinal* (1-10): "And it came to pass, that, while Apollos was at Corinth, Paul having passed through the upper country came to Ephesus,

and found certain disciples: and he said unto them, Did
ye receive the Holy Spirit when ye believed? And
they said unto him, Nay, we did not so much as hear
whether the Holy Spirit was given. And he said, Into
what then were ye baptized? And they said, Into John's
baptism. And Paul said, John baptized with the baptism of repentance, saying unto the people that they
should believe on him that should come after him, that
is, on Jesus. And when they heard this, they were
baptized into the name of the Lord Jesus. And when
Paul had laid his hands upon them, the Holy Spirit
came on them; and they spake with tongues, and prophesied. And they were in all about twelve men. And
he entered into the synagogue, and spake boldly for
the space of three months, reasoning and persuading as
to the things concerning the kingdom of God. But
when some were hardened and disobedient, speaking evil
of the Way before the multitude, he departed from them,
and separated the disciples, reasoning daily in the school
of Tyrannus. And this continued for the space of two
years; so that all they that dwelt in Asia heard the
word of the Lord, both Jews and Greeks.'' If the Deity,
the Father and the Son and the Holy Spirit, were not,
neither could the Way be. The perfect reality and
glorious outcome of the Way conclude positively all
controversy as to the eternal existence of the Godhead,
out of whose supreme wisdom and absolute knowledge
came the Bible and the gospel and ''the kingdom of
God'' and ''the word of the Lord.'' The question
Paul asked of the disciples he found in Ephesus, ''Did
ye receive the Holy Spirit when ye believed?'' discovered the defect in their conversion, as it will lay bare
any imperfection in all professed changes from the
natural to the spiritual state. Faith and repentance

and confession and baptism are the practical application of the gospel, which Luke makes plain and simple and emphatic and imperative by much repetition. Neither repentance nor confession nor baptism follows faith as something distinct from faith, for each one of these acts is really a part of faith, a deed of faith, and all of them together perfect faith primarily. In every instance of conversion or the new birth in Acts of Apostles, if only belief or faith, as is the case here, is mentioned, belief or faith stands for the whole process and includes repentance and confession and baptism. That these Ephesians had not received the Holy Spirit when they were baptized, showed their baptism spurious; John's baptism, into which they had been baptized, carried no promise of the Holy Spirit, as did the baptism that Jesus placed at the door of His church, which they obeyed immediately when they learned about it. Some would make a distinction between the kingdom of God and the kingdom of heaven and the church of Christ, for any technical discussion of which, being like splitting hairs, we have neither space nor taste; suffice it to say that the Scriptures use these terms with practical synonymy. There can be no kingdom without a king: Jesus was never King in this world, but following His life and death and resurrection on earth He ascended to heaven, where He was crowned King; and His first official act was the creation of His church in the original twelve apostles on Pentecost. Verily, that was the beginning of the divine kingdom in this world: into what it shall grow through the years of time and the eons of eternity is ''above all that we ask or think'' or hope or imagine.

*"The Way"* *sprang out of providence and miracle* (11-22): "And God wrought special miracles by the

hands of Paul: insomuch that unto the sick were carried away from his body handkerchiefs or aprons, and the diseases departed from them, and the evil spirits went out. But certain also of the strolling Jews, exorcists, took upon them to name over them that had the evil spirits the name of the Lord Jesus, saying, I adjure you by Jesus whom Paul preacheth. And there were seven sons of one Sceva, a Jew, a chief priest, who did this. And the evil spirit answered and said unto them, Jesus I know, and Paul I know; but who are ye? And the man in whom the evil spirit was leaped on them, and mastered both of them, and prevailed against them, so that they fled out of that house naked and wounded. And this became known to all, both Jews and Greeks, that dwelt at Ephesus; and fear fell upon them all, and the name of the Lord Jesus was magnified. Many also of them that had believed came, confessing, and declaring their deeds. And not a few of them that practiced magical arts brought their books together and burned them in the sight of all; and they counted the price of them, and found it fifty thousand pieces of silver. So mightily grew the word of the Lord and prevailed. Now after these things were ended, Paul purposed in the spirit, when he had passed through Macedonia and Achaia, to go to Jerusalem, saying, After I have been there, I must also see Rome. And having sent into Macedonia two of them that ministered unto him, Timothy and Erastus, he himself stayed in Asia for a while.'' God takes care of His universe by His providence, and releases a miracle when it is impossible to accomplish His purpose otherwise. However, the providential and the miraculous seem to be close together: either one of them, especially both of them, should awe the sons of men into the worship of the great God. It is just as easy to believe these "special miracles by the hands of Paul" as it is to believe any miracles; "the King is eternal, immortal, invisible, the only God," and to limit His power is to destroy His deity. It is striking and amazing how the Lord exposed and humiliated the tramp Jews who claimed the power to cast out demons; verily, this double miracle glorified "the name of the Lord Jesus," sent many in faith to confess their sins, and made a public bonfire, to the extent of fifty thousand pieces of silver, of the false-record books of the mere wizards. It is no wonder that "mightily grew the word of the Lord and prevailed." It is not possible that, since formerly Paul was forced by the Lord into Europe and not allowed to go into Asia where he was permitted to remain "for a while" at this time, he made up his mind independently of the Lord to go to Jerusalem or to Rome; but he made this purpose "in the Spirit." Hardly had sin become an awful fact, when Jehovah God set out in His providence, using His miraculous power when necessary, of which we have an illustration in this chapter, to reveal His highway through the patriarchs and the prophets and John the Baptist and Jesus of Nazareth, which He brought to the fullness of glory on the first Pentecost after His resurrection by the creation of the church of Christ in the original twelve apostles; from that time till this, sections of the gospel train over the railway of heaven have reported, and shall continue to do so, with new citizens of the eternal city.

*"The Way" is elevated and practical* (23-41) : "And about that time there arose no small stir concerning the Way. For a certain man named Demetrius, a silver-smith, who made silver shrines of Diana, brought no little business unto the craftsmen; whom he gathered

together, with the workmen of like occupation, and said,
Sirs, ye know that by this business we have our wealth.
And ye see and hear, that not alone at Ephesus, but
almost throughout all Asia, this Paul persuaded and
turned away much people, saying that they are no
gods, that are made with hands: and not only is there
danger that this our trade come into disrepute; but also
that the temple of the great goddess Diana be made of
no account, and that she should even be deposed from
her magnificence whom all Asia and the world wor-
shippeth. And when they heard this they were filled
with wrath, and cried out, saying, Great is Diana of
the Ephesians. And the city was filled with the confusion: and they rushed with one accord into the theatre,
having seized Gaius and Aristarchus, men of Macedonia,
Paul's companions in travel. And when Paul was
minded to enter in unto the temple, the disciples suffered him not. And certain also of the Asiarchs, being
his friends, sent unto him and besought him not to
adventure himself into the theatre. Some therefore
cried one thing, and some another: for the assembly was
in confusion; and the more part knew not wherefore
they were come together. And they brought Alexander
out of the multitude, the Jews putting him forward.
And Alexander beckoned with the hand, and would have
made a defence unto the people. But when they perceived that he was a Jew, all with one voice about the
space of two hours cried out, Great is Diana of the
Ephesians. And when the townclerk had quieted the
multitude, he saith, Ye men of Ephesus, what man is
there who knoweth not that the city of the Ephesians
is the temple-keeper of the great Diana, and of the
image which fell down from Jupiter? Seeing then that
these things cannot be gainsaid, ye ought to be quiet,

and to do nothing rash. For ye have brought hither these men, who are neither robbers of temples nor blasphemers of our goddess. If therefore Demetrius, and the craftsmen that are with him, have a matter against any man, the courts are open, and there are pro-consuls: let them accuse one another. But if ye seek anything about other matters, it shall be settled in the regular assembly. For indeed we are in danger to be accused concerning this day's riot, there being no cause for it: and as touching it we shall not be able to give account of this concourse. And when he had thus spoken, he dismissed the assembly.'' Of course, Paul, in promoting ''The Way,'' had to take square issue with the gross idolatry in the midst of which he found himself; and this excited the skilled mechanics, whose object was material gain, and through them the populace. Verily, it required a hard blow to dislodge this incrusted, aggravated false worship; but Paul smote Diana, the false Ephesian goddess, and this meant her eventual destruction and annihilation. Demetrius and his associate silversmiths led the people into this riot, which the most of them did not understand at all. The townclerk showed himself adept in handling the multitude, whom he quieted and dismissed; but he really glossed over the idolatry, which ''The Way'' is entirely too elevated and practical to tolerate at all. ''The Way'' is high in the realm of righteousness, and is in direct opposition to any traffic that leaves men in gross ignorance of God and beclouds their minds and damns them in body and soul and spirit. The devil has shifted to the liquor traffic, which is the worship of the appetite and the belly. ''The Way'' is both providential and miraculous; ''The Way'' is defined by the divine doctrine and emerges in the lives of Christians.

# XX

## SPIRITUAL PASSION

### (Acts 20)

*Passion means power.* The passionate man is always
intense and zealous, with all the power in him available.
Here is a striking event in the life of Jesus: "And the
passover of the Jews was at hand, and Jesus went up
to Jerusalem. And he found in the temple those that
sold oxen and sheep and doves, and the changers of
money sitting: and he made a scourge of cords, and
cast all out of the temple, both the sheep and the oxen;
and he poured out the changers' money, and overthrew
their tables; and to them that sold the doves he said,
Take these things hence; make not my Father's house
a house of merchandise. His disciples remembered that
it was written, Zeal for thy house shall eat me up"
(John 2:13-17). The prime requisite of spiritual passion is the Holy Spirit Himself, who came upon Jesus
at His baptism; and in Nazareth He applied Isaiah's
wonderful Messianic prophecy to Himself, which we
are glad to quote as follows:

"The Spirit of the Lord is upon me,
  Because he anointed me to preach good things to
    the poor:
  He hath sent me to proclaim release to the
    captives,
  And recovering of sight to the blind,
  To set at liberty them that are bruised,

To proclaim the acceptable year of the Lord''
(Luke 4 : 18, 19).

In the whole history of the world, in all the story of the human race, no other mind ever shone, no other heart ever glowed, no other spirit ever blazed, equal to that of Jesus of Nazareth, the Son of the Living God, in whom the Holy Spirit found perfect accord and infinite achievement. Verily, He stands forever as the great human Exemplar and the divine Saviour and Guide of all that accept and follow Him! And standing up closest to Him are the twelve original apostles, in whom the Holy Spirit miraculously created the church, His church, on the first Pentecost after His resurrection from the dead. But this priority or precedence of the Twelve was from necessity, for the sake of service; and is in no sense classific in the church of the Lord Jesus Christ. The church, like the human race, having no antecedents, had to be created to come into existence; but when the church was once launched, the law of birth became supreme and universal in it, as it had already prevailed in the human race. Methuselah, who was born, lived longer than Adam, who was created; likewise Paul, who was born a Christian, in some respects surpassed the original Twelve, who were created Christians. But the same Holy Spirit that created the church originally on Pentecost, and begat the three thousand who were born on that day through the gospel Peter and his associates preached, and baptized Paul to make him an apostle also, has likewise brought or shall bring through the same gospel every Christian into existence in the world, and is the source of spiritual passion and power in the church forever through the New Testament of our Lord and Saviour Jesus Christ.

### Paul's Spiritual Passion (vs. 1-38)

*Paul's spiritual passion flamed in action* (1-16):
"And after the uproar ceased, Paul having sent for
the disciples and exhorted them, took leave of them,
and departed to go into Macedonia. And when he had
gone through those parts, and had given them much
exhortation, he came into Greece. And when he had
spent three months there, and a plot was laid up against
him by the Jews as he was about to set sail for Syria,
he determined to return through Macedonia. And there
accompanied him as far as Asia, Sopater of Berœa, the
son of Pyrrhus; and of the Thessalonians, Aristarchus
and Secundus; and Gaius of Derbe, and Timothy; and
of Asia, Tychicus and Trophimus. But these had gone
before, and were waiting for us at Troas. And we
sailed away from Philippi after the days of unleavened
bread, and came unto them to Troas in five days; where
we tarried seven days. And upon the first day of the
week, when we were gathered together to break bread,
Paul discoursed with them, intending to depart on the
morrow; and prolonged his speech until midnight. And
there were many lights in the upper chamber where
we were gathered together. And there sat in the window
a certain young man named Eutychus, borne down with
deep sleep; and as Paul discoursed yet longer, being
borne down by his sleep he fell down from the third
story, and was taken up dead. And Paul went down,
and fell on him, and embracing him said, Make ye no
ado; for his life is in him. And when he was gone up,
and had broken the bread, and eaten, and had talked
with them a long while, even till break of day, so he
departed. And they brought the lad alive, and were
not a little comforted. But we, going before to the ship,

set sail for Assos, there intending to take in Paul: for so he had appointed, intending himself to go by land. And when he met us at Assos, we took him in, and came to Mitylene. And sailing from thence, we came the following day over against Chios; and the next day we touched at Samos; and the day after we came to Miletus. For Paul had determined to sail past Ephesus, that he might not have to spend time in Asia; for he was hastening, if it were possible for him, to be at Jerusalem the day of Pentecost." Paul's life was always full of movement, while at the same time he is especially famous for his power of speech and oratory; indeed, action may legitimately include words. As an evangelist, Paul could appraise a climax; he knew that the time had come for him to leave Ephesus, where he had released an influence that would go right on in his absence in the destruction of the idolatrous worship of Diana; while he betook himself to the work of the Lord in other communities. Taking orderly leave of his Ephesian brethren, he set his face again toward the provinces of Macedonia and Greece, where, having previously preached the gospel primarily, his activity at this particular visit seems to have been hortatory. In Greece, however, where he spent three months, but had not traveled extensively before, Paul and his associates probably broke new ground. Now, while Paul's very deeds bore the stamp of his spiritual passion, the course of his action was characteristically heroic. The conspiracy "laid against him by the Jews as he was about to set sail for Syria" in no wise deterred him; and "he determined to return through Macedonia," where his enemies would have better opportunity to harm him than on the Mediterranean Sea. Moreover, Paul's intensity and the attraction and power of his message

are reflected in his comrades—such men as Sopater and
Aristarchus and Secundus and Gaius and Timothy and
Tychicus and Trophimus—who waited for Paul and
Luke at Troas, where the whole company "tarried seven
days." And during that week stirring and significant
events occurred. Here the custom of the primitive
church crops out in these simple words of Luke: "And
upon the first day of the week, when we were gathered
together to break bread, Paul discoursed with them";
this is clearly reference to the weekly observance of
the Lord's Supper, which is an authoritative example
for the church to follow in all the world forever. The
purpose of the weekly assembly of the church in Troas
was "to break bread," to observe the Lord's Supper,
to remember Jesus in His own appointed way, rather
than to hear Paul preach. Of course, both Paul and
his audience knew that his time was limited in Troas
on this occasion, when he was so vehement and they
were so eager, that he could not but preach "until midnight," yea "even till break of day." The "upper
chamber" in which Paul preached was brilliantly
lighted; but Eutychus, sleeping heavily "in the window," "fell down from the third story, and was taken
up dead." But for Paul's miraculous power as apostle
of Jesus Christ, this accident might have been calamitous
to the meeting in Troas. However, Paul's wonderful,
merciful act of raising this young man from the dead
exceeded the eloquence of mere words. There are times
when any man with the depth of Paul's spirit seeks
seclusion; and Paul, allowing his allies to sail from
Troas to Assos, made the journey alone by land on foot.
Paul kept his life well planned and orderly arranged,
and economized his time; his sharp objective on this
particular occasion was "to be at Jerusalem the day

of Pentecost.'' And so he and his company sailed
rapidly from Assos to Mitylene and Chios and Samos
and Miletus, passing by Ephesus in Asia, where he had
recently spent three years; ''for he was hastening, if it
were possible for him, to be at Jerusalem the day of
Pentecost.'' It is good and wholesome and inspiring,
as we go through this text, to note how Paul's spiritual
passion flamed in action. The Spirit of the Lord, the
Holy Spirit, dominated him and led him and stimulated
him and empowered him.

*Paul's spiritual passion blazed in word* (17-38):
''And from Miletus he sent to Ephesus, and called to
him the elders of the church. And when they were
come to him, he said unto them, Ye yourselves know,
from the first day that I set foot in Asia, after what
manner I was with you all the time, serving the Lord
with all lowliness of mind, and with tears, and with
trials which befell me by the plots of the Jews; how
I shrank not from declaring unto you anything that
was profitable, and teaching you publicly, and from
house to house, testifying both to Jews and to Greeks
repentance toward God, and faith toward our Lord
Jesus Christ. And now, behold, I go bound in the
spirit unto Jerusalem, not knowing the things that shall
befall me there: save that the Holy Spirit testifieth
unto me in every city, saying that bonds and afflictions
abide me. But I hold not my life of any account as
dear unto myself, so that I may accomplish my course,
and the ministry which I received from the Lord Jesus,
to testify the gospel of the grace of God. And now,
behold, I know that ye all, among whom I went about
preaching the kingdom, shall see my face no more.
Wherefore I testify unto you this day, that I am pure
from the blood of all men. For I shrank not from

declaring unto you the whole counsel of God. Take
heed unto yourselves, and to all the flock, in which the
Holy Spirit hath made you bishops, to feed the church
of the Lord which he purchased with his own blood.
I know that after my departing grievous wolves shall
enter in among you, not sparing the flock; and from
among your own selves shall men arise, speaking perverse things, to draw away the disciples after them.
Wherefore watch ye, remembering that by the space of
three years I ceased not to admonish every one night
and day with tears. And now I commend you to God,
and to the word of his grace, which is able to build you
up, and to give you the inheritance among all them that
are sanctified. I coveted no man's silver, or gold, or
apparel. Ye yourselves know that these hands ministered unto my necessities, and to them that were with
me. In all things I gave you an example, that so labor-
ing ye ought to help the weak, and to remember the
words of the Lord Jesus, that he himself said, It is
more blessed to give than to receive. And when he had
thus spoken, he kneeled down and prayed with them
all. And they all wept sore, and fell on Paul's neck
and kissed him, sorrowing most of all for the word
which he had spoken, that they should behold his face
no more. And they brought him on his way unto the
ship.'' Paul's words here are neither accidental nor
incidental, nor did they relate to a side-issue; they are
fundamental and central to his own heart and to his
own work in Ephesus and to the elders and the life of
that congregation and to the church of the Lord Jesus
Christ everywhere: in no other way could Paul or any
other man breathe forth words of such fiery, eternal
significance! Not having time to visit the church itself
in Ephesus, Paul called the elders of this congregation

to see him in Miletus, and challenged them to witness
in their own hearts that he spoke the truth about his
own wonderful work in Asia, where he had served the
Lord with great humility and affection and heroism and
completeness. Paul preached and taught the gospel
"publicly, and from house to house, testifying both to
Jews and to Greeks repentance toward God, and faith
toward our Lord Jesus Christ." Both the Jews and
the Gentiles knew something about the great God,
through the law and nature and the light of their own
being, but they had sinned against that knowledge; and
Paul called on them to repent toward the mighty
Jehovah whose law they had transgressed. But it is
practically impossible for any man, whether Jew or
Gentile, to have any satisfactory or adequate faith in
the eternal, immortal, invisible God, who rejects the
revelation of the Lord Jesus Christ; and so Paul
preached and taught to all men "faith toward our
Lord Jesus Christ." Verily, there is absolutely no
other way for any man to be saved than by "the gospel of
the grace of God," which Paul testified. Even though
the Holy Spirit had revealed to Paul that "bonds and
afflictions" awaited him in Jerusalem, he was determined to go to this great city, because he was "bound
in the spirit" to go, and he held not his life of any
account as dear unto himself, so that he might accomplish his course, and the ministry which he received
from the Lord Jesus, "to testify the gospel of the grace
of God." Paul could have lived quietly and com-
fortably among his brethren, in the midst of whom he
was, the rest of his life; but his heroic spirit rose up
to go to Jerusalem and to Rome, braving all danger, to
preach the gospel of the Son of God there. Paul knew
that he was bidding the elders of Ephesus final fare-

well, who were looking on his face the last time; and he called them to witness that he had saved himself "from the blood of all men" by declaring "the whole counsel of God." With the certain prophetic gift, Paul saw the future swiftly coming on; and he admonished the elders, "Take heed unto yourselves, and to all the flock, in which the Holy Spirit hath made you bishops, to feed the church of the Lord which he purchased with his own blood." He saw ravening wolves seeking to slay the sheep of the Lord, and false leaders rising up in the church; and urged his brethren to copy his tender watch-care for three years. Then he commended them to the grace of God, that they might have the inheritance of the sanctified, which he himself had sought by eschewing mere material wealth, taking care of himself and helping the weak, thus furnishing them and us an example, and rescuing from oblivion the incomparable words of the Lord Jesus, "It is more blessed to give than to receive." Surely the brethren that surrounded Paul had never seen a more solemn occasion than this, which reached its climax in prayer and great show of personal affection and extreme sadness "that they should behold his face no more. And they brought him on his way unto the ship," but the work of the Lord went right on with increasing power.

## XXI

## THE DOMINANCE OF THE DIVINE WILL

### (Acts 21)

*Both the safety and the perpetuity of the universe rest in the hands of God.* Surely everybody above infancy or idiocy must know that there is a conflict of wills in this world; and along the broadest possible lines, but in the deepest, straitest sense, the Bible calls this conflict *sin.* With the Deity, there is no such thing as time or space as these conditions obtain in our limited, temporary realm: the great uncreated God knows all things all the time and is everywhere forever, whether we can comprehend that or not. Even Jehovah God yearned for fellowship, which He did not always have; it would seem that He was not sufficient unto Himself for His own happiness. But the self-existent and eternal God knew the risk that He must take in the creatures of His own creation; and from the beginning, even before the beginning, of His universe He safeguarded mankind from their own rebellion against Him, by the ascendancy of His own will. But salvation from sin is physical and moral and spiritual in harmony with the mercy of the Lord and the law of man's life, and can not be arbitrary or mechanical or claptrap. No being has any will in the first birth; the Creator has to thrust this initial life upon him, which makes him but the creature of God. But without definite choice there can be no second birth, which is the only way any man can become a child of God. In the gospel,

the Lord says to man, "Do you like the temporary life
I have given you in your physical birth? If you will
be born again, of water and the Spirit, you may live
forever." We are all sinners, because we are not always in harmony with the will of the Deity, which
must of necessity prevail, even though all the impeni-
tent, hardened, depraved sinners are swallowed up of
the second death and perish forever. Hear John, the
beloved" (1 John 1: 5-10): "And this is the message
which we have heard from him and announce unto you,
that God is light, and in him is no darkness at all.
If we say that we have fellowship with him and walk in
the darkness, we lie, and do not the truth: but if we
walk in the light, as he is in the light, we have fellowship one with another, and the blood of Jesus his Son
cleanseth us from all sin. If we say that we have no sin,
we deceive ourselves, and the truth is not in us. If we
confess our sins, he is faithful and righteous to forgive
us our sins, and to cleanse us from all unrighteousness.
If we say that we have not sinned, we make him a liar,
and his word is not in us." Now, as we study the
chapter before us, we shall be happy to discover the
divine will dominant in Paul, and inspired to look for
the hand of the Lord in our own lives. There is rebellion
against the supreme Being in high places; but all the
devils and sinners and rebels and dictators can not
dethrone the Lord, who will maintain His own suprem-
acy and have His own way.

### "The Will of the Lord Be [Was] Done" in Paul
### (vs. 1-40)

*"The will of the Lord be [was] done" in Paul in his
going to Jerusalem* (1-16): "And when it came to
pass that we were parted from them and had set sail,

we came with a straight course unto Cos, and the
next day unto Rhodes, and from thence unto Patara:
and having found a ship crossing over unto Phœnicia,
we came aboard, and set sail. And when we had
come in sight of Cyprus, leaving it on the left hand,
we sailed unto Syria, and landed at Tyre; for there
the ship was to unlade her burden. And having
found the disciples, we tarried there seven days:
and these said to Paul through the Spirit, that he
should not set foot in Jerusalem. And when it came
to pass that we had accomplished the days, we departed and went on our journey; and they all, with
wives and children, brought us on our way till we
were out of the city: and kneeling down on the beach,
we prayed, and bade each other farewell; and we
went on board the ship, but they returned home
again. And when we had finished the voyage from
Tyre, we arrived at Ptolemais; and we saluted the
brethren, and abode with them one day. And on the
morrow we departed, and came unto Cæsarea: and
entering into the house of Philip the evangelist, who
was one of the seven, we abode with him. Now this
man had four virgin daughters, who prophesied. And
as we tarried there some days, there came down from
Judæa a certain prophet, named Agabus, and coming
to us, and taking Paul's girdle, he bound his own
feet and hands, and said, Thus saith the Holy Spirit,
So shall the Jews at Jerusalem bind the man that
owneth this girdle, and shall deliver him into the
hands of the Gentiles. And when we heard these
things, both we and they of that place besought him
not to go up to Jerusalem. Then Paul answered,
What do ye, weeping and breaking my heart? for
I am ready not to be bound only, but also to die at

Jerusalem for the name of the Lord Jesus. And
when he would not be persuaded, we ceased, saying,
*The will of the Lord be done.* And after these days
we took up our baggage and went up to Jerusalem.
And there went with us also certain of the disciples
from Cæsarea, bringing with them one Mnason of
Cyprus, an early disciple, with whom we should
lodge.'' Here Luke wrote veritable history; his story
is so set among real things that it must be true: indeed, this is characteristic of the whole Bible. It
was the will of the Lord that Paul should go to
Jerusalem for Pentecost, one of the greatest occasions
that ever came to that religious center; which would
widen and deepen Paul's influence for Christianity.
But the Holy Spirit dealt fairly with Paul, apprising
him that his public appearance in Jerusalem when
his enemies would be there in large numbers would
give them opportunity to persecute him, if not even
to slay him; in truth, this warning came to Paul
both directly and repeatedly through his brethren
en route to Jerusalem. Paul and his party, having
bidden their Ephesian brethren an affectionate farewell at Miletus, immediately resumed their voyage to
Jerusalem, passing rapidly by Cos and Rhodes and
Patara, real places still on the map. At the last-
named place, they boarded a ship that was bound
for Phœnicia, and sailed right on by the Island of
Cyprus till they came to the country of Syria, and
landed at Tyre, where the ship was unloaded, and
where they spent a week with their brethren, who
urged Paul "through the Spirit" not to go to Jerusalem at all. Of course, this made the situation very
serious and tense; and when Paul and his associates
departed to resume their journey to Jerusalem, whole

families accompanied them out of Tyre and bade them an ardent adieu in prayer on the beach, watching them "board the ship" and returning to their homes. From Tyre, Paul and his company sailed a short way to Ptolemais, where they saluted members of the church and spent one day with them. The very next day they arrived in Cæsarea, and became the guests "of Philip the evangelist, who was one of the seven" deacons originally selected in the great first church in Jerusalem. Luke had left Philip in Cæsarea, where, following his victory in Samaria and with the Ethiopian eunuch in the desert, he had evidently established his home. Philip had a most interesting, remarkable family; his four daughters were virgins and prophetesses. Now, while Paul was the guest of Philip in Cæsarea, the strongest, most spectacular influence to prevent him from going to Jerusalem was precipitated by a Judean prophet "named Agabus." While all admonitions were based on truth that came to Paul through his brethren and he knew the danger ahead of him better than anybody else, he was certain that it was the will of the Lord for him to go to Jerusalem, and he was determined to go. Paul recognized that his brethren were opposed to his cherished desire to be in Jerusalem on Pentecost, because of their natural human fear that he would be oppressed or murdered by his wicked enemies; but Paul's comfort and life were not nearly so important to him as the prosperity of the church of the Lord Jesus Christ. Agabus so climaxed this negative entreaty to keep Paul away from Jerusalem on Pentecost, by his scenic display in the use of Paul's girdle, that both the church in Cæsarea and the members of Paul's party, including Luke, were swept off their feet; but Paul was absolutely unmoved, except to cry out, "What do ye, weeping and breaking my heart? for I am ready not to be bound only, but also to die at Jerusalem for the name of the Lord Jesus." Then it was borne in upon those that were with Paul, that day, that he was right and they were wrong: and they could not but exclaim, "The will of the Lord be done." And with this question finally thus settled, Paul and his fellow missionaries made the last stage of their journey on foot to Jerusalem, which was not far away, carrying their baggage; and some of the members of the church in Cæsarea accompanied them: all of whom were entertained in Jerusalem by Mnason of Cyprus.

*The will of the Lord prevailed in what happened to Paul in Jerusalem* (17-40): "And when we were come to Jerusalem, the brethren received us gladly. And the day following Paul went in with us unto James; and all the elders were present. And when he had saluted them, he rehearsed one by one the things which God had wrought among the Gentiles through his ministry. And they, when they heard it, glorified God; and they said unto him, Thou seest, brother, how many thousands there are among the Jews of them that have believed; and they are all zealous for the law: and they have been informed concerning thee, that thou teachest all the Jews who are among the Gentiles to forsake Moses, telling them not to circumcise their children, neither to walk after the customs. What is it therefore? they will certainly hear that thou art come. Do therefore this that we say to thee: We have four men that have a vow on them; these take, and purify thyself with them, and be at charges for them, that they may shave their heads: and all shall know that there is no truth in the things whereof they have been informed concerning thee; but that thou thyself also walkest orderly, keeping the law. But as touching the Gentiles that have believed, we wrote, giving judgment that they should keep themselves from things sacrificed to idols, and from blood, and from what is strangled, and from fornication. Then Paul took the men, and the next day purifying himself with them went into the temple, declaring the fulfillment of the days of purification, until the offering was offered for every one of them. And when the seven days were almost completed, the Jews from Asia, when they saw him in the temple, stirred up all the multitude and laid hands on him, crying out, Men of Israel, help: This is the man that teacheth all men everywhere against the people, and the law, and this place; and moreover he brought Greeks also into the temple, and hath defiled this holy place. For they had before seen with him in the city Trophimus the Ephesian, whom they supposed that Paul had brought into the temple. And all the city was moved, and the people ran together; and they laid hold on Paul, and dragged him out of the temple: and straightway the doors were shut. And as they were seeking to kill him, tidings came up to the chief captain of the band, that all Jerusalem was in confusion. And forthwith he took soldiers and centurions, and ran down upon them: and they, when they saw the chief captain and the soldiers, left off beating Paul. Then the chief captain came near, and laid hold on him, and commanded him to be bound with two chains; and inquired who he was, and what he had done. And some shouted one thing, some another, among the crowd: and when he could not know the certainty for the uproar, he commanded him to be brought into the castle. And when

he came upon the stairs, so it was that he was borne of
the soldiers for the violence of the crowd; for the multitude of the people followed after, crying out, Away
with him. And as Paul was about to be brought into
the castle, he saith unto the chief captain, May I say
something unto thee? And he said, Dost thou know
Greek? Art thou not then the Egyptian, who before
these days stirred up to sedition and led out into the
wilderness the four thousand men of the Assassins? But
Paul said, I am a Jew, of Tarsus in Cilicia, a citizen of
no mean city: and I beseech thee, give me leave to speak
unto the people. And when he had given him leave,
Paul, standing on the stairs, beckoned with the hand
unto the people; and when there was made a great
silence, he spake unto them in the Hebrew language,
saying, Brethren and fathers, hear ye the defence which
I now make unto you.'' The day Paul and his party
walked into the city of Jerusalem, there was no portent
of danger to any of them; on the contrary, their fellow
Christians received them with confident gratification.
And the very next day, Paul greeted James and the
elders, and reported to them in detail his work among
the Gentiles; which provoked them to glorify God, but
also drew out of them their fear for Paul's safety in
Jerusalem at that particular time. No one can really
know any city or place by a flying visit; it requires
time to discover the deeper, hidden currents of life in
any locality. However, the ringleaders against Paul at
that time were ''the Jews from Asia,'' rather than those
that lived in Jerusalem. Paul's purifying himself in
the temple, on the advice of James and the elders of
the church in Jerusalem, according to the law of Moses,
with ''four men that had a vow on them,'' was not required of him by any principle of the Christian religion,

as is evinced by the instruction to Gentile Christians, repeated here; but it was a matter of expediency, to allay, if possible, the bitter criticism of Paul's enemies, indicating that they had actually lied about him. This adroit management, however, fell far short of its purpose; for the Asian Jews, Paul's most daring adversaries, stole a march on him in the temple, accusing him of being antagonistic everywhere to the interests of the Jewish people in the law and the temple, of defiling the temple by bringing Greeks into it, and of exciting, right in the temple, a mob that was about to murder him precipitately. But before these false, wicked descendants of Judah and Israel and Abraham could execute their vile purpose, the Lord came in His providence by the great Roman nation, personified in the chief captain and soldiers and centurions, and rescued Paul and saved his life. The chief captain did not know who Paul was, but Paul soon told him in the Greek language; and then, with the permission of this great Roman officer, Paul, "standing on the stairs," lifted his hand, silenced even his enemies, and delivered in the Hebrew tongue to the Jews themselves one of the most remarkable pleas in all the records of the human race.

# XXII

## THE COMPLETEST CHANGE

### (Acts 22)

*This world is marked by constant, incessant change; however* (Heb. 13:8) *"Jesus Christ is the same yesterday and to-day, yea and for ever."* The change of evolution is supposed always to mark growth and development; but *involution* is a fitter description of sin, every step in which is downward, and means declination and deterioration and degeneration and destruction and damnation and death! Change is impossible in the Lord Jesus Christ, because He cannot sin, and He has reached the very acme of perfection. It is bald supposition, if not the sheerest superstition, that the first man and the first woman, the created couple, were originally naked, without sense enough to recognize their nudity; before their disobedience, they must have been clothed in light, like the angels, and the Son of God and Moses and Elijah on the mount of transfiguration, which sin lost them, and made them ashamed. The progenitor of the human race was not the savage, barbarous, brutish creature some of his vain, modern presumptuous descendants have imagined him to be. He originated the names of all the lower animals, whose creation preceded his own—a feat which his descendants could not have done with all their vaunted, ostensibly superior learning, with all their boasted modernism. Indeed, the radical process of sin makes conversion from sin the completest of all changes. Sin swept Adam and Eve from their

original goodness, together with all their descendants
save One, into guiltiness, so that only God is good now;
sin planted the seeds of death in man's body, and has
impaired all his faculties; sin banished man from the
garden of Eden, and God guarded its entrance by the
cherubim with a flaming sword. The ravages of sin
are everywhere in the earth today. Said Paul (Rom.
8: 18-25), "For I reckon that the sufferings of this
present time are not worthy to be compared with the
glory which shall be revealed to us-ward. For the earnest expectation of the creation waiteth for the revealing
of the sons of God. For the creation was subjected to
vanity, not of its own will, but by reason of him who
subjected it, in hope that the creation itself also shall
be delivered from the bondage of corruption into the
liberty of the glory of the children of God. For we
know that the whole creation groaneth and travaileth
in pain together until now. And not only so, but ourselves also, who have received the first-fruits of the
Spirit, even we ourselves groan within ourselves, waiting for our adoption, to wit, the redemption of our body.
For in hope were we saved: but hope that is seen is not
hope: for who hopeth for that which he seeth? But
if we hope for that which we see not, then do we with
patience wait for it." Sin, spawned in hell, hatched pesti-
lence on the earth, to rot the human body and pollute
the soul of man; and our only hope is the Lord Jesus
Christ, the great Physician, the only Saviour from sin!

### Paul's Conversion from Sin Was the Completest Change (vs. 2-30)

*Paul's conversion from sin was the completest change,
which Luke recounted graphically here for the second
time, quoting Paul's own words* (2-16): "And when

they heard that he spake unto them in the Hebrew
language, they were the more quiet: and he saith, I am
a Jew, born in Tarsus of Cilicia, but brought up in this
city, at the feet of Gamaliel, instructed according to
the strict manner of the law of our fathers, being zealous for God, even as ye all are this day: and I persecuted this Way unto the death, binding and delivering
into prisons both men and women. As also the high
priest doth bear me witness, and all the estate of the
elders: from whom also I received letters unto the
brethren, and journeyed to Damascus to bring them
also that were there unto Jerusalem in bonds to be
punished. And it came to pass, that, as I made my
journey, and drew nigh unto Damascus, about noon,
suddenly there shone from heaven a great light round
about me. And I fell unto the ground, and heard a
voice saying unto me, Saul, Saul, why persecutest thou
me? And I answered, Who art thou, Lord? And he
said unto me, I am Jesus of Nazareth, whom thou persecutest. And they that were with me beheld indeed
the light, but they heard not the voice of him that spake
to me. And I said, What shall I do, Lord? And the Lord
said unto me, Arise, and go into Damascus; and there
it shall be told thee of all things which are appointed
for thee to do. And when I could not see for the glory
of that light, being led by the hand of them that were
with me, I came into Damascus. And one Ananias, a
devout man according to the law, well reported of by
all the Jews that dwelt there, came unto me, and standing by me said unto me, Brother Saul, receive thy sight.
And in that very hour I looked upon him. And he
said, The God of our fathers hath appointed thee to
know his will, and to see the Righteous One, and to
hear a voice from his mouth. For thou shalt be a

witness for him unto all men of what thou hast seen and heard. And now why tarriest thou? arise, and be baptized, and wash away thy sins, calling on his name.'' Paul had personality—magnetic, impressive, popular, persistent, powerful; he was a linguistic scholar, speaking with equal ease and facility in both the Hebrew and the Greek language; he compelled the attention of even his bitterest enemies. The completest, the most radical change the world ever saw was the conversion of Saul of Tarsus into Paul the Apostle; indeed, this transformation proves forever the power of the gospel to save the sinful. And those who pronounce impossible a change so radical are driven to the denial of the identity of Saul and Paul. I heard a bold pseudo-philosopher say that Paul the Apostle was not a Jew at all, neither did he ever persecute Christians. It is pitiable that a man will marry himself to a pet theory, and close his eyes to indisputable facts, and despicable that one so foolish will affect superiority. That Paul was technically trained by Gamaliel, one of the greatest teachers of Israel, was important, of course, in the development of his intellect; but this element has been overdone in estimating Paul's education to preach. With all the instruction Saul had received from any source, Jewish or Greek, he was definitely and radically on the wrong side, arrayed against the Lord Jesus Christ; and today many so-called well and highly educated people apparently have missed the right way, and are traveling the road to hopeless death as fast as the wheels of time can carry them. After his conversion to Christ, Paul realized that that was where he was going while he lived in sin; and he sounded this note of peril in all his preaching, the absence of which in much modern advocacy has smitten it with weakness

and emasculation and sterility.  Hear me now: If the
church is not brave enough and heroic enough and
faithful enough to preach the truth to the lost and
warn the sinful, it shall sink into the bottomless pit,
too.  When Paul preached, he discarded what he had
learned from Gamaliel, and determined to know nothing, and to preach nothing, but "Jesus Christ and him
crucified."  Any college or university or seminary grad-
uate that rejects the Bible as inspired revelation and
the New Testament as the instrument of the Lord Jesus
Christ, and mouths the vapid imaginations of faithless
professors, will not be worth his salt as a preacher.  It
is impossible to obscure the marvelous change that made
Saul, the Jewish fanatic, the chief of sinners, into Paul
the Apostle and the Christian, which based itself in
well known facts and began in the glaring light of
midday.  Saul's vision was both objective and subjective: he both saw the heavenly light that eclipsed the
noonday sun, in which the Lord appeared to him, and
heard His voice; while his traveling companions witnessed the miraculous light, but heard no voice.  Of
course, Saul did not recognize his mysterious Visitant,
who identified Himself as "Jesus of Nazareth, whom
thou persecutest": this opened Saul's eyes, who thought
he was punishing obscure men and women to destroy a
dangerous Jewish heresy.  This startling appearance
of the Lord Jesus Christ to Saul of Tarsus was not
merely to save him from sin, but rather to qualify him
for the apostolate; if the Lord would directly reveal
Himself to one man to save him from sin, He would
be obligated thus to deal with all sinners.  It is also
significant that the Lord did not Himself tell Saul what
to do to be saved, but commanded him to go into
Damascus, where He sent to Saul an honorable Jew

and a humble Christian, named Ananias, who preached the gospel to Saul, the same gospel Saul as Paul later pressed on the attention of the world, the only gospel, "Brother Saul, receive thy sight. . . . And now why tarriest thou? arise, and be baptized, and wash away thy sins, calling on his name." Before Jesus Christ returned to heaven, He gave into the hands of His apostles, into the hands of men, the work of telling the sinful world what to do to be saved; and He would not take it out of their hands, and be inconsistent with Himself, to accommodate Saul of Tarsus.

*Paul's conversion from sin was the completest change, but his enemies refused his testimony* (17-30): "And it came to pass, that, when I had returned to Jerusalem, and while I prayed in the temple, I fell into a trance, and saw him saying unto me, Make haste, and get thee quickly out of Jerusalem; because they will not receive of thee testimony concerning me. And I said, Lord, they themselves know that I imprisoned and beat in every synagogue them that believed on thee: and when the blood of Stephen thy witness was shed, I also was standing by, and consenting, and keeping the garments of them that slew him. And he said unto me, Depart: for I will send thee forth far hence unto the Gentiles. And they gave him audience unto this word; and they lifted up their voice, and said, Away with such a fellow from the earth: for it is not fit that he should live. And as they cried out, and threw off their garments, and cast dust into the air, the chief captain commanded him to be brought into the castle, bidding that he should be examined by scourging, that he might know for what cause they so shouted against him. And when they had tied him up with the thongs, Paul said unto the centurion that stood by, Is it lawful for you to

scourge a man that is a Roman, and uncondemned?
And when the centurion heard it, he went to the chief
captain and told him, saying, What art thou about to
do? for this man is a Roman. And the chief captain
came and said unto him, Tell me, art thou a Roman?
And he said, Yea. And the chief captain answered,
With a great sum obtained I this citizenship. And
Paul said, But I am a Roman born. They then that
were about to examine him straightway departed from
him: and the chief captain also was afraid when he
knew that he was a Roman, and because he had bound
him. But on the morrow, desiring to know the certainty
whereof he was accused of the Jews, he loosed him, and
commanded the chief priests and all the council to come
together, and brought Paul down and set him before
them.'' Some seem impervious to the gospel, because
of their apathy or ignorance or prejudice or perfidy or
wickedness; no appeal can move any man who has
nothing in him to respond. God made man like Himself,
because He foresaw the necessity of making Himself
like man: thus He laid the foundation of the gospel in
the very beginning. Now, if sin has completely destroyed the divine image out of any human being, his
salvation is impossible. Paul yearned in his heart that
every Jew might become a Christian; but many of his
contemporary Jews were so incensed at him for desert-
ing what they regarded as their cause, that they resisted
his influence to the utmost. Immediately after Paul's
return to Jerusalem, following his conversion in
Damascus, the Lord saw fit to warn him in a dream,
''Make haste, and get thee quickly out of Jerusalem;
because they will not receive of thee testimony concerning me'': and ignoring Paul's argument that he might
stay in Jerusalem, the Lord commanded him, ''Depart:

for I will send thee forth far hence to the Gentiles.''
The gospel is the greatest test of character, which Paul,
in the narration of his own remarkable conversion, set
before his Jewish audience in Jerusalem, with all its
colors and contrasts without even denting them, save
to excite in them the mob spirit. What this turbulent,
lawless bunch called Paul—an inferior, worthless person, fit for destruction—only mirrored the source from
which it came, leaving Paul absolutely unscathed. However, this mob, crazed by the intoxication of the devil,
wildly stripped off their clothing, filling the welkin with
their savage shouts and beclouding the air with dust,
and would have murdered Paul, but for the timely intervention of the chief captain. This responsible Roman
officer, determined, if possible, to find out why the Jews
were bitter against Paul, was about to lash him painfully, when Paul, an intelligent Roman citizen himself
who knew his rights, struck terror to the centurion that
had him in charge by the revelation of his proud citizenship in the great Roman Empire. Now, this captain
of a hundred soldiers instantly carried his alarm to his
superior officer, the chief captain, who was amazed to
learn that Paul was a Roman. This chief captain had
bought his Roman citizenship with a large sum of money,
but Paul was born in the Roman Empire. From this
time on, these Roman soldiers, whose duty was to enforce
Roman law, and protect every Roman citizen in his
rights and privileges, fearful Paul might go above them
in appeal for redress, treated him with great respect,
and set him at liberty, in the midst of the chief priests
and all the Jewish council, who had been called together
for the express purpose of giving consideration to Paul's
case. The sorriest creature on the earth is the sinner,
lacking intellectual discernment, devoid of moral sen-

sibility, destitute of spiritual insight, unaware of his lost condition, heedless of all appeals, plunging headlong into the abyss of hell! It seems that Paul's enemies had sunk that low! Verily, conversion from sin is so radical a change that it is the new birth, being born again of water and of the Spirit. Paul illustrated in his own experience every fundamental of the gospel that he preached to others, both Jews and Gentiles— the same gospel that he sent ringing down the years of time forever: (1) He heard the gospel; (2) he believed on the Lord Jesus Christ; (3) he repented of his sins; (4) he confessed Jesus to be the Christ and the only Saviour of sinners; (5) he was baptized into Christ, in the likeness of His death and burial and resurrection; (6) he lived faithful till death. Divine in its conception, miraculous in its creation, profound in its depths, human in its appeal the gospel is the embodiment of simplicity in its practical application. And anybody and everybody may be saved who wants to be saved.

# XXIII

## THE COMPASS OF CONSCIENCE

### (Acts 23)

*The compass of conscience should be clearly defined.*
A good conscience means integrity; a conscientious man
is a whole man. Yet, however sincere one may be, he
may also be wrong; his conscientiousness recommends
him, but is no guarantee of his being right. Conscience
has no absolute independence, but is the creature of
education; conscience is produced by teaching, training,
development, growth. Perhaps there is in the history
of the human race no better example as to what conscience is than Saul of Tarsus, Paul the apostle, Paul
the Christian. Saul believed he was doing right when
he sympathized with the murderers of Stephen and
struck terror to the church of the Lord Jesus Christ
by persecuting its members wherever he could find them;
but in reality his hands were red with innocent human
blood. However, his sincerity recommended him to
the Lord, who saw in him the possibility of a great,
heroic servant, and called him to be the vehicle of His
grace to the whole Gentile world. The function of conscience is to urge its possessor to do right, and hold him
back from doing wrong; but as to the real distinction
between right and wrong, one must look beyond his
conscience. Conscience is not merely the product of
any school or system; conscience is ultimately the truth
of God, or the lie of the devil. One is not right simply
because he thinks he is right; he is right because he has

accepted the standard of the Lord Jesus Christ. And yet the only way to guide any man is through his own conscience, which must be educated by the Word of God. Everyone should harken to the voice of his own conscience, and keep it inviolate; the constant violation of conscience will destroy moral sense and spiritual insight. Hear Jesus, the great Creator of the Christian conscience (John 6:43-51): "Jesus answered and said unto them, Murmur not among yourselves. No man can come to me, except the Father that sent me draw him: and I will raise him up in the last day. It is written in the prophets, And they shall all be taught of God. Every one that hath heard from the Father, and hath learned, cometh unto me. Not that any man hath seen the Father, save he that is from God, he hath seen the Father. Verily, verily, I say unto you, He that believeth hath eternal life. I am the bread of life. Your fathers ate the manna in the wilderness, and they died. This is the bread which cometh down out of heaven, that a man may eat thereof, and not die. I am the living bread which came down out of heaven: If any man eat of this bread, he shall live forever: yea and the bread which I will give is my flesh, for the life of the world." Most assuredly, this is the "inner light," which all may have who follow the leadership of the Lord Jesus Christ, whom God approved by raising Him from the dead, which those that reject Him can not have at all.

## Conscience Is Really Man Himself, a Dependent (vs. 1-35)

*After he was born again, the good conscience in which Paul lived was Paul himself, inspired by the Lord Jesus Christ* (1-11): "And Paul, looking stedfastly on the

council, said, Brethren, I have lived before God in all
good conscience until this day.  And the high priest
Ananias commanded them that stood by him to smite
him on the mouth.  Then said Paul unto him, God shall
smite thee, thou whited wall: and sittest thou to judge
me according to the law, and commandest me to be
smitten contrary to the law?  And they that stood by
said, Revilest thou God's high priest?  And Paul said,
I knew not, brethren, that he was high priest: for it is
written, Thou shalt not speak evil of a ruler of thy
people.  But when Paul perceived that the one part
were Sadducees and the other Pharisees, he cried out
in the council, Brethren, I am a Pharisee, a son of
Pharisees: touching the hope and resurrection of the
dead I am called in question.  And when he had so said,
there arose a dissension between the Pharisees and Sadducees; and the assembly was divided.  For the Sadducees say that there is no resurrection, neither angel,
nor spirit; but the Pharisees confess both.  And there
arose a great clamor: and some of the scribes of the
Pharisees' part stood up, and strove, saying, We find
no evil in this man: and what if a spirit hath spoken
to him, or an angel?  And when there arose a great
dissension, the chief captain, fearing lest Paul should
be torn in pieces by them, commanded the soldiers to
go down and take him by force from among them, and
bring him into the castle.  And the night following the
Lord stood by him, and said, Be of good cheer: for as
thou hast testified concerning me at Jerusalem, so must
thou bear witness also at Rome.''  Of course, Paul
thought he was right before he became a Christian;
but, like all other Jews that persecuted Christ and His
church, he was led by the devil.  The high priest,
Ananias, showed himself unworthy of his office, and

hypocritical, as Paul indicated, by the humiliating personal indignity he sought to impose on Paul; but so delicate was Paul's conscience, that when he learned that Ananias was high priest, he apologized for calling him a "whited wall," even though individually, if not officially, Ananias lived up to that description. And yet Paul had no qualm about arraying the Sadducees and the Pharisees against each other, to state the truth and break any possible unity among them against him. The characteristic difference between these two leading classes among the Jews was, that the Pharisees believed that life is restored to the dead and that both angels and spirits exist; while the Sadducees were in stout opposition to all these cardinal doctrines. And when Paul declared himself a Pharisee of the most radical type, there arose a vehement contention between the Pharisees and the Sadducees in the council, before whom Paul had been brought by the chief captain, the responsible Roman officer; and immediately some of the Pharisee scribes sprang to the defense of Paul as a fellow Pharisee, declaring that they discovered nothing wrong in him, and that a spirit or an angel may have spoken to him. Thereupon the strife between the Pharisees and the Sadducees became so fierce as to endanger Paul's life; and again he was rescued by the Roman soldiers, and placed in the castle for protection. Like all other men, Paul was naturally a dependent creature; and it was impossible for him to know anything about the future except by revelation. And "the Lord," knowing that, in the midst of these bitter persecutions that constantly endangered his life, Paul needed encouragement, "the night following stood by him, and said, Be of good cheer: for as thou hast testified concerning me at Jerusalem, so must thou bear witness also at Rome." The

apostolate qualified Paul to be a direct, immediate witness of the Lord Jesus Christ; but did not make special
revelations like this, which was about his own personal
future, which the Lord wanted him to know.  Only the
independent, uncreated, self-existent, eternal, immortal,
invisible God can know everything in the past and in
the present and in the future and in all time and in all
eternity.  Wise and happy is the man that lives his
life in humble recognition of his own dependence, and
knows that no man, no set of men, ever could have
created the sacred Scriptures, or invented the story of
the life of Jesus or the miraculous creation and marvelous growth of His church.  Talk about the conscience
of man! Man knows, can know, only what he has learned.
what has been revealed to him through the Word of God.
Will Rogers said all he knew he read in the papers; all
we know we read in the Bible.  It is impossible for God
to lie.  The devil took issue with Jehovah and deliberately lied—he is the first liar and the father of lies!  Evidently, the Lord revealed to Paul through his subjective
mind at night while his objective mind was asleep, that
he should witness for Him in Rome: in this same way
other divine communications are recorded in both Testaments.  The subjective mind must be the soul or the
spirit, which will come into complete consciousness when
the objective mind perishes by the death of the body.

*The Jewish enemies of Paul were poisoned in con-
science by Satan* (12-22): "And when it was day, the
Jews banded together, and bound themselves under a
curse, saying that they would neither eat nor drink till
they had killed Paul.  And they were more than forty
that made this conspiracy.  And they came to the chief
priests and the elders, and said, We have bound ourselves under a great curse, to taste nothing until we

have killed Paul. Now therefore do ye with the council signify to the chief captain that he bring him down unto you, as though ye would judge of his case more exactly: and we, before he comes near, are ready to slay him. But Paul's sister's son heard of their lying in wait, and came and entered into the castle and told Paul. And Paul called unto him one of the centurions, and said, Bring this young man unto the chief captain; for he hath something to tell him. So he took him, and brought him to the chief captain, and saith, Paul the prisoner called me unto him, and asked me to bring this young man unto thee, who hath something to say to thee. And the chief captain took him by the hand, and going aside asked him privately, What is it that thou hast to tell me? And he said, The Jews have agreed to ask thee to bring down Paul tomorrow unto the council, as though thou wouldest inquire somewhat more exactly concerning him. Do not therefore yield unto them: for there lie in wait for him of them more than forty men, who have bound themselves under a curse, neither to eat nor to drink till they have slain him: and now are they ready, looking for the promise from thee. So the chief captain let the young man go, charging him, Tell no man that thou hast signified these things to me.'' Because of man's very dependence, to cling close to the Lord is his only safety; otherwise, he is certain to become the prey of the devil. There is only one standard of righteousness, the origination or creation of which, possible only to the independent, self-sufficient God, is as high above dependent man as heaven is exalted above the earth, and as impossible to the devil as darkness is to light. Luke does not name any leader among the more than forty Jews that made themselves execrable without food or drink to kill Paul, but we know that Satan had his rings in their noses. No doubt these fellows felt themselves especially smart and brave, but they were all most miserable, murderous wretches. It is interesting and exhilarating to note how God in His providence defeated their vile purpose through Paul's unnamed nephew, who, learning of their wicked plot, walked right into the Roman castle, where Paul was being protected, and told him about it; and Paul requested a centurion to take his nephew to the chief captain, because he had a very important revelation to make to this officer, who was answerable for Paul's life as a prisoner. The manner in which this military tribune received this young man as Paul's messenger, taking him by the hand aside for a secret conference, and then cautioning him to keep strictly to himself their conversation, would indicate that he was duly impressed by the gravity of the situation. This dark conspiracy was as diabolical as the devil could make it: these Jewish scapegraces had planned to request the Roman officer in charge of Paul to deliver him again the very next day to their council, as if to "inquire somewhat more exactly concerning him," that they might have opportunity to murder Paul while he was in transit. But there must have been more than forty devilish apes that suffered excruciating pain from hunger and thirst, if indeed they did not even expire for want of food and water!

*The Romans had conscience and character enough to protect Paul as their prisoner* (23-35): "And he called unto him two of the centurions, and said, Make ready two hundred soldiers to go as far as Cæsarea, and horsemen threescore and ten, and spearmen two hundred, at the third hour of the night: and he bade them provide beasts, that they might set Paul thereon, and bring him safe unto Felix the governor. And he wrote a letter after this form: Claudius Lysias unto the most excellent governor Felix, greeting. This man was seized by the Jews, and was about to be slain of them, when I came upon them with the soldiers and rescued him, having learned that he was a Roman. And desiring to know the cause wherefore they accused him, I brought him down unto their council: whom I found to be accused about questions of their law, but to have nothing laid to his charge worthy of death or of bonds. And when it was shown to me that there would be a plot against the man, I sent him to thee forthwith, charging his accusers also to speak against him before thee. So the soldiers, as it was commanded them, took Paul and brought him by night to Antipatris. But on the morrow they left the horsemen to go with him, and returned to the castle: and they, when they came to Cæsarea and delivered the letter to the governor, presented Paul also before him. And when he had read it, he asked of what province he was; and when he understood that he was of Cilicia, I will hear thee fully, said he, when thine accusers also are come: and he commanded him to be kept in Herod's palace.'' For the first time in his history, Luke gives the name of the very important officer to whom he had many times referred as "the chief captain"—Claudius Lysias, who proceeded with dispatch and remarkable executive skill in the further defense of Paul against his depraved enemies that thirsted for his blood: he commanded two of his trusted subordinates to have two hundred soldiers, with seventy horsemen and two hundred spearmen, ready "at the third hour of the night," and escort Paul, furnishing him a beast on which to ride, "and bring him safe unto Felix the governor" in Cæsarea; to whom Claudius Lysias wrote a dignified note, apprising the governor

Felix of the salient features of Paul's case, that the
Jews were about to kill Paul, a Roman, and forced him
as "the chief captain" to save Paul's life by the Roman
soldiers.  This letter also advised Felix that these Jews
had charges against Paul "about questions of their law"
only, who had done nothing worthy of death or of bonds;
and he was sending Paul to him as governor, because
his enemies were conspiring to kill him, before whom
also he had charged his enemies to speak.  The two
hundred soldiers went as far as Antipatris by night,
where they left Paul with the horsemen, who delivered
him the next day, together with Claudius Lysias' letter
of explanation, to Felix as governor in Cæsarea.  The
governor, having learned he was of Cilicia, promised to
hear Paul fully when his accusers arrived, and protected him in Herod's palace.  The Lord Himself is
the Judge of all men.  However, we can not but see
that the consciences of these Roman officers and soldiers
stand out in great superiority above the Jews who did
their utmost to kill Paul, and would have succeeded,
but for the providence of God through the strong arm
of the mighty Roman Empire.

## XXIV

## THE WAY OF IMMORTALITY

### (Acts 24)

*Nothing short of immortality will ever be satisfactory.* There is small gratification for the ego in the philosophy that man dies, but his influence is eternal. Influence does not float in the air and hit one in the back as he turns the corner; influence emanates from personality: God is the fountainhead of all good; the devil is the primal source of all evil. The low order of sin grovels in the dust, to which even the Christian is exposed in this world; and death stands in the way of the so-called social gospel. It never will suffice merely to change or amend or patch or improve or reorganize the social structure of the human race; immortality demands a new birth and a new life and a new, perfect environment. Here we carry much baggage, which impedes our progress and must be cast into the sea of oblivion. There is, there can be, no eternal life for the world or the nation or the state or the county or the community or the tribe or the family; there will be no United States of America or British Empire or commonwealth or clan or clique in heaven. The doctrine that the race of man is everlasting because of the endless coming and going of the generations by birth and death is superficial, and leaves the individual utterly forgotten, if not annihilated. The truth is, that the individual soul or spirit is the only thing in this sinful world that can live forever. The gospel addresses itself primarily to the individual, and deals with the crowd only one by one. The individual is the only entity, without which there can be neither group nor collection nor assembly nor crowd nor multitude—all of which are merely aggregations of individuals. If the individual can not be saved, then the whole creation falls into a heap of ruins; and God's glory is a fading glory. But the individual is being saved in large numbers, and the glory of the Lord is eternal. But nobody can steal into heaven in a group or a collection or an assembly or a crowd or a multitude of individuals. Men come into this world one by one through birth, and they go out of it in the same way by death. Initial life is thrust on man in this world, but immortality must be chosen; not even the Creator can force any creature to live forever against his will. The only way sinful man can choose exemption from death is to take it as a gift from the Lord Jesus Christ by believing on Him as the Son of God and repenting of his sins and confessing Christ before men and by being baptized into Him in the likeness of His death and burial and resurrection, and living faithful till death. The way of immortality is the way of choice—the way of belief and penitence and confession and baptism—the way of trust and obedience—the way of faith and hope and love—the way of complete satisfaction and absolute happiness and eternal life.

## Immortality Bridges Death by the Resurrection (vs. 1-27)

*There was striking contrast between Tertullus and Paul* (1-21): "And after five days the high priest Ananias came down with certain elders, and with an orator, one Tertullus; and they informed the governor against Paul. And when he was called, Tertullus began

to accuse him, saying, Seeing that by thee we enjoy
much peace, and that by thy providence evils are corrected for this nation, we accept it in all ways and in
all places, most excellent Felix, with all thankfulness.
But, that I be not further tedious unto thee, I entreat
thee to hear us of thy clemency a few words. For we
have found this man a pestilent fellow, and a mover
of insurrections among all the Jews throughout the
world, and a ringleader of the sect of the Nazarenes:
who moreover assayed to profane the temple: on whom
also we laid hold: from whom thou wilt be able, by
examining him thyself, to take knowledge of all these
things whereof we accuse him. And the Jews also joined
in the charge, affirming that these things were so. And
when the governor had beckoned unto him to speak,
Paul answered, Forasmuch as I know that thou hast
been of many years a judge unto this nation, I cheer-
fully make my defence: seeing that thou canst take
knowledge that it is not more than twelve days since I
went up to worship at Jerusalem: and neither in the
temple did they find me disputing with any man or
stirring up a crowd, nor in the synagogues, nor in the
city. Neither can they prove to thee the things whereof
they now accuse me. But this I confess unto thee, that
after the Way which they call a sect, so serve I the
God of our fathers, believing all things which are according to the law, and which are written in the prophets; having hope toward God, which these also themselves look for, that there shall be a resurrection both
of the just and unjust. Herein I also exercise myself
to have a good conscience void of offence toward God
and men always. Now after some years I came to bring
alms to my nation, and offerings: amidst which they
found me purified in the temple, with no crowd, nor

yet with tumult: but there were certain Jews from Asia
—who ought to have been here before thee, and to make
accusation, if they had aught against me. Or else let
these men themselves say what wrongdoing they found
when I stood before the council, except it be for this
one voice, that I cried standing among them, Touching
the resurrection of the dead I am called in question
before you this day.'' Tertullus, orator that he was,
lawyer that he must have been, was smooth and suave
and politic; and while he was bold in his accusation of
Paul, on behalf of the Jewish high priest and elders
with whom he came to Jerusalem, and whom he represented, yet both he and they were entirely without evidence to prove their disgraceful charges against Paul,
whose life as a Christian and an apostle of the Lord
Jesus Christ, was an open book, against whom it would
be impossible for all the orators and lawyers and witnesses on earth to sustain an indictment for wrongdoing. Of course, the Jews did their utmost to prove
the accusation of Tertullus as their representative against
Paul; but this whole case, absolutely unsupported by
any fact whatsoever, simmers down to nothing but
bitter, relentless, unreasonable, devilish persecution of
perhaps the greatest man that ever lived save the Lord
Jesus Christ only. Tertullus, with all his astuteness and
oratorical skill and legal training and practical experience, shows much inferiority in his sharp contrast
with Paul, whose speeches Luke records side by side.
Paul was even more expert and proficient in presenting
his own plight than Tertullus was in his vain effort to
make the complicated situation a crisis to Paul. Making
short shrift of Tertullus' strenuous endeavor to fasten
crime on him, Paul revealed the real issue between him
and his Jewish enemies in these words to the governor,

who "beckoned unto him to speak"; "But this I confess
unto thee, that after the Way which they call a sect, so
serve I the God of our fathers, believing all things
which are according to the law, and which are written
in the prophets; having hope toward God, which these
also themselves look for, that there shall be a resurrection both of the just and unjust." Paul had kept nothing under cover in his life, neither was he afraid of
any of his enemies or of all of them. The real instigators of Paul's trouble and persecution in Jerusalem
were Jews from Asia, who should have come to Cæsarea
and stated their case against him before the governor
whom Paul himself addressed in his own defense. In
their absence, Paul knew that the Jews present could
say nothing against him, unless it be to quote what he
had said before the Jewish council; namely, "Touching
the resurrection of the dead I am called in question
before you this day." At the time when Paul made
this statement originally, both the Pharisees and the
Sadducees were against him; but this drew a sharp line
between them, placing the Pharisees, who believed the
doctrine of the resurrection, with Paul, and probably
saved his life. Here is the crucial point in this chapter
—the resurrection of the dead, all the dead, the just
and the unjust, the good and the bad, the righteous and
the sinful—the way of immortality! Back of this agita-
tion against Paul and persecution of the church of
Christ is the old devil himself, the propagator of darkness and gloom and doom and death! Following the
death of the body—every individual—all men are to be
manifested for judgment; and manifestation means embodiment, thus necessitating the resurrection or the restoration of the human body. But after this will come
the second death, which will probably swallow up,

annihilate, both the bodies and the spirits of the incorrigibly wicked. As long as we live in the flesh, the chasm of death is before us, but immortality has spanned it by the resurrection or the restoration of life.

*Felix was a trifler* (22-27) : "But Felix, having more exact knowledge concerning the Way, deferred them, saying, When Lysias the chief captain shall come down, I will determine your matter. And he gave order to the centurion that he should be kept in charge, and should have indulgence; and not to forbid any of his friends to minister unto him. But after certain days, Felix came with Drusilla, his wife, who was a Jewess, and sent for Paul, and heard him concerning the faith in Christ. And as he reasoned of righteousness, and self-control, and the judgment to come, Felix was terrified, and answered, Go thy way for this time; and when I have a convenient season, I will call thee unto me. He hoped withal that money would be given him of Paul: wherefore also he sent for him the oftener, and communed with him. But when two years were fulfilled, Felix was succeeded by Porcius Festus; and desiring to gain favor with the Jews, Felix left Paul in bonds." Out of the Old Testament comes the doctrine of the resurrection, the endurance of consciousness, the resumption, the restoration, of life, the way of immortality; Paul believed "all things which are according to the law, and which are written in the prophets," and hoped for the resurrection. This most ancient of all dogmas is the groundwork and frame of the divine house; it is the fundamental principle that binds the Testaments and all the books of the Bible and holds them in unity forever. "But Felix, having more exact knowledge concerning the Way," trifled with it, and dallied with Paul and Tertullus and the Jews, holding their case in indefinite abeyance, with the subterfuge, "When Lysias the chief captain shall come down, I will determine your matter." Felix was a selfish, unprincipled, mercenary politician currying everybody's favor in the hope of taking tribute of him: he knew perfectly well that Paul was innocent and entitled to the liberty of a loyal Roman citizen, yet he kept Paul in prison to please his Jewish enemies; he trusted Paul and honored him, and visited with him often, hoping that Paul would give him money to gain complete release from jail. But Felix did not fool Paul, who must have read him like a book, and terrified his fickle heart by the startling truth of the gospel. Felix, in company with Drusilla, his Jewish wife, feigned interest in "the faith in Christ Jesus," and Paul, "reasoning of righteousness, and self-control, and the judgment to come," shook him to his shallow depths, making him cry out, "Go thy way for this time; and when I have a convenient season, I will call thee unto me." Evidently, "a convenient season" never came to this superficial, foolish trifler, who toyed with his soul, till it splashed into the sea of oblivion, after two years of purposelessness, when Porcius Festus pushed him off the scene of action in the Roman Empire, and took his place as governor in Cæsarea. Now, while the Old Testament had the idea of immortality, as stated above, and the New Testament did not originate it, yet the New Testament did define it and demonstrate it and illustrate it and prove it by the resurrection of Jesus, and amplify and particularize the Way of immortality by the Great Commission in this very Book of Acts of Apostles.

## XXV

## THE SOURCE OF POWER

### (Acts 25)

*Leadership means power.* The power of the leader comes from his followers. The devil is the god of this world, because all worldlings follow him; if all men rejected his leadership, he would be shorn of his power. However, the power of the great God the Creator is absolute and eternal; if the whole world should deny Him, He would still be supreme and dominant. Why (Rom. 4:17), "God giveth life to the dead, and calleth the things that are not, as though they were!" Indeed, God could blot an obstreperous race out of existence, as He did by the flood, and go on with His plan. It puts no strain on the power of the Deity to restore life to the dead; and when He summons things that do not exist, they spring into being! And yet Jehovah has endowed His creatures with certain powers. Even the lower animals have leaders, who guide their fellows in migratory motions, and largely determine their destiny. And for man there can be no community life without some sort of simple organization. But the position or power of the leader among all creatures, whether natural or official, is relative and temporary: one may lead successfully and brilliantly for a while, and then be thrust back among the followers. Still one must be a good follower in order to be a good leader. The leader must always know the cause or interest in which he is to lead his associates; otherwise, he will be in

danger of the abuse of his power, which will cause his
dethronement. The human race has only one supremely great Leader—Jesus of Nazareth, now the Lord Jesus
Christ forever. He was elevated above all men by His
death and by His resurrection from the dead, by His
ascension to heaven and by His coronation at the right
hand of God. He can never be dethroned or shelved.
For all time to come, He has furnished men the standard
of real, genuine leadership in every human relationship.
He created His church on the first Pentecost after His
resurrection to represent Him in the world till the end
of time. The ideal for His church is the hope of the
human race. All the positions of trust and honor and
service in business and government should be filled by
Christians. Leaders are inevitable in all walks of life,
in every grade of society, in every human interest and
relationship, in every calling and vocation, in every
business and activity, in every relaxation and diversion.
And never will the highest and best interests of the
people be conserved and protected and safeguarded and
developed till all human leaders are really and genuine-
ly Christian. What men should be in the church of
Christ is precisely what they should be in the whole
world. The Lord Jesus Christ has defined what human
life should be by the life that He Himself lived; He
lived and died not for a favored few, but for the entire
race of men.

## The Source of Power Is Life Itself (vs. 1-27)

*Paul Before Festus Appealed to Cæsar* (1-12):
"Festus, therefore, having come into the province, after
three days went up to Jerusalem from Cæsarea. And
the chief priests and the principal men of the Jews informed him against Paul; and they besought him, asking

a favor against him, that he would send for him to
Jerusalem; laying a plot to kill him on the way. Howbeit Festus answered, that Paul was kept in charge at
Cæsarea, and that he himself was about to depart thither
shortly. Let them therefore, saith he, that are of power
among you go down with me, and if there is anything
amiss in the man, let them accuse him. And when he
had tarried among them not more than eight or ten
days, he went down unto Cæsarea; and on the morrow
he sat on the judgment seat, and commanded Paul to be
brought. And when he was come, the Jews that had
come down from Jerusalem stood round about him,
bringing against him many and grievous charges which
they could not prove; while Paul said in his defense,
Neither against the law of the Jews, nor against the
temple, nor against Cæsar, have I sinned at all. But
Festus, desiring to gain favor with the Jews, answered
Paul and said, Wilt thou go up to Jerusalem, and there
be judged of these things before me? But Paul said,
I am standing before Cæsar's judgment seat, where I
ought to be judged: to the Jews have I done no wrong,
as thou also very well knowest. If then I am a wrong-
doer, and have committed anything worthy of death, I
refuse not to die; but if none of those things is true
whereof these accuse me, no man can give me up unto
them. I appeal unto Cæsar. Then Festus, when he
had conferred with the council, answered, Thou hast
appealed unto Cæsar: unto Cæsar shalt thou go.'' Out
of the life of the Jewish people came power, foisted on
them by wicked leaders, with which Paul was forced to
reckon; in the Roman nation arose superior power, which
held Jewry in leash, and protected Paul's life as a
citizen-member of that political organization. This
change of the Roman governorship from Felix to Festus

was unfortunate for Paul, taking him out of the hands of the former, who understood the status between Paul and his Jewish enemies, and placing him in the power of the latter, who was under the necessity of informing himself, thus still further deferring any decision in Paul's case, which had already been postponed for two years by Felix' trifling neglect. Here we recall that Lincoln said, ''It is not wise to swap horses while fording a stream.'' But often human government proceeds ponderously, with irritating delay and disappointing circumlocution, with vexatious slowness. However, when, within three days after occupying his throne in Cæsarea, Festus came to Jerusalem, the Jewish leaders seized the very first opportunity to poison his mind against Paul, asking him to return Paul to Jerusalem for trial, that they might execute their plot to slay him en route. Yet, while Festus liked to please these powerful leaders among the Jews who were in his territory as governor, and might make trouble for him if he went counter to their prejudice, he was too shrewd to grant this sly, sinister request; and he politely advised these murderous wretches that the only course open to them was to go with him to Cæsarea, to which he was almost ready to return, where Paul was incarcerated, and bear witness against him there. Now, while evidently Festus was not as well informed as Felix, yet neither was he a dilatory trifler; for, after a brief visit in Jerusalem, he ordered Paul brought before his court the very next day following his return to Cæsarea. There Paul saw again his enemies from Jerusalem, and realized that in the interval of the two years that had passed, they had lost none of their venomous hatred for him; they were as vociferous against him, but utterly without evidence, as they had always been. It is one thing to accuse a man

of crime; it is quite another thing to prove that serious
and disgraceful charge. In the absence of credible witness, it was sufficient for Paul in his defense to make
this simple, plain disavowal: "Neither against the law
of the Jews, nor against the temple, nor against Cæsar,
have I sinned at all." Festus knew that he had no
legal right to take Paul away from the Roman capital
of the province, Cæsarea, and try him in Jerusalem,
where the atmosphere was morbid and poisoned against
him by the sinful leaders of the Jews; Festus must have
been certain also that Paul was absolutely innocent, and
entitled to the fullness of liberty. But, politician that
he was, Festus' sense of justice was eclipsed by his
desire for popularity; and instead of dealing honestly
with Paul, he sought to placate Paul's enemies. However, Paul knew his privileges as a Roman citizen, upon
which he stood firmly, burning all the bridges behind
him, and appealing to the highest tribunal in the Empire
in the world at that time, the court of Cæsar himself.
Paul saw clearly that he would never receive justice
before any "judgment seat" that his enemies could
influence, who wanted to kill him without trial or evidence or guilt, by mobocracy or in any way at all. By
this time, it must have been apparent to Festus that he
had a most extraordinary prisoner on his hands, who
was eminently above crime and absolutely innocent of
any kind of wrongdoing. But these lawless Jews put
all the pressure on Festus they could; and in his perplexity it was not clear to him what course to take in
regard to Paul, who forced him to a final decision by
appealing to the imperial court, thus taking his case out
of the hands of the local tribunal in Cæsarea or elsewhere. Surely everybody before Festus that day must
have felt the tenseness of the situation and sensed the

excitement and temper in this climax of the drama of
Paul's trial, when Festus, having talked with the council, said to Paul, ''Thou hast appealed unto Cæsar:
unto Cæsar shalt thou go.''

*Festus brought Paul to the attention of King Agrippa*
(13-27): ''Now when certain days were passed, Agrippa
the king and Bernice arrived at Cæsarea, and saluted
Festus. And as they tarried there many days, Festus
laid Paul's case before the king, saying, there is a certain man left a prisoner by Felix; about whom, when
I was at Jerusalem, the chief priests and the elders of
the Jews informed me, asking for sentence against him.
To whom I answered, that it is not the custom of the
Romans to give up any man, before that the accused
have the accusers face to face, and have had opportunity
to make his defence concerning the matter laid against
him. When therefore they were come together here, I
made no delay, but on the next day sat on the judgment
seat, and commanded the man to be brought. Concerning whom, when the accusers stood up, they brought no
charge of such evil things as I supposed; but certain
questions against him of their own religion, and of one
Jesus, who was dead, whom Paul affirmed to be alive.
And I, being perplexed how to inquire concerning these
things, asked whether he would go to Jerusalem and
there be judged of these matters. But when Paul had
appealed to be kept for the decision of the emperor, I
commanded him to be kept till I should send him to
Cæsar. And Agrippa said unto Festus, I could wish
to hear the man myself. Tomorrow, saith he, Thou
shalt hear him. So on the morrow, when Agrippa was
come, and Bernice, with great pomp, and they were
entered into the place of hearing with the chief captains
and the principal men of the city, at the command of

Festus Paul was brought in. And Festus saith, King Agrippa, and all men who are here present with us, ye behold this man, about whom all the multitude of the Jews made suit to me, both at Jerusalem and here, crying that he ought not to live any longer. But I found that he had committed nothing worthy of death: and as he himself appealed to the emperor I determined to send him. Of whom I have no certain thing to write unto my lord. Wherefore I have brought him forth before you, and especially before thee, king Agrippa, that, after examination had, I may have somewhat to write. For it seemeth to me unreasonable, in sending a prisoner, not withal to signify the charges against him.'' Power may be a vain ambition, a staggering, crushing, fatal responsibility. We have just seen the curtain fall on Felix, hiding him in obscurity, burying him in the wickedness of his career, because of his inability, inefficiency, incapacity to carry the heavy load of accountability in the position he occupied as governor in Cæsarea—on account of his abuse of power. Felix trifled with power, and it slew him like electricity. Now we observe the authority of this same position bearing heavily on Festus, straining, confusing, embarrassing, exasperating him. Festus took advantage of King Agrippa's congratulatory visit to him at this time, in the very beginning of his gubernatorial office, to learn through Agrippa's better knowledge of affairs among the Jews. This distinguished visitor brought with him his sister Bernice, who belonged to the reigning family of the Herods (the wife of Felix, Drusilla, also was member of this family, being sister of Agrippa and Bernice): the Herod who killed James and imprisoned Peter was their father; Bernice, then a widow, living with her brother, Agrippa, had been the wife of her

own uncle; the Herod who beheaded John the Baptist
and mocked Jesus, was their uncle; while the Herod
who sought to slay Jesus in His infancy was their great-
grandfather. Festus, in placing before Agrippa the
suit of the Jews against Paul, evinced his determination
to meet the responsibility in this case according to
Roman custom or law, in spite of the counter influence
of Paul's enemies; whom he forced to face Paul as his
accusers, and give him the opportunity to defend himself. However, when they came to look Paul in the
face, their charges against him were not nearly so wicked
as they had led Festus to believe they would be; but
they amounted to a religious question, which found its
essence in Jesus, to whom Festus referred as "one
Jesus," as if he had never heard of Him before, "who
was dead" to Festus, but alive to Paul. Festus acknowledged to Agrippa that he did not know just how to
proceed with a question of this kind, and wanted to go
to Jerusalem with it; but Paul took it out of his power
by forcing it to the imperial court. Now, this young
Herod, Agrippa, would not have deigned to go to the
temple or a synagogue or any other public place merely
to hear Paul preach; but he saw an opportunity to
gratify his curiosity to hear Paul in the privacy of the
pretorium where Paul was in prison, without lowering
the dignity of his station. And with alacrity Felix
made the opportunity for Agrippa the very next day,
with one of the most august assemblies in the history of
the local court in Cæsarea, in which were the king and
his sister and "the chief captains and the principal
men of the city." This was certainly not the first time
Agrippa, and many others before Festus on that occasion, had heard the name of Jesus or Paul, who must
have been amazed at the ignorance of Festus! But the

inability of Festus to formulate, or reduce to writing, the charges against Paul, to send along with him to Cæsar, was not due to his ignorance. Paul was examined before Felix and twice before Festus, at the last examination king Agrippa being present also; and absolutely nothing was found against Paul. Festus could write no charge to Cæsar against Paul, because there was no charge to write. Paul believed and preached the doctrine of the resurrection of the dead, as illustrated and demonstrated and proved by the Lord Jesus Christ, which is always offensive to the devil and his henchmen. The source of power is life, and the source of life is power: (Heb. 7:11-25) Jesus was made a Priest forever ''after the power of an endless life,'' which Paul's faith gave him, and which ours will give us, as certainly as Jesus arose from the dead and is enthroned forever at the right hand of power!

# XXVI

## "THE HEAVENLY VISION"

### (Acts 26)

*Vision is absolutely essential to the life and the happiness of man.* The human body has eyes with which to see material things, and the human heart has eyes with which to see spiritual things. "Blessed are the pure in heart; for they shall see God." "Where there is no vision, the people cast off restraint; but he that keepeth the law, happy is he." Usually, to label a man as visionary is to eliminate him from consideration in the practical world, but practice is the product of vision; the visionless "cast off restraint," but the visionary keep the law. Of course, vision is of the imagination; but imagination is another name for faith, which is the requisite of all real vision. Like Joseph in Egypt nearly four thousand years ago, who had corn when the furious famine came with blighting power in Egypt and all over the world, the faithful dreamer always sees the future. To the man who believes, God is everywhere—in the heavens above him, in the air round about him, in the earth beneath his feet, in the creatures of His handiwork and in the Word of His inspiration; and this vital view transforms the faithful into the divine image. Oh, to behold the Lord, and see God! But that is a daring request! Moses, the man of God, cried out to view the divine Glory, which would have consumed him. To see the face of God would strike the body of flesh in death. Jehovah protected Moses "in a cleft of the rock," and covered him with His hand while He passed by; then He removed His hand, and let Moses look upon His back. (See Ex. 33:17-22.) "No man hath seen God at any time; the only begotten Son, who is in the bosom of the Father, he hath declared him" (John 1:18). Job proclaimed (Job 23:8, 9),

> "Behold, I go forward, but he is not there;
> And backward, but I cannot perceive him;
> On the left hand, when he doth work, but I
>     cannot behold him;
> He hideth himself on the right hand, that I
>     cannot see him."

We can not see the Lord directly and immediately in the flesh, but we can behold "with unveiled face," "as in a mirror," His glory as revealed in His life and reflected in His church and manifested in His world. We can not attain His superior excellence or perfection at a step or a leap or a bound, but we grow into His image "from glory to glory." Let us see Him in His prophecy, in His biography, in the history of His church, in the letters of His apostles, in the revelation of His home, in the heaven above us, in the earth beneath us, in the towering mountain, in the reaching valley, in the rolling, roaring sea, in the flowing river, in the flashing lightning, in the sailing cloud, in the pattering rain, in the falling snow, in the standing tree, in the growing lily, in the waving grain, in the ripening fruit, in the singing bird, in the shining sun, in the gleaming moon, in the shimmering star, in the stilling darkness, in His disciples living and dying and ascending, and grow into this glorious likeness! There are two forms—the form of God and the form of man. The form of God is the spirit and the form of man is the flesh. There are two bodies, the natural body and the spiritual body; "the blood is the life" of the natural body, the spirit must be the life of the spiritual body.

## "The Heavenly Vision" Is a Divine Revelation (vs. 1-32)

*"The heavenly vision" was a divine revelation to Paul* (1-23): "And Agrippa said unto Paul, Thou art permitted to speak for thyself. Then Paul stretched forth his hand, and made his defence: I think myself happy, king Agrippa, that I am to make my defence before thee this day touching all the things whereof I am accused by the Jews: especially because thou art expert in all customs and questions which are among the Jews: wherefore I beseech thee to hear me patiently. My manner of life then from my youth up, which was from the beginning among mine own nation and at Jerusalem, know all the Jews; having knowledge of me from the first, if they be willing to testify, that after the straitest sect of our religion I lived a Pharisee. And now I stand here to be judged for the hope of the promise made of God unto our Fathers; unto which promise our twelve tribes, earnestly serving God night and day, hope to attain. And concerning this hope I am accused by the Jews, O king! Why is it judged incredible with you, if God doth raise the dead? I verily thought with myself that I ought to do many things contrary to the name of Jesus of Nazareth. And this I also did in Jerusalem: and I both shut up many of the saints in prisons, having received authority from the chief priests, and when they were put to death I gave my vote against them. And punishing them oftentimes in all the synagogues, I strove to make them blaspheme; and being

exceedingly mad against them, I persecuted them even unto foreign cities. Whereupon as I journeyed to Damascus with the authority and commission of the chief priests, at midday, O king, I saw on the way a light from heaven, above the brightness of the sun, shining round about me and them that journeyed with me. And when we were all fallen to the earth, I heard a voice saying unto me in the Hebrew language, Saul, Saul, why persecutest thou me? it is hard for thee to kick against the goad. And I said, Who art thou, Lord? And the Lord said, I am Jesus whom thou persecutest. But arise, and stand upon thy feet: for to this end have I appeared unto thee, to appoint thee a minister and a witness both of the things wherein thou hast seen me, and of the things wherein I will appear unto thee; delivering thee from the people, and from the Gentiles, unto whom I send thee, to open their eyes, that they may turn from darkness to light and from the power of Satan unto God, that they may receive remission of sins and an inheritance among them that are sanctified by faith in me. Wherefore, O king Agrippa, I was not disobedient unto the heavenly vision: but declared both to them of Damascus first, and at Jerusalem, and throughout all the country of Judæa, and also to the Gentiles, that they should repent and turn to God, doing works worthy of repentance. For this cause the Jews seized me in the temple, and assayed to kill me. Having therefore obtained the help that is from God, I stand unto this day testifying both to small and great, saying nothing but what the prophets and Moses did say should come; how that the Christ must suffer, and how that he first by the resurrection of the dead should proclaim light both to the people and to the Gentiles.'' It is perfectly evident that Paul told the truth about what he saw and heard on the way to Damascus, even as he spoke the facts in regard to any other experience in his life to which he referred; and if "the heavenly vision" was as he described it, there can no longer be any question about the glorious reality of the life and resurrection of the Lord Jesus Christ! It gave Paul ecstatic joy to defend himself before Agrippa, who took charge of the court when Festus finished his statement and sat down, knowing that Agrippa could understand him better than Claudius Lysias or Felix or Festus, and feeling that it might be possible even to show the young king, Agrippa, a scion of the Herod family, all of whom had been bitter enemies of Jesus of Nazareth, the eternal light of the risen Lord and Saviour Jesus Christ. It was well known that Paul was born and trained a Hebrew or an Israelite or a Jew, and that he had lived the rigid life of a Pharisee, as a member of "the straitest sect" among the Jews; and the truth was, that the persecution in the midst of which Agrippa found him, was originally stirred up, and kept alive, by the Sadducees, the old Jewish skeptics, unto whom "the promise [of the resurrection of the dead] made of God unto our fathers," meant nothing, though the faithful of the twelve tribes hoped to attain it, for which Paul was accused of the Jews. That was the kind of Jew Paul had been, and a ringleader in the terrible persecution of the Christians, till something happened to him, and he became a Christian himself. Now what happened to Saul, "the heavenly vision," was the appearance of the risen Lord to him, which revolutionized him, making him a follower and an apostle of the Lord Jesus Christ. This miraculous appearance of the Lord is of the greatest possible moment; indeed, it is a part of the gospel, according to Paul's own luminous analysis. We have been saying that the gospel consists of three facts to be believed; namely, (1) the death, (2) the burial, (3) the resurrection of Christ. But we have misread Paul here (1 Cor. 15:3-8): "For I delivered unto you first of all that which also I received: [1] that Christ died . . . ; [2] and that he was buried; and [3] that he hath been raised . . . ; and [4] that he appeared to Cephas; then to the twelve; then he appeared to above five hundred at once . . . ; then he appeared to James; then to all the apostles; and last of all, as to the child untimely born, he appeared to me also." Paul connects all four of these facts, the death and the burial and the resurrection and the appearance of Christ, by the co-ordinate conjunction *and*. If, after arising from the grave, Jesus had gone to heaven without appearing to anybody, the world never could have known what became of Him; consequently, His selection of, and appearance to, witnesses is an essential, fundamental part of His gospel. This "heavenly vision," unto which Paul was not disobedient, included what he heard as well as what he saw, and made him a witness for the risen Lord "both to them of Damascus first, and at Jerusalem, and throughout all the country of Judæa, and also to the Gentiles, that they should repent and turn to God, doing works worthy of repentance."

*"The heavenly vision" was not merely for Paul, but for the world; that anybody will reject it as divine revelation is tragic* (24-32): "And as he thus made his defence, Festus saith with a loud voice, Paul, thou art mad; thy much learning is turning thee mad. But Paul saith, I am not mad, most excellent Festus; but speak forth words of truth and soberness. For the king knoweth of these things, unto whom I also speak freely: for I am persuaded that none of these things is hidden from

him; for this hath not been done in a corner. King Agrippa, believest thou the prophets? I know that thou believest. And Agrippa said unto Paul, With but little persuasion thou wouldst fain make me a Christian. And Paul said, I would to God, that whether with little or with much, not thou only, but also all that hear me this day, might become such as I am, except these bonds. And the king rose up, and the governor, and Bernice, and they that sat with them: and when they had withdrawn, they spake one to another, saying, This man doeth nothing worthy of death or of bonds. And Agrippa said unto Festus, This man might have been set at liberty, if he had not appealed unto Cæsar.'' He who was born into this world as Jesus of Nazareth had prior existence in the ''form of God'' before He took the form of man. (See Phil. 2: 5-11.) Evidently, He has the power to assume at will either the form of God or the form of man. When He appeared to the original twelve apostles after His resurrection, they saw Him in human form so that they could identify Him as they knew Him in the flesh. But in ''the heavenly vision'' Paul, who never knew Him in human form, must have seen Him in the form of God; for the light of His face eclipsed the light of the noonday sun. There are visions and visions. But Paul's ''heavenly vision'' is unique in the history of the world, surpassing what Moses, or any other man, ever beheld. Both for himself and the human race, Paul saw the risen Jesus in the form of God; why, ''the heavenly vision'' felled him to the earth, put his eyes out, leaving him in prayer and without food for three days, and but for divine mercy would have slain him, as it would have slain Moses! (See Ex. 33: 17-23.) This augments the tragedy of any human being's rejecting Paul's ''heavenly vision'' as divine revelation. Paul's speech before Agrippa is called his defense, which it was incidentally, but really and fundamentally it is one of the most wonderful gospel sermons ever preached. Paul forgot himself, and was transported in rapture, in the hope of persuading King Agrippa especially, or anybody else who sat before him, to become a Christian! Why, the poor old heathen Festus thought Paul had gone stark mad, and talked right out "in meeting," disturbing Paul in his speech, so excited was he; while Agrippa saw Paul's point and felt the pressure of his power, and he cried out, "With but little persuasion thou wouldst fain make me a Christian. And Paul said, "I would to God, that whether with little or much, not thou only, but also all that hear me this day, might become such as I am, except these bonds." Paul's reference to Agrippa and Festus made him conscious of his chains, which he wanted nobody else ever to have to wear. And as these distinguished auditors interrupted Paul and withdrew from his audience, they bore witness of his innocence and power.

## XXVII

## ANGELIC MINISTRY

### (Acts 27)

*Nothing could be more interesting or more beautiful
than the ministry of the angels.* However, like men,
angels are both good and bad. Some of the angels fell
and were imprisoned: Peter (2 Pet. 2:4) declared,
"God spared not angels when they sinned, but cast them
down to hell, and committed them to pits of darkness,
to be reserved unto judgment." But what Paul wrote
in Eph. 2:2, "wherein ye once walked according to the
course of this world, according to the prince of the powers
of the air, of the spirit that now worketh in the sons of
disobedience," seems to indicate that God has not yet
finally judged some evil angels, who still have liberty to
lead men astray. Amenable angels served the Lord, whose
law they announced, and who conveyed His messages
and inflicted divine penalties and protected His people;
yea, the angels are "ministering spirits, sent forth to
do service for the sake of them that shall inherit salvation" (Heb. 1:14). Gabriel revealed to Zacharias that
he and Elisabeth should have a great son, John the
Baptist, to turn many of the children of Israel to the
Lord their God, and apprised Mary that she was to be
the mother of the Son of God and name Him Jesus, whose
miraculous birth was proclaimed to the shepherds by
the angels of heaven. How gracious, how fitting, that
angels declared the birth of the Son of God and protected Him from the irate king who sought His life,

264

fed Him following His victory over the tempter, held themselves ready to come to Him in the twinkling of an eye in Gethsemane when His enemies sought to overcome Him, preached His Second Coming when a cloud of glory received Him out of the view of His disciples! The doctrine is sound and exhilarating that every penitent, obedient believer in the Lord Jesus Christ has his own guardian angel to protect and inspire him in the way of life. No Christian may ever know all the angels do for him in this world. Surely this angelic ministry shows the proximity of the two worlds—the visible and the invisible, earth and heaven—and suggests that the form of God and the form of man may be more closely related than we now know. Like the Lord, whose they are and whom they serve, the angels appear and disappear mysteriously; that we can not see them with our bodily eyes is no evidence at all that they are not present with us, any more than this same negative, physical proof evinces the absence of the great God and the Lord Himself. One must accept the testimony of faith, and see with the eyes of one's heart, even to be a Christian; what any man can see or hear or touch naturally is as limited as the little world in which he lives, but faith puts him in touch with eternity and the great God Himself, entitling him to be served by the angels.

### An Angel of God Ministered to Paul (vs. 1-44)

*This angel revealed to Paul his own future and that of his associates* (1-26) : "And when it was determined that we should sail for Italy, they delivered Paul and certain other prisoners to a centurion named Julius, of the Augustan band. And embarking in a ship of Adramyttium, which was about to sail unto the places on the coast of Asia, we put to sea, Aristarchus, a Mace-

donian of Thessalonica, being with us. And the next
day we touched at Sidon: and Julius treated Paul kindly,
and gave him leave to go unto his friends and refresh
himself. And putting to sea from thence, we sailed
under the lee of Cyprus, because the winds were contrary. And when we had sailed across the sea which
is off Cilicia and Pamphylia, we came to Myra, a city
of Lycia. And there the centurion found a ship of
Alexandria sailing for Italy; and he put us therein.
And when we had sailed slowly many days, and were
come with difficulty over against Cnidus, the wind not
further suffering us, we sailed under the lee of Crete,
over against Salmone; and with difficulty coasting along
it we came unto a certain place called Fair Havens; nigh
whereunto was the city of Lasea. And when much time
was spent, and the voyage was now dangerous, because
the fast was now already gone by, Paul admonished them,
and said unto them, Sirs, I perceive that the voyage will
be with injury and much loss, not only of the lading and
the ship, but also of our lives. But the centurion gave
more heed to the master and to the owner of the ship,
than to those things which were spoken by Paul. And
because the haven was not commodious to winter in, the
more part advised to put to sea from thence, if by any
means they could reach Phœnix, and winter there;
which is a haven of Crete, looking northeast and south-
east. And when the south wind blew softly, supposing
that they had obtained their purpose, they weighed
anchor and sailed along Crete, close inshore. But after
no long time there beat down from it a tempestuous
wind, which is called Euraquilo: and when the ship
was caught, and could not face the wind, we gave way
to it, and were driven. And running under the lee of
a small island called Cauda, we were able, with diffi-

culty, to secure the boat: and when they had hoisted it up, they used helps, undergirding the ship; and, fearing lest they should be cast upon the Syrtis, they lowered the gear, and so were driven. And as we labored exceedingly with the storm, the next day they began to throw the freight overboard; and the third day they cast out with their own hands the tackling of the ship. And when neither sun nor stars shone upon us for many days, and no small tempest lay on us, all hope that we should be saved was now taken away. And when they had been long without food, then Paul stood forth in the midst of them, and said, Sirs, ye should have hearkened unto me, and not have set sail from Crete, and have gotten this injury and loss. And now I exhort you to be of good cheer; for there shall be no loss of life among you, but only of the ship. For there stood by me this night an angel of the God whose I am, whom also I serve, saying, Fear not, Paul; thou must stand before Cæsar: and lo, God hath granted thee all them that sail with thee. Wherefore, sirs, be of good cheer: for I believe God, that it shall be even so as it hath been spoken unto me. But we must be cast upon a certain island.'' Now at length Luke, in his plain, perfect narrative, presented Paul on the way to Rome, without miraculous intervention, but by a remarkable chain of providence, in which there were such links as Jewish plots, the covetousness of Felix, the vacillation of Festus, the discretion of Paul and the protection of citizens by the Roman Empire. ''Paul and certain other prisoners,'' together with Luke and other allies, left Cæsarea in the care of Julius, a centurion, whose band of Roman soldiers was named Augustan for the Emperor. The first ship in which they sailed ''touched at Sidon,'' and penetrated the sea beyond Cyprus, till they ''came to

Myra, a city of Lycia''; where the centurion changed to another ship bound for Italy, which, on account of unfavorable wind and weather, was barely able to reach Fair Havens on the island of Crete. Here ''much time was spent, and the voyage was now dangerous''; and Paul warned that immediate continuation of the journey meant loss of life and property. However, with the centurion, whose authority was supreme as representative of Rome, the advice of the master and the owner of the ship was weightier than Paul's; and the majority of the passengers, lulled by a soft, south wind, which proved the prelude of an unprecedented storm, were in favor of leaving the incommodious harbor of Fair Havens to spend the winter in Phœnix. This they could not do, on account of the terrible wind, which we would call ''Northeaster,'' which swept down on them from the mountains of Crete, and blew them far to sea in the direction of ''the Syrtis,'' quicksand near Africa, darkened the heavens day and night ''for many days,'' lost all freight on the ship, which it utterly demolished, swallowing all hope of life. Right here is the point in the revelation of the angel to Paul: The only way any man, whether patriarch or priest or prophet or king or apostle, can know the future is by divine inspiration or revelation; and God sent His angel to Paul in the very face of death in the dark, turbulent sea, to reveal to him that even the elements of nature could not interfere with the divine plan for him to preach the gospel ''before Cæsar,'' and therefore God would spare both his life and the lives of all that sailed with him. Of course, this was good news to Paul, because he believed it, and with it he cheered all on board the ship. What an awful picture this last ship presents to all the world! What a blessed experience it was to be saved from it!

The old ship of Satan has sprung a leak, and shall go down to the bottom of the sea. Let all sinners on board this wicked vessel believe the gospel, the good news preached originally by Paul and the other apostles, transfer to the lifeboat of the Lord Jesus Christ, and be saved and live forever. Paul's belief of the revelation of the angel made it good news to him; nothing, not even the one gospel itself, is good news to anybody who does not believe it.

*This angelic ministry gave Paul supreme elevation among all others on the ship* (27-44) : "But when the fourteenth night was come, as we were driven to and fro in the sea of Adria, about midnight the sailors surmised that they were drawing near to some country: and they sounded, and found twenty fathoms; and after a little space, they sounded again, and found fifteen fathoms. And fearing lest haply we should be cast ashore on rocky ground, they let go four anchors from the stern, and wished for the day. And as the sailors were seeking to flee out of the ship, and had lowered the boat into the sea, under color as though they would lay out anchors from the foreship, Paul said to the centurion and to the soldiers, Except these abide in the ship, ye can not be saved. Then the soldiers cut away the ropes of the boat, and let her fall off. And while the day was coming on, Paul besought them all to take some food, saying, This is the fourteenth day that ye wait and continue fasting, having taken nothing. Wherefore I beseech you to take some food: for this is your safety: for there shall not a hair perish from the head of any of you. And when he had said this, and had taken bread, he gave thanks to God in the presence of all; and he break it, and began to eat. Then were they all of good cheer, and themselves also took food. And we were in all in

the ship two hundred threescore and sixteen souls. And
when they had eaten enough, they lightened the ship,
throwing out the wheat into the sea. And when it was
day, they knew not the land: but they perceived a certain bay with a beach, and they took counsel whether
they could drive the ship upon it. And casting off the
anchors, they left them in the sea, at the same time loosing the bands of the rudders; and hoisting up the fore-
sail to the wind, they made for the beach. But lighting
upon a place where two seas met, they ran the vessel
aground; and the foreship struck and remained un-
movable, but the stern began to break up by the violence
of the waves. And the soldiers' counsel was to kill the
prisoners, lest any of them should swim out, and escape.
But the centurion, desiring to save Paul, stayed them
from their purpose; and commanded that they who
could swim should cast themselves overboard, and get
first to the land; and the rest, some on planks, and some
on other things from the ship. And so it came to pass,
that they all escaped safe to the land.'' After being
tossed fourteen nights in the sea of Adria, which covered
then a greater space than it does now, the opinion of
the sailors that they were approaching land, probably
based on the sound of distant breakers, proved true by
their measuring the depths of the sea, which showed a
rapid decrease from one hundred and twenty feet to
ninety feet; and the precaution was taken, to prevent
being ''cast ashore on rocky ground,'' of casting ''four
anchors from the stern,'' and praying for the light of
day. At this point, Paul discovered the plan of the
sailors to abandon the ship, and warned the centurion
and the soldiers that a scheme so unworthy and faithless
would be fatal to them; whereupon they promptly made
it impossible, by dropping the boat into the sea. Now

in the dawning of the fourteenth fateful day, Paul urged
his associates on board the ship, to be able to make necessary draft on their strength and meet the responsibility
of new life to be granted them beyond this awful crisis
in the sea, to break their long fast; and set the proper
example before them by eating himself, with thanksgiving to God. Thus the two hundred and seventy-five
people on board the ship with Paul (there were two
hundred and seventy six, counting him), became cheerful
under the leadership of Paul and the food they ate,
though their situation in the sea seemed to get worse.
With the light of day upon them, they could not recognize the land toward which they were being blown.
However, having lightened the ship by throwing the
wheat into the sea, and discarding the anchors, and
loosing the rudder bands, they unfurled the sail, and
sought to drive the ship upon the beach of a bay they
had discovered; but the foreship grounded fast, and the
stern was crushed by "two seas," or two giant waves,
which completely stranded the ship. The soldiers showed
themselves as unfeeling as the sailors in their desire
to kill Paul with the other prisoners, lest he swim ashore
and escape with his life. But Julius met this base in-
gratitude with quick rebuff, and spared everybody's life
on board the ship: some swam to the land; "and the
rest, some on planks, and some on other things from the
ship. And so it came to pass, that they all escaped safe
to the land." No more fortunate thing could have happened to Paul during this memorable, terrible sea voyage, than the revelation of the angel to him that the
divine purpose already made known to him was to be
executed, that he should go to Rome and preach the
gospel there; and, while the ship was to be lost, all of the
two hundred and seventy-six souls on board the ship

were to be saved. Paul exceeded the seasoned seamen, the sailors and the soldiers, in his coolness and calm deliberation in that fateful, eventful disturbance of the elements of nature because he accepted the message of the angel as the most certain Word of God. Yet, Paul was not presumptuous, neither would he suffer presumption in any other on the ship, that the Lord would or could save him without his full co-operation. Verily, the supreme part Paul played in the scenes of that stirring, exciting, almost sleepless, nearly foodless voyage, could not but give him pre-eminence over the master and the owner of the ship and Lucius the Roman centurion and soldier responsible to Cæsar and absolutely everybody else on board the ship! Aside from the Lord Jesus Christ Himself only, Paul has shown himself the supreme leader of the human race; since Paul came on the stage of action or speech Luke has scarcely written a scene in which Paul did not come quickly and permanently to the front.

# XXVIII

## PAUL THE APOSTLE

### (Acts 28)

*Paul is not merely AN apostle; he is unique; he is
really THE apostle.* Now we hasten to disclaim any
trespass on the domain of the original twelve apostles,
who, because the church was primarily created in them,
and they bore the first witness of the risen, glorified
Lord, have precedence and priority over Paul and all
other human beings, as the very first Christian fathers.
Of course, the article *the* is definite and distinct, and
can not properly be used to modify a noun or a name
common to two or more objects of the same class; in
that case, the indefinite article *a* or *an* should be employed. But Paul is in a class by himself, the only
apostle of his kind the world has ever seen. And this
difference is more than temperamental or adjunctive.
So far as we know or can find out, Paul is the only
apostle who ever saw the risen Jesus in the form
of God. In a way, or so to speak, Paul is balanced
against all the other apostles: they saw the Conqueror
of death in the form of man, which was essential and
sufficient, because they had known Him as Jesus of
Nazareth; Paul beheld Him in the contour of the Deity,
never having seen Him otherwise, and being unable to
identify Him in the flesh of man. And so the fourth
fact of the gospel, the appearance of Jesus after His
resurrection from death, which has been slurred over,
without co-ordination with the first three facts of His

death and burial and resurrection (see 1 Cor. 15:1-11) has been doubly buttressed and strengthened forever against unbelief and skepticism and infidelity and modernism and all the contrary winds that blow on the shores of time. It is just as legitimate or pertinent or germane to say "Paul *the* Apostle" as "John *the* Baptist" or "Jesus *the* Christ." That John was *"the* Baptist" expresses or means, more than simply that he *baptized* or was a *baptizer;* under God he created baptism and baptized Jesus of Nazareth, thus leading to the divine visible, audible introduction and announcement of Him to the Jews and to the whole world as the Son of God. It would be false and ridiculous to call Jesus *a* Christ; He is *the* Christ. Likewise, it lacks propriety and precision and force and exact description to classify Paul only as *one* of the apostles; he is *the* apostle—*the* apostle that saw the Lord Jesus Christ in His divine eternal form, *the* apostle that had to obey the gospel, and be born again, *the* apostle that was sent to the Gentiles, and that labored more abundantly than all the other apostles. That man Saul had everything the world or nature could give—wealth and social standing and Hebrew blood and Jewish training and Greek education and Roman citizenship, and energy and talent and genius—all of which he laid on the altar for "the great God and our Saviour Jesus Christ"; and as *the* apostle he became the most remarkable and the most influential character in history, under Christ; and made Christianity the universal religion. *Saul* was his original Jewish name; *Paul* became his Greek or Gentile name as *the* greatest of all the apostles and servants and exponents and advocates of the Lord Jesus Christ to all the world forever!

### Paul Is the Apostle to the Gentiles (vs. 1-31)

*Paul ministered to Gentiles and finished his passage to Rome* (1-16): "And when we were escaped, then we knew that the island was called Melita. And the barbarians showed us no common kindness: for they kindled a fire, and received us all, because of the present rain, and because of the cold. But when Paul had gathered a bundle of sticks and laid them on the fire, a viper came out by reason of the heat, and fastened on his hand. And when the barbarians saw the venomous creature hanging from his hand, they said one to another, No doubt this man is a murderer, whom, though he hath escaped from the sea, yet Justice hath not suffered to live. Howbeit he shook off the creature into the fire, and took no harm. But they expected that he would have swollen, or fallen down dead suddenly: but when they were long in expectation and beheld nothing amiss come to him, they changed their minds, and said that he was a god. Now in the neighborhood of that place were lands belonging to the chief man of the island, named Publius; who received us, and entertained us three days courteously. And it was so, that the father of Publius lay sick of fever and dysentery: unto whom Paul entered in, and prayed, and laying his hands on him healed him. And when this was done, the rest also that had diseases in the island came, and were cured: who also honored us with many honors; and when we sailed, they put on board such things as we needed. And after three months we set sail in a ship of Alexandria which had wintered in the island, whose sign was the twin brothers. And touching at Syracuse, we tarried there three days. And from thence we made a circuit, and arrived at Rhegium: and after one day a south wind

sprang up, and on the second day we came to Puteoli;
where we found brethren, and were entreated to tarry
with them seven days: and so we came to Rome. And
from thence the brethren, when they heard of us, came
to meet us as far as the market of Appius and the three
taverns; whom when Paul saw, he thanked God, and
took courage. And when we entered into Rome, Paul
was suffered to abide by himself with the soldier that
guarded him.'' Wherever went Paul the Apostle, he
always found his clientele. On the rather small island
of Melita, to which two hundred and seventy-six men
escaped from the lost ship in the sea, presumably there
was neither synagogue nor Jewish nucleus for a church;
but there were Gentiles all around him, with whom Paul
leveled himself in humble, practical service. It must
have been a heroic task to provide a fire right out in the
open to warm nearly three hundred men who came out
of the sea in the cold rain of that never-to-be-forgotten
morning in which Paul the Apostle, a hero always, was
bound to have a part. Now Paul's miraculous escape
from a poisonous snake bite, as he sought to replenish
the burning, roaring fire on the seashore, swept the
rustic barbarians around him from the false conclusion
that he was a murderer to the opposite extreme that
he was a god. Near where the ship was lost, whose
occupants reached the shore alive, was Publius, the ruler
of the island of Melita (now called Malta), who gracious-
ly took all the two hundred and seventy-six men who had
escaped alive from the lost ship, as his guests for three
days. But Publius was abundantly rewarded for this
remarkable hospitality by Paul the Apostle, who miraculously cured his father of a very dangerous fever. Of
course, it was inevitable that this supernatural healing
should become known all over Melita, the happy result

of which was that all the sick of the island came to Paul, and he restored them all to health, also. Naturally, this widespread beneficence on the part of the apostle reflected great credit on the whole company with which he was associated, all of whom the islanders honored; in so much that when, three months after the storm had cast these men on the island, they sailed away, their benefactors presented them with everything they needed. However, Luke does not bother to inform us what arrangement was made for the entertainment of the apostle and his company during the remainder of their three months' sojourn in Melita, after lodging with Publius for three days. Neither does Luke even mention any ceremony Paul used in restoring to health the ill of the island, but we know that Paul always accomplished this wonderful work in the name of the Lord Jesus Christ. Now we just can not imagine Paul's making the bodies of these Gentiles whole without his ministering also to their minds and souls and hearts and spirits, though our historian offers no estimate of any achievement along this line. Perhaps Luke's silence here may be due to the fact that the apostle found this part of the world entirely without any preparation for Christ by the law of Moses or the prophets of Israel, there being no evidence that Jews lived on this island, where a church would have been inopportune, if not impossible, at the time. Finally the company whose record Luke wrote, being himself a member of the assemblage, bade their generous friends adieu on Melita, and resumed their passage to Rome, as soon as possible, on an Alexandrian ship, with the sign, the twin brothers, named Castor and Pollux, for the fabled sons of Jupiter, the special guardians of sailors. This ship went to Syracuse, a distance less than one hundred miles, in less than

twenty-four hours, where it tarried three days, either
on account of contrary winds, or to unload freight.
Next, probably on account of unfavorable winds, it cir-
cuited to Rhegium, now called Reggio, and at last it
went to Puteoli, which now has been superseded by
Naples, a distance of one hundred and eighty miles, in
one day, helped by a south wind.    Of course, the
rest of the distance to Rome, Paul and his associates
traveled by land.    That Paul found brethren in Puteoli
indicates that the gospel had already been preached in
Italy; and that Julius would allow Paul to tarry with
his brethren in Puteoli for one whole week evinces the
respect with which this Roman centurion had come to
regard the apostle.    Happily, this period of seven days
included a Lord's Day, affording Paul and his companions the blessed privilege of celebrating the Lord's
Supper with their fellow Christians in Puteoli.    It
greatly encouraged the apostle for his brethren to meet
him at the market of Appius and the three taverns,
and relieved him to be allowed "to abide by himself with
the soldier that guarded him."

*Paul revealed the very genius of his apostleship*
(17-31): "And it came to pass, that after three days
he called together those that were the chief of the Jews:
and when they were come together, he said unto them,
I, brethren, though I had done nothing against the
people, or the customs of our fathers, yet was delivered
prisoner from Jerusalem into the hands of the Romans:
who, when they had examined me, desired to set me at
liberty, because there was no cause of death in me.
But when the Jews spake against it, I was constrained
to appeal unto Cæsar; not that I had aught whereof
to accuse my nation.    For this cause therefore did I
entreat you to see and to speak with me: for because

of the hope of Israel I am bound with this chain. And
they said unto him, We neither received letters from
Judæa concerning thee, nor did any of the brethren
come hither and report or speak any harm of thee. But
we desire to hear of thee what thou thinkest: for as
concerning this sect, it is known to us that everywhere
it is spoken against. And when they had appointed him
a day, they came to him into his lodging in great number; to whom he expounded the matter, testifying the
kingdom of God, and persuading them concerning Jesus,
both from the law of Moses and from the prophets, from
morning till evening. And some believed the things
which were spoken, and some disbelieved. And when
they agreed not among themselves, they departed after
that Paul had spoken one word, Well spake the Holy
Spirit through Isaiah the prophet unto your fathers,
saying,

"Go thou unto this people, and say,
    By hearing ye shall hear, and shall in no wise
        understand;
    And seeing ye shall see, and shall in no wise
        perceive:
    For this people's heart is waxed gross,
    And their ears are dull of hearing,
    And their eyes they have closed;
    Lest haply they should perceive with their eyes,
    And hear with their ears,
    And understand with their heart,
    And should turn again,
    And I should heal them.

"Be it known therefore unto you, that this salvation
of God is sent unto the Gentiles: they will also hear.
And when he had said these words, the Jews departed,

having much disputing among themselves. And he abode two whole years in his own hired dwelling, and received all that went in unto him, preaching the kingdom of God, and teaching the things concerning the Lord Jesus Christ with all boldness, none forbidding him.'' It is of the very essence of this Christian apostleship that it gratefully acknowledges its inception in God's chosen, ancient people, called Hebrews for Abraham or Israelites for Jacob, or Israel, or Jews for Judah. It would have been impossible for Paul to be the apostle to the Gentiles, if he had not been himself a Hebrew or an Israelite or a Jew; and at no stage of his great, creative work as the apostle, could he ignore his own people, his own Jewish brethren. That is precisely why ''he called together those that were the chief of the Jews,'' within three or four days after his arrival in the great supreme city of Rome. The apostle knew that the Jews knew that he had just been escorted into this world capital as an imperial prisoner, and he sought to state to them directly and immediately the true status of his own case. It is easily on the surface of this explicit summary of Paul's own legal situation, that he could bring suit in the Roman court of justice, against the Jews for persecuting him; but he repeatedly disclaimed any desire to do that sort of thing. Yea, the great apostle seemed to take pride in this persecution— in being bound with a chain for ''the hope of Israel,'' which is elaborated in Christianity, as the apostles mediated it to the whole world, both Jews and Gentiles. But Paul learned, perhaps to his surprise, that his Jewish brethren in Rome had no animus or prejudice against him. However, they were curious to learn his estimate of what they called a ''sect,'' which had sprung up among the Jews everywhere, and was in every place "spoken against." Of course, that was too large a task to be performed quickly in a limited meeting, which required a whole day and the largest audience possible of assembly. But this committee of chief Jews, with whom Paul was in conference, promptly selected a time, when they crowded his lodging with eager listeners. The apostle met this challenge by interpreting Christianity, "testifying the kingdom of God, and persuading them concerning Jesus, both from the law of Moses and from the prophets, from morning till evening."( Now there happened here what always came to pass when Paul or anybody else preached the gospel—"some believed the things which were spoken, and some disbelieved." The great apostle was keenly sensitive to this common, ordinary, but tragic, division in his audience; and before his listeners left him, he quoted to them that most remarkably graphic and descriptive passage of poetic prophecy given to the world through Isaiah, which the Lord Jesus Christ had used to picture His own generation, and announced to them that the divine salvation he had elaborated to them was sent unto the Gentiles also. "And he abode two whole years in his own hired dwelling, and received all that went in unto him, preaching the kingdom of God, and teaching the things concerning the Lord Jesus Christ with all boldness, none forbidding him." Thus Paul the Apostle has made plain another fundamental characteristic of the gospel; namely, that it offers salvation to all men, and the reason all are not saved who hear the proffer is, that some will not accept it: they have gross hearts, and see without perceiving, and hear without understanding. The heart of Paul was rich and strong and powerful, and enslaved to the stupendous, tremendous task of making the gospel universally known.